The Complete Book of Microwave Cooking

The Complete Book of Microwave Cooking

Carol Bowen

HAMLYN

Other books by the same author

Hamlyn All Colour Book of Main Dishes
Hamlyn All Colour Book of Puddings and Desserts
Hamlyn All Colour Book of Home Baking
No Need to Cook Book
Barbecue Cookbook

The author and publishers would like to thank the following for lending the backgrounds, crockery and cutlery shown in the photographs:
Astrohome Ltd, Neal Street, London
Argenta Gallery, Fulham Road, London
David Mellor, James Street and Sloane Square, London

Photography by James Jackson
Line illustrations The Hayward Art Group
Two-colour illustrations by Ann Rees

First published in 1983 by
Hamlyn Publishing
Astronaut House, Feltham, Middlesex, England
© Copyright Hamlyn Publishing 1983, a division of The Hamlyn Publishing Group Limited

Fifth impression 1984

All rights reserved. No part of this publication may be reproduced, stored in a retrieval system, or transmitted in any form or by any means, electronic, mechanical, photocopying, recording or otherwise, without the permission of Hamlyn Publishing.

ISBN 0 600 32327 7

Set in 11pt Apollo by Servis Filmsetting Limited, Manchester

Printed in Italy

Contents

USEFUL FACTS AND FIGURES

Notes on Metrication

In this book quantities are given in metric and Imperial measures. Exact conversion from Imperial to metric measures does not usually give very convenient working quantities and so the metric measures have been rounded off into units of 25 grams. The table below shows the recommended equivalents.

Ounces	*Approx g to nearest whole figure*	*Recommended conversion to nearest unit of 25*
1	28	25
2	57	50
3	85	75
4	113	100
5	142	150
6	170	175
7	198	200
8	227	225
9	255	250
10	283	275
11	312	300
12	340	350
13	368	375
14	396	400
15	425	425
16 (1 lb)	454	450
17	482	475
18	510	500
19	539	550
20 (1¼ lb)	567	575

Note: When converting quantities over 20 oz first add the appropriate figures in the centre column, then adjust to the nearest unit of 25. As a general guide, 1 kg (1000 g) equals 2.2 lb or about 2 lb 3 oz. This method of conversion gives good results in nearly all cases, although in certain pastry and cake recipes a more accurate conversion is necessary to produce a balanced recipe.

Liquid measures The millilitre has been used in this book and the following table gives a few examples.

Imperial	*Approx ml to nearest whole figure*	*Recommended ml*
¼ pint	142	150 ml
½ pint	283	300 ml
¾ pint	425	450 ml
1 pint	567	600 ml
1½ pints	851 ml	900 ml
1¾ pints	992	1000 ml (1 litre)

Spoon measures All spoon measures given in this book are level unless otherwise stated.

Can sizes At present, cans are marked with the exact (usually to the nearest whole number) metric equivalent of the Imperial weight of the contents, so we have followed this practice when giving can sizes.

Notes for American and Australian users

In America the 8-oz measuring cup is used. In Australia metric measures are now used in conjunction with the standard 250-ml measuring cup. The Imperial pint, used in Britain and Australia, is 20 fl oz, while the American pint is 16 fl oz. It is important to remember that the Australian tablespoon differs from both the British and American tablespoons; the table below gives a comparison. The British standard tablespoon, which has been used throughout this book, holds 17.7 ml, the American 14.2 ml, and the Australian 20 ml. A teaspoon holds approximately 5 ml in all three countries.

British	*American*	*Australian*
1 teaspoon	1 teaspoon	1 teaspoon
1 tablespoon	1 tablespoon	1 tablespoon
2 tablespoons	3 tablespoons	2 tablespoons
3½ tablespoons	4 tablespoons	3 tablespoons
4 tablespoons	5 tablespoons	3½ tablespoons

An Imperial/American guide to solid and liquid measures

Imperial	*American*
Solid measures	
1 lb butter or margarine	2 cups
1 lb flour	4 cups
1 lb granulated or caster sugar	2 cups
1 lb icing sugar	3 cups
8 oz rice	1 cup
Liquid measures	
¼ pint liquid	⅔ cup liquid
½ pint	1¼ cups
¾ pint	2 cups
1 pint	2½ cups
1½ pints	3¾ cups
2 pints	5 cups (2½ pints)

NOTE: WHEN MAKING ANY OF THE RECIPES IN THIS BOOK, ONLY FOLLOW ONE SET OF MEASURES AS THEY ARE NOT INTERCHANGEABLE.

It isn't every day, or even every year, that a new cooking appliance hits the headlines with promises of super-quick meals, 'cool' cooking procedures and the ability to 'unfreeze' meals in a fraction of the time it normally takes. Such was the dramatic debut of the microwave oven – but has it lived up to these promises? The answer is an unquestionable yes from those thousands of owners who now cook meals in minutes rather than hours, enjoy food from the freezer at a moment's notice and really do appreciate a cool kitchen and reduced risk of burning from hot dishes and cookers.

However, like any other appliance, the microwave oven does have a few limitations and there are some people who are sceptical of this cooking method. No one appliance has ever proved perfect in all cooking operations and problems can possibly occur through unfamiliarity with the way in which a microwave oven cooks. It was with these thoughts in mind that *The Complete Book of Microwave Cooking* was born, so I have set out to answer all those questions that are likely to be asked by would-be and experienced microwave owners alike. A basic section on how the microwave oven works, backed up with a section on techniques for getting the very best results, will arm you with all the knowledge you need to achieve perfect microwave meals. The recipe section that follows will provide a springboard to give you a good launch into the delights of microwave cooking.

Many of my friends, family and colleagues have passed on their favourite recipes and handy hints for this book. Many thanks go to them all, too numerous to mention, but especially to my sister Jackie Goodwin, whose help in testing and double-checking the recipes has been immeasurable. I should also like to offer my grateful thanks to Philips Electronics for kindly supplying the microwave oven in which all testing was done for this book.

Special thanks also go to Bridget Jones who carefully edited the book, Claire James who typed and made sense of some of my early draft recipes and to my husband Peter for his quick wit and sense of humour when things occasionally went wrong!

Introduction

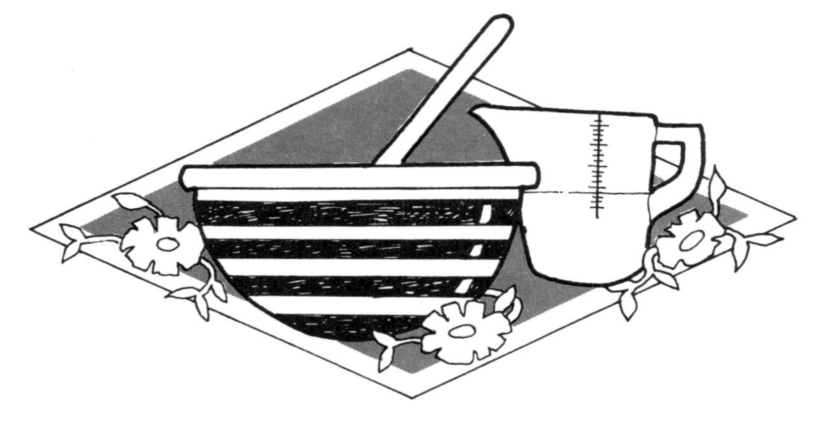

The chances are, if you are a freezer owner or a busy cook, you will welcome the arrival of the domestic microwave oven. With a microwave oven in your home, you will be able to cook or defrost food, keep prepared dishes warm or reheat them in just minutes instead of hours.

Microwave cooking resulted from radar research during the second world war, and in 1945 General Electric produced the first microwave oven for cooking commercial fast food. For some twenty years these microwave ovens were used extensively in hospitals and catering establishments. The fifties saw the introduction of several microwave ovens for domestic use, some combining microwave cooking and conventional cooking in one operation.

Consumer enthusiasm increased dramatically in the sixties, especially in the United States, and brought with it a surge of developments in the domestic microwave oven market. The major development was the introduction of variable power cooking which included defrost power and made it possible to cook delicate and heat-sensitive foods in the microwave.

Over the last twenty years there have been many new developments. Temperature probe cooking was among the first advances in microwave cooking: a temperature probe inserted into the food means that a pre-selected final temperature can be chosen and when that temperature is reached the probe automatically signals to the oven to stop cooking. Other developments include microwave cooking combined with forced air convection for quick cooking and browning in one operation.

Simmer and cook, one of the latest techniques for temperature-controlled, slow microwave cooking, allows for the defrosting and cooking of food in one operation. Along with new and future developments – like two-tier or multiple level cooking zones which enable you to cook foods at different power settings, in the oven at the same time, and computerised cooking programmes with touch control features and memory recall – the domestic microwave oven market is becoming an increasingly sophisticated one.

Microwave Facts

What are microwaves? Microwaves are electro-magnetic waves, converted from electrical energy. Microwave energy is a type of high frequency radio wave positioned at the top end of the radio band. The waves are of a very short length and high frequency – hence the name 'microwaves'. They are not, however, as powerful as infra-red rays and are far removed from x-rays, gamma rays and ultra violet rays which are all known to damage human cells.

How are microwaves produced in the microwave oven? The mechanics of microwave cooking are simple. Inside the microwave oven there is a magnetron vacuum tube. This converts ordinary household electrical energy into high frequency microwaves. These waves are then channelled into the oven cavity through a wave guide. A stirrer fan distributes the microwaves evenly. If the oven has a turntable this will also ensure the foods are evenly cooked.

How do microwaves cook the food? Once produced, the microwaves can do one of three things –

a) They can be reflected off a surface. Metals reflect microwaves, which is why they are safely contained within the oven cavity and why cooking utensils must be non-metallic.

b) They can pass through certain materials. Glass, pottery, china, paper, wood and most plastics allow the waves to pass through. These materials stay cool which is why they make ideal cooking utensils.

c) The microwaves can be absorbed by some substances. They are absorbed by the moisture molecules – water, fat and sugar – in the food causing them to vibrate rapidly, and in turn producing heat to cook the food. Imagine the boy scout rubbing sticks together to produce heat: the same is true of microwave cooking. The molecules vibrate millions of times per second – precisely 2,450 million times per second – producing an extremely intense heat. This intense heat accounts for the speed of microwave cooking. This heat-producing activity spreads from the initial point of penetration which is 5 cm/2 in into the food. Microwave ovens do not need preheating like conventional ovens, as the microwave energy produces heat inside the food molecules immediately the waves are produced by the magnetron.

Microwaves produce heat within the food and not within the utensils. Compared with conventional methods this is a completely different form of cooking and, as such, needs a fundamentally different approach. The dishes may, however, become warm by normal conduction through contact with the hot food.

Are microwave ovens safe? The microwave oven is one of the safest kitchen appliances around. It does not get very hot so you are unlikely to get a burn or scald from the oven. It is also heavy enough not to tip over like a hot saucepan. Worries about safety arise because of the unusual operation of the microwave oven and that confusing word 'radiation'.

There are two types of radiation – ionising and non-ionising. The ionising type can be hazardous but the non-ionising type, like microwaves, does not damage human cells. Despite this and to reassure public confidence, manufacturers also ensure that all microwaves stay within the oven cavity by employing a number of checks on all microwave oven doors.

To back these up the presence of the British Electrotechnical Standard label (checked by the British Electrotechnical Board) is a guarantee that your oven is perfectly safe. This states that your microwave oven complies with BS 3456: Part 2: Section 2:33:1976 'Microwave Ovens' which lays down an absolute maximum microwave oven leakage of 5 milliwatts per square centimetre at a distance of 5 centimetres from the oven door throughout the life of the oven.

To put the safety aspects into perspective, one eminent professor of electrical engineering specialising in microwave energy rates the chances of harmful exposure to microwave energy from a domestic microwave oven as likely as getting a suntan from the moon!

The Microwave Oven

At first glance, the range of microwave ovens available and their many different features can seem intimidating or even alarming. After consideration and inspection, however, you will see that the basic microwave oven comprises an almost universal basic unit as shown below.

The basic unit comprises a door **8**, magnetron **4**, wave stirrer **6**, power supply **1** and controls. Some have additional sophistications such as a browning element, variable power control, oven turntable or temperature probe, but the basis upon which they all work remains the same.

1 The *plug* is inserted into the socket and the electricity flows to
2 the *power transformer* which increases the ordinary household voltage. This passes into
3 a *high-voltage rectifier and capacitor* which changes the high directional voltage to indirectional voltage. The indirectional voltage is applied to
4 the *magnetron* which converts electrical energy into electro-magnetic or microwave energy. This energy is then passed through to
5 the *wave guide* which directs the microwave energy into the oven cavity.

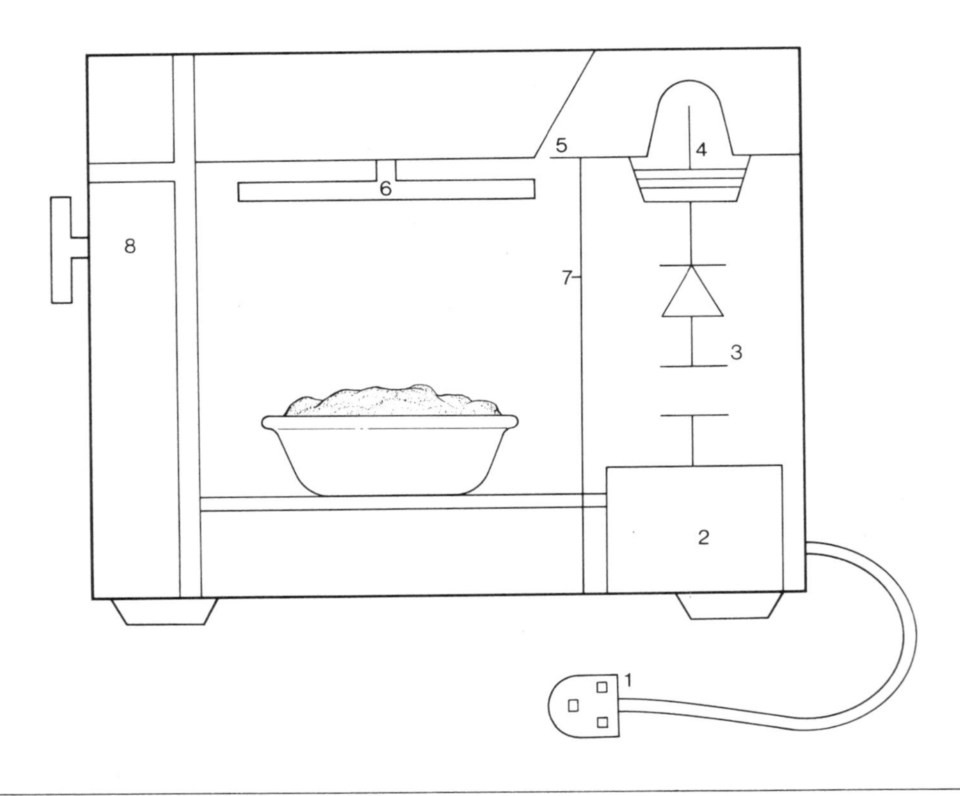

6 The *wave stirrer* turns slowly to distribute the microwaves in an even pattern around the oven.
7 The *oven cavity* is made of metal so as to contain the microwaves safely and deflect them from the walls and base of the oven to be absorbed by the food.
8 The *oven door* and the door frame are fitted with special seals to ensure that the microwaves are safely contained within the oven. Up to seven cut-out devices are incorporated so that the microwave energy is cut off automatically whenever the door is opened.

Beyond the basic unit the features are numerous and each is worth discussing.

A The *timer control* – available sometimes as a slide control rather than a dial. This timer controls the cooking period and may be either mechanical or of the digital type. It is set to the required number of minutes (or sometimes seconds) and when the cooking time is completed a bell or buzzer usually sounds to indicate this. The timer will also automatically shut off the microwave energy. Care should always be taken to set the timer accurately.

B The *cook* or *start* control. This does not operate until the oven door has been closed. When the door is opened during cooking, the microwave energy is automatically cut off. To re-start cooking, this button must be pushed again. Often, before this button can be operated the

C *On/Off* or *Power On* button must be pressed. Some basic ovens combine the *power on* and *cook* control buttons as one device. As well as alerting the cooking operation, this control often switches on the cooling fan and the interior light.

D The *variable power* or *power level* control is available on variable control ovens only. This feature offers greater flexibility and its nearest equivalent on the conventional oven is the temperature control. In the microwave oven this control means, very simply, that you can choose to decrease the microwave energy, introducing a 'slower' cooking rate for delicate items or foods that require longer cooking. The number of settings on this control vary widely between models and are described in various ways. For example, to name just a few, some manufacturers use a numerical scale of 2–10 or 1–7, others describe the power settings as LOW, MEDIUM, HIGH or FULL, and some refer to cooking methods such as SIMMER, ROAST, REHEAT and BAKE. Whichever control your oven has, the highest setting will be equivalent to FULL POWER or 100% energy input.

E *Indicator lights* are often incorporated as a useful reminder that a cooking operation has been set, is in progress, or has been completed. In most ovens this generally refers to FULL POWER or DEFROST POWER settings.

F A *cooking guide* is sometimes given on a panel on the side or top of the oven. It is the manufacturer's way of supplying at-a-glance information for cooking or defrosting basic, everyday foods.

G Some microwave ovens have a *turntable* instead of, or as well as, the wave stirrer. The turntable ensures that the waves are distributed evenly through the food, so reducing the effects of hot and cold spots. When a turntable is available in an oven, there is generally no need to turn or rotate dishes during cooking or the necessity is at least reduced to a minimum. Turntables are made of toughened ceramic glass and are often removable for cleaning. If the revolving turntable cannot be removed it may restrict the size and shape of dishes that can be used in the microwave.

Never use a dish which knocks against the oven walls as it rotates on the turntable during the cooking operation – this will only strain the turntable motor. Check your manufacturer's instructions to see if the microwave turntable can be removed and if the oven can be used without it in position.

There are some portable turntables that work on rechargeable batteries and these are useful for the owner of a microwave oven without a turntable, particularly for making heat-sensitive dishes, such as cakes and pastries, where even cooking is essential.

H A *browning element* or *integral grill*, somewhat like a radiant electric grill, is sometimes incorporated in the roof of the microwave oven. This can be used to pre-brown food or to crisp and brown food after cooking; or, in some cases, it can be used during microwave cooking. If you already have a good separate grill on your conventional oven, then it is not a particularly useful feature.

I On most microwave ovens the *door* has a side opening but some are available with drop down or slide up doors (some automatically open when the cooking operation is complete). The door often has a transparent mesh covering so that you can see the food cooking.

J An *interior light* usually lights up as soon as the appliance is turned on and this enables you to see the food as it cooks. Some models have a switch for the light, others have the light switch incorporated with the cook control. Follow the manufacturer's instructions for changing the bulb if necessary.

K Some microwave ovens have a *removable floor* or *base*, made of special ceramic glass or plastic, which acts as a spillage plate. Wash this in warm soapy water when necessary.

L All ovens have some sort of *vent* either positioned at the back or at the top of the oven. The vent allows moisture to escape from the oven during cooking. Some models also have a *filter* which allows air into the oven to cool the working components.

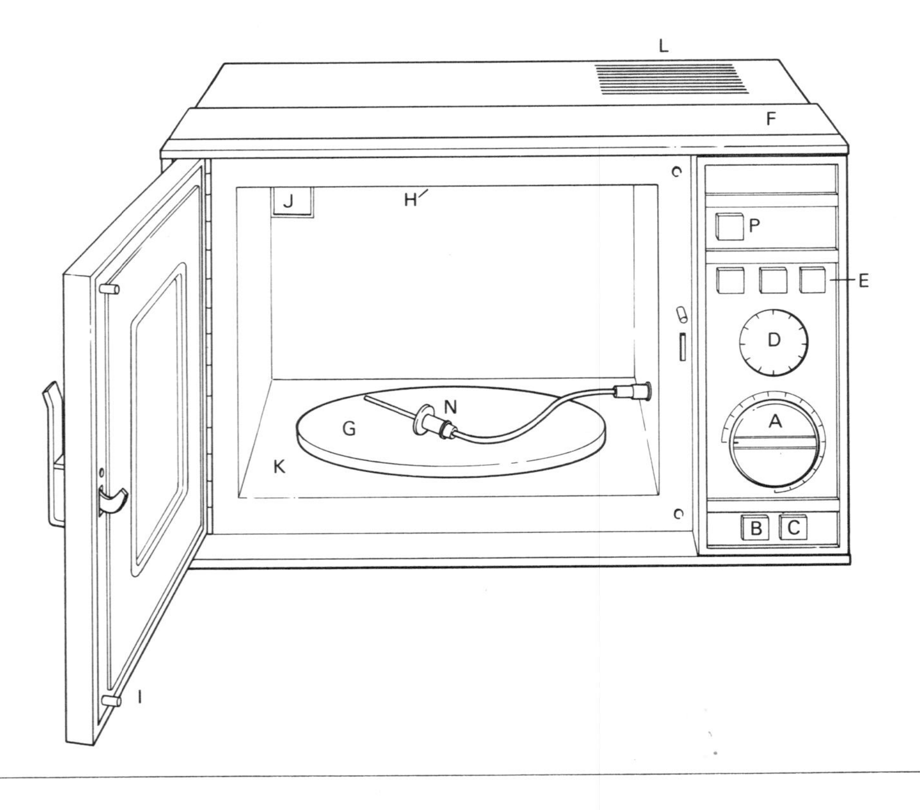

Generally, the filter is removable and should be checked and cleaned regularly according to the manufacturer's instructions.

M Sometimes the wave stirrer has a special *splash guard* to protect it from food spatterings. Remove and clean this regularly according to the manufacturer's instructions.

N Some models of microwave oven have an *integral thermometer* or *temperature probe*. This enables you to cook foods by their internal temperature, rather than by time. This is especially useful when cooking meat and poultry roasts. The probe has a flexible lead which connects inside the oven cavity. The point of the probe is positioned inside the thickest part of the food being cooked and the desired temperature is selected, rather than setting a timer. When the temperature is reached the oven switches off or keeps the food warm on a low setting. The beauty of this device is that it takes the guesswork out of timing dishes. Use it along with more conventional methods of testing foods for never-fail results.

O Since the conventional thermometer cannot be used in the microwave oven some manufacturers supply a special *microwave thermometer* for use in cooking foods.

P An increasing number of microwave ovens now have a *defrost control*. This control enables foods to defrost evenly by giving a short burst of energy followed by a rest period, then repeating the process until the food is evenly thawed. In ovens without a defrost control this procedure must be done manually. It is a very useful feature for freezer owners.

Additional Special Features

Keep warm/stay hot controls These controls are based on a very low power setting and enable food to be kept warm for up to 1 hour without further cooking.

Touch controls These function just like more conventional controls but only require a finger tip touch to operate.

Memory controls These are one of the latest developments and enable the cook to select various power settings with different timings for accurate cooking. For example a defrost setting may be selected initially to defrost food automatically, followed by a cooking setting to cook the same food all in one operation.

Dual level or multiple level cooking The microwave energy is fed into these ovens from the sides rather than from the top or base. The oven may have one or more racks, rather like a conventional oven, and this allows foods to be cooked at different power levels. Normally the foods in the higher positions or on the racks receive more microwave energy than those on the floor of the oven. So, place those foods which require longer cooking on the racks and those which simply need reheating or keeping warm on the base. This facility is useful as it allows you to cook an entire meal in the microwave in one operation, but it does require careful planning.

Types of Microwave Oven

There are three types of microwave oven on the market, the countertop or portable model, the double oven model and a combination model. The choice you make will depend upon a good number of factors including price, size, features available and what you expect the microwave to do.

When choosing an oven consider your present and future needs and the type of cooking you and your family prefer, then look for a microwave oven to fit in with your other appliances. It is wise to consider your microwave as an adjunct to, rather than a replacement for your existing appliances.

Having noted these requirements, look at the models available: do they meet your demands? Does the oven carry the BEAB mark of safety or the Electricity Council's 'approved for safety' label? Does it have a guarantee, or full, or limited warranty? Check too the guarantee period, if any, for the magnetron and any servicing arrangements. Inspect the model for good overall design and you should be able to make a sensible choice.

Portable microwave ovens Also called countertop models, these simply require a 13 or 15 amp plug. They will sit neatly on a work surface or trolley or can be carried from room to room. This is useful for quickly reheating food in the dining room or for use with an extension lead out of doors. Some portable or countertop models can be built into your kitchen or dining room units. Your microwave manufacturer will give the best advice on this and your kitchen unit manufacturer will supply details of the ideal fixing kit. Follow the guidelines on page 18 for siting and ventilating a portable or countertop model.

Double oven microwave cookers These are available in two forms: firstly as a freestanding cooker with a conventional oven under the hob and a microwave oven at eye-level; or as a built-in, double oven unit comprising a microwave oven and a separate conventional oven. The grill is usually situated in the top of the conventional oven. The advantages of the double oven unit incorporating a microwave oven are enormous because they allow you to use these complementary methods of cooking efficiently. You can, however, use your countertop model with your existing conventional oven in the same way.

Combination ovens These ovens have the facility to cook conventionally and by microwave energy, either separately, or in sequence, as preferred. In some models it is also possible to grill and cook by microwave energy at the same time. The advantages of combination ovens are numerous, and fast cooking by microwave coupled with conventional browning is hard to beat!

In such combination models the microwave oven output is usually lower than that in countertop or double oven models.

Factors Which Affect Microwave Cooking

Starting temperature of food The colder the food the longer it will take to heat up or cook and vice versa. For best results, defrost frozen foods first, then cook them. Remember, too, that room temperatures may differ appreciably during the year so adjust your cooking times accordingly. Cooking times given in the recipes refer to the starting temperature of the foods as they are normally stored.

Density of food The denser the food the longer it takes to cook. For example, a dense piece of meat or vegetable will take longer to defrost, reheat or cook than light, porous foods such as bread, cakes and puddings.

Remember that when cooking both a dense and light substance together extra care is needed to apply more energy to the denser mass of food. For example, when cooking a pie, insert a rolled-up piece of brown paper about 2.5 cm/1 in. in length into the pie to direct the energy into the filling rather than to the crust.

Composition of food Fats and sugars absorb microwave energy faster than other liquids and so they will cook faster and reach a higher temperature than water-based foods. It takes longer to cook foods which are high in moisture like meats and vegetables than it does to cook those with little water like bread, cakes and biscuits.

Quantity of food In both conventional and microwave cooking, small amounts of food usually take less time to cook than large ones. This is most apparent with microwave cooking, where timings are directly related to the number of servings. If you double the amount of food being cooked in the microwave the cooking time will increase by about half as much again.

Size of food In both conventional and microwave cooking, small pieces of food cook faster than large ones. Portions that are similar in size and shape cook more evenly (see diagram below).

Shape of food In both conventional and microwave cooking, thin areas of food cook faster than the thick areas. This can be controlled in microwave cooking by placing thick pieces to the outer edge of the dish with thin pieces towards the centre (see diagram below).

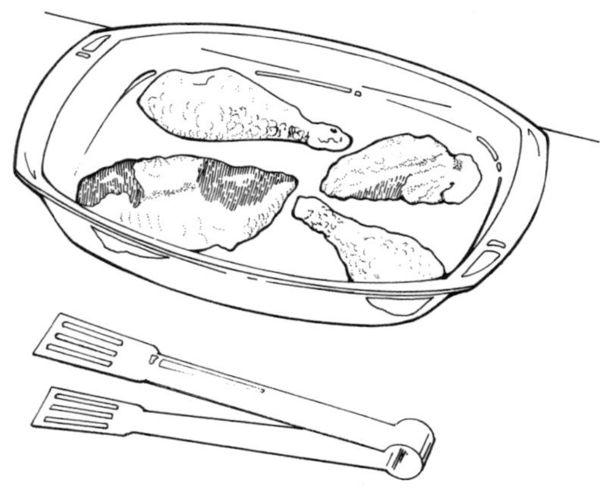

Round and ring shapes cook more evenly than square or oval shapes where the energy seems to concentrate in the corners and causes overcooking. Protect such corners with small pieces of foil to shield them during cooking.

Height in oven In both microwave and conventional cooking, areas which are closest to the source of heat or energy cook faster. For even cooking, turn over, rotate or shield vulnerable areas during cooking.

Bones in meat Bone conducts heat in food. Wherever possible, for even cooking remove the bone and roll the meat, tying it securely into a neat shape with string. If a piece of meat is cooked with the bone in, remember that the meat next to the bone will cook faster. Shield this area of meat with a little foil after about half of the cooking time to prevent overcooking.

Pricking foods to release pressure Steam builds up pressure in foods which are tightly covered by a skin or membrane. Prick potatoes, egg yolks and livers or giblets with a fork before cooking to prevent them from bursting (see diagram below). Likewise if covering food with cling film during cooking, prick or snip two holes in the top of the covering to prevent it from ballooning up during cooking. Also, remove the cling film carefully after cooking – the build-up of steam means the air inside is very hot.

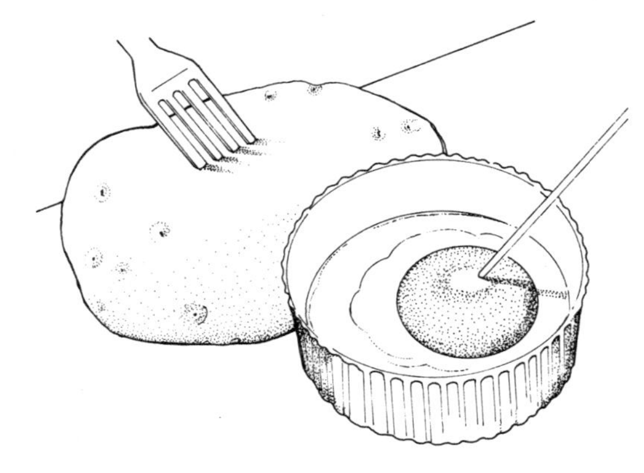

Vulnerable foods Bury vulnerable foods which attract microwave energy, such as cheese or meat, in less vulnerable foods during cooking. For example cover them with a sauce or with vegetables as shown below.

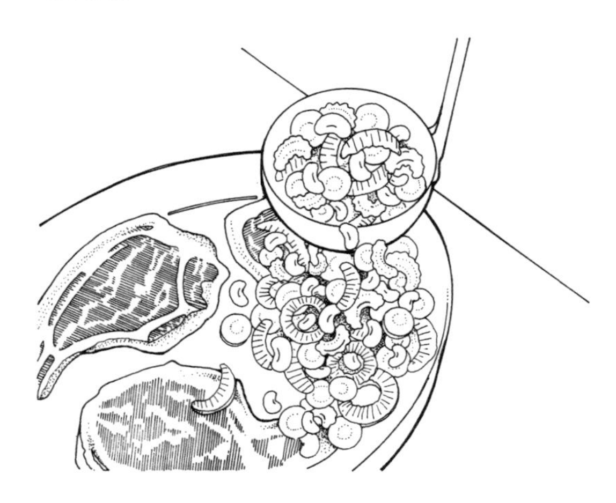

Standing time Due to residual heat, all food continues to cook for a little while after it has been removed from the oven, whether cooked by the microwave or by a conventional method. With microwave cooking it is important to observe this standing time and also to under cook foods a little to allow for the fact that the residual heat will continue to cook it. Leave to stand before deciding whether to cook the food a little longer.

It is especially important to note the standing times quoted when cooking meats. Wrap the meat in foil to keep it warm during this period. After the standing time meat will carve more easily than before.

Browning The brown colouring on the surface of foods is achieved over a period of time by a chemical reaction between food sugars and amino acids with the application of heat. Because of the speed of microwave cooking the surface temperature of the food does not change sufficiently to enable this process to occur significantly. So most foods cooked in the microwave lack the brown appearance expected of them. If you prefer browned foods, there are several ways to overcome this lack of colour.

1 Brown the food under the grill prior to cooking in the microwave.

2 Brown foods after cooking, either under the grill or in the conventional oven.

3 Cover meats and poultry, as well as vegetables, with rich sauces and dark-coloured gravies.

4 Cakes, breads or biscuits can be coated with frosting, icing or nuts, or sprinkled with a dark spice mixture before cooking.

5 Pre-brown certain foods on a browning dish specially designed for the microwave.

6 Coat meat and poultry lightly with a little well-coloured seasoning. For example try a mixture of butter and paprika, a packet of seasoned coating mix, browned breadcrumbs, soy sauce, brown sauce, tomato ketchup, Worcestershire sauce, barbecue sauce, herbs, crumbled beef stock cubes, dry soup mixes (like onion and mushroom), jams and marmalades, crushed crisps or crumbled cooked bacon.

Why Have a Microwave Oven?

Microwave ovens, once thought the extravagant playthings of the cook, have quickly found a useful place in the kitchen. Not least of all because of their advantages over conventional cooking.

Speed You can save up to three-quarters of normal cooking times, but generally microwave cooking takes about one-third to one-quarter of the conventional cooking time. Variations occur according to the starting temperature of the food, its density, shape and the quantity being cooked.

Economy Since the cooking time is so short you are bound to save money. If you have any doubts simply compare the electricity or gas you would use to bake a jacket potato in the conventional oven against the small amount of electricity used to cook a jacket potato in 5–6 minutes in the microwave oven.

Installation costs are often negligible with portable or countertop models. Since the energy is available for immediate use there is no costly heat-up period to observe. When the microwave oven is switched off the food will still continue to cook by means of its residual conducted heat.

Efficiency The energy in the microwave oven is directed straight to the food so there is no heat loss into the kitchen itself and it is thought to be up to four times as efficient as cooking conventionally.

Smells or cooking odours These are reduced to a minimum because of the quick cooking time and because they are largely contained within the oven cavity.

Coolness As explained earlier, the microwave oven and its utensils stay cool when cooking, so the kitchen itself will stay cooler than with conventional cooking, and there is less chance of having a nasty burn from the microwave oven. With very short cooking times oven gloves are not even required for handling dishes.

Washing-up Because most microwave cooking is moist you are unlikely to come across baked-on and difficult to clean dishes thereby reducing the washing up time. It is recommended that you cook and serve food in the same container and this reduces washing up considerably.

Cleanliness Cooking in the microwave oven is faster, there often tends to be less spattering, baking-on and general spill-overs so your kitchen stays a cleaner place. Oven walls will simply need a wipe with a soapy cloth.

Defrosting The freezer is a wonderful help with menu planning if, of course, you remember to take foods out of the freezer in advance of requiring them. If you have a microwave oven this necessity becomes a thing of the past: simply defrost, then cook in one simple operation for perfect results at a moment's notice.

Reheating The problem of conventional cooking is that you need to eat when foods are cooked or soon afterwards. Traditional 'keeping warm' tactics often result in dried out foods that both look and taste that way. Reheating in the microwave brings food to the table minutes or even hours after cooking without the slightest trace of having been cooked before. This is especially useful for families with an unreliable eating routine.

Nutritional value and flavour Because it is important to time foods accurately for microwave cooking it is unlikely that you overcook foods and therefore reduce their nutritional value. Colour, flavour and texture are likely to be at their very best.

Versatility Don't forget that as well as producing super meals your microwave oven will also cope with those niggly little chores in basic food preparation like dissolving gelatine, melting chocolate, roasting nuts and reheating liquids in super quick time. This adds a new dimension that conventional cooking can't hope to match.

Mobility It's difficult – impossible – to move your conventional cooker into the garden or dining room, but not so with the microwave. Look upon it as your portable cooking appliance for super efficiency in all parts of the house and garden.

Overcooking With careful timing this is likely to become a thing of the past. No need to keep foods warm for long periods either; simply turn off until required then quickly reheat for delicious piping hot food that is not dried out.

Disadvantages of Microwave Cooking

Browning Since there is no direct surface heat, food does not brown readily in the microwave oven within the short cooking times. Browning aids such as brown sauce, soy sauce, seasoning sauces and spices will help to overcome this if it worries you. Often the best procedure, however, is to pop the cooked dish under a hot grill.

Metals You simply *must* forget your traditional metal cookware. Metals reflect microwave energy back to the magnetron and can damage it, so do not use them. Having said that, the materials that can be used in the microwave range from paper through to plastic and china so you can often use a much wider choice of cooking vessels than you could for traditional cooking.

Impossible foods You cannot cook certain foods successfully in the microwave oven. Hard-boiled eggs cannot be cooked since the pressure that builds up in the shells causes them to explode. Meringues do not dry out sufficiently, Yorkshire puddings fall flat and pancakes will not go brown or cook satisfactorily. It was once thought to be impossible to cook soufflés in the microwave. However, if the basic sauce is adjusted and stabilised by using evaporated milk this can be done.

Where Should I Position the Microwave Oven?

Introducing a microwave oven of the portable kind into your kitchen is surprisingly easy. All that is required is a fused power socket outlet to match the plug, a strong, stable surface on which to stand the cooker or a firm base if the oven is of the built-in kind, and sufficient space between the vent and adjoining surface or a suitable venting outlet. If the vents are at the back of the cooker remember not to push it too close to a wall or if they are on top do not squeeze it into a cupboard where there is no chance of ventilation. If in any doubt always refer to the manufacturer's instructions.

How Should I Clean the Microwave Oven?

The microwave is very easy to clean because the oven walls stay cool during cooking and so there is less baked-on or scorched food to deal with. Always wipe up spills immediately or they will continue to absorb microwave energy and thereby slow down the cooking operation. Disconnect

Top: Wilted Lettuce Salad (page 127); *Below:* Sausage-stuffed Potatoes, Crispy Bacon-stuffed Potatoes, Seafood-stuffed Potatoes and Stuffed Potatoes with Blue Cheese (page 122)

the oven from the electricity supply when cleaning.

Wipe over the exterior and interior with a damp, soapy cloth at regular intervals or use a microwave oven cleaner as recommended by the manufacturer.

Removable bases and shelves should always be cleaned regularly as, too, should the door seals. To remove any cooking smells which may linger inside the oven, place a bowl containing 3 parts water to 1 part lemon juice in the oven and cook for 5–10 minutes. Wipe the oven dry after cooking.

Take care when washing the outside not to splash water over the exterior vents. These should also be wiped over occasionally to remove any condensation. Clean any air filters or stirrer fan guards regularly as recommended by the manufacturer.

Also remember to have the microwave checked or serviced by a qualified engineer every 12 months, or as recommended by the manufacturer.

Microwave Cooking Techniques

Most of the techniques used in microwave cooking are the same as those employed in conventional cooking, but because of the speed they have to be followed carefully and employed at regular intervals for good cooking results. Most of the following techniques either quicken the cooking process or promote even heating.

Turning over We turn foods over in conventional cooking and this is also important in microwave cooking to ensure even results. Turning is often used with the following three techniques – stirring, rotating and rearranging.

Top: Mexican Salami Medley (page 135);
Below: Silverside Summer Salad (page 136)

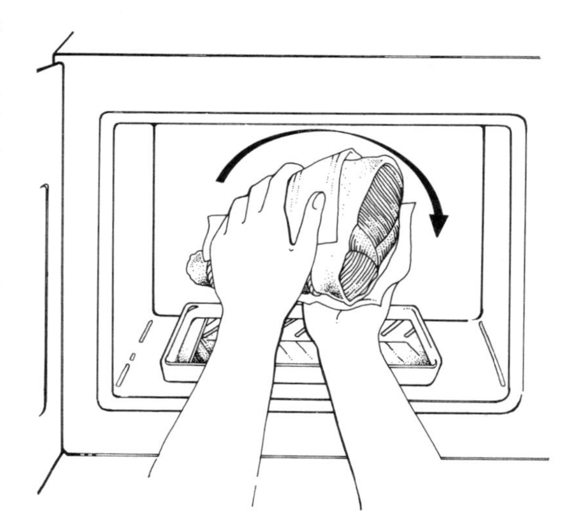

Stirring Stirring helps to distribute the heat evenly through the food throughout the cooking period. Always stir from the outside of the dish (as shown in the diagram below), where the food seems to cook first, bringing the outer cooked portions into the centre.

Rotating When the food cannot be stirred or turned over the dish should be rotated in the oven. This is necessary when the microwave oven does not have a turntable and is particularly important when cooking cakes and large items such as meat roasts.

Rearranging To ensure even cooking, foods can be rearranged in the dish during cooking or defrosting. In most cases this is generally only necessary once during the cooking or defrosting time.

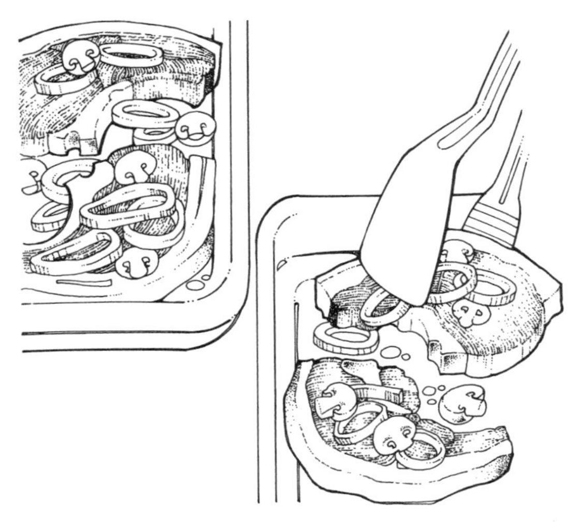

Covering foods Covering foods during cooking can speed up the cooking and retain the moisture. A loose cover will also prevent spattering on the oven walls, especially from fatty foods like bacon and chops.

A tight-fitting lid to a dish, cling film, greaseproof paper, roasting bags without the metal ties (use an elastic band or a piece of string to secure), absorbent kitchen paper, or an inverted plate will all prove useful covers while cooking.

Arranging foods When cooking in the microwave, arrange foods in one of the following ways.

a) If you are cooking several items of the same food then arrange them in a ring shape, leaving the centre empty for even heating. The centre of a dish receives less microwave energy while the sides receive equal amounts.

b) Unevenly shaped foods like chicken pieces, whole fish or chops should be placed with the thinner parts to the centre where they will receive less energy.

Shielding Shielding is protecting vulnerable parts of the food from overcooking. This is the only time when small pieces of foil can be introduced into the microwave oven. Make sure that the area uncovered is greater than the area covered with foil or the microwaves may arc. The foil will reflect the microwaves from sensitive areas including the wings and tips of poultry and game, the head and tails of fish, the breast bone of poultry and the bone ends of chops.

Variable Control Cooking

Conventional cooking uses different temperature settings to control the rate of cooking food. In a basic on/off microwave oven, the rate of cooking can only be controlled by timing. Variable control models, however, can exercise more control over the cooking procedure by their variable control power settings.

Manufacturers can alter the power setting in the microwave oven in two different ways.They can either pulse in the microwave energy on FULL POWER for a short time, then switch it off automatically at variable intervals to achieve an overall lower cooking speed, or they can reduce the microwave energy entering the oven for the entire cooking period without switching on or off. Both are efficient methods of reducing the power levels to below full power.

Variable control offers the cook a greater amount of flexibility in cooking operations like defrosting, reheating, keeping warm, roasting and simmering.

Use of the power control dial

LOW (1, KEEP WARM, LOW or 2)
The energy is on for about 25% of the time. It is used for keeping foods warm for up to about 30 minutes. It is also useful for softening butter, cream cheese, melting chocolate, proving yeast and very gentle cooking.

DEFROST (3, STEW, MEDIUM/LOW or 4)
The energy on this setting is on for about 40% of the time. It is used for defrosting meat, poultry and fish and for cooking slow-cooking casseroles and less tender cuts of meat. It is also useful for cooking rich fruit cakes and for cooking some delicate egg dishes.

MEDIUM (4, DEFROST, MEDIUM or 6)
The energy is on for about 50% of the time on this power setting. It is used for roasting meats and poultry if not on full power. It is also useful for cooking pâtés and yeast doughs.

MEDIUM/HIGH (6, ROAST, MEDIUM/HIGH or 7–8)
The energy is on for about 60–75% of the time. It is a useful setting for reheating.

FULL (7, FULL/HIGH or 10)
The energy is on for 100% of the time. This is the only setting available on basic on/off microwave models. It is the prime cooking level and is used for quick cooking of meats, fish, poultry, eggs, cheese, pasta, rice, cakes and desserts.

Note Use the settings above in relation to the chart given on page 27 which shows comparable descriptions of variable control power settings for popular microwave ovens and gives a guide to adjusting the cooking time.

Microwave Cooking Utensils

There is little doubt that the range of cooking utensils that can be used in the microwave oven is wider than those that can be used for cooking conventionally. Dishes which are suitable for microwave cooking should not act as a barrier to microwave energy nor should they absorb the energy.

Since metal reflects microwave energy you should not use it in the microwave oven. Even small amounts will reflect the energy, so check that plates and china do not have metal trims, that casseroles do not have metal bases, that glass is not of the lead crystal type, that dishes do not have metal screws or attachments and that freezer, cooking or roasting bags do not have metal ties.

In addition to the material, the shape of the dish is also important. Round and ring shapes give the most even cooking results, whereas square and oval shapes have a tendency to overcook in the corners. Since the penetration of microwave energy is to a depth of about 5 cm/2 in, shallow dishes give better cooking results than deeper dishes. A straight-sided container is also better than a curved one, as the microwaves can penetrate more evenly.

China, glass and pottery Ovenproof china, pottery and glass are suitable for the microwave oven. Check that there is no metallic trim, no glued-on handles and, in the case of pottery, that the dish is non-porous. To check if the dish is non-porous, heat it in the microwave for 15–20 seconds. If the dish feels warm to the touch then it should not be used for microwave cooking.

Paper Paper is ideal for quick cooking or low power cooking such as reheating, defrosting or short cooking of foods with a low sugar, fat or water content. Paper plates, absorbent kitchen paper, napkins, paper cups, cartons and paper pulp board all have their uses. Absorbent kitchen paper and greaseproof paper are especially useful for covering foods and preventing spattering on the oven walls.

Wax-coated paper plates and cups should be avoided since the high temperatures in foods will cause the wax to melt. They can however be used when defrosting cold foods like desserts and frozen cakes.

Plastics 'Dishwasher Safe' is a useful indicator as to the suitability of a plastic container for the microwave cooker, but do not use them for cooking foods with a high fat or sugar content since the temperatures reached in cooking such foods are extremely high. Other plastics like foam cups, baby bottles, plastic cling film and boil-in-the-bags are also suitable for microwave oven use. Melamine, however, is not recommended for microwave cooking since it absorbs enough energy to cause charring. If a plastic cling-film cover, plastic cooking pouch or bag is used for microwave cooking, remember to puncture it to allow the steam to escape.

Cotton and linen Cotton and linen napkins can be used for short reheating purposes; for example, warming bread rolls, but check that the material is 100% cotton or linen and that it does not contain any synthetic fibres.

Straw and wood These are only suitable for short reheating purposes since the moisture in them will tend to dry out causing cracking and charring in time. Wooden spoons can be left in the oven for short cooking periods – for example, when cooking a sauce.

Clay pots Part-glazed or unglazed earthenware cooking pots which are soaked in water prior to cooking can be used effectively in the microwave. They are especially useful for pot-roasting less tender cuts of meat and whole chickens or game birds, as the microwave energy is attracted to the moisture held in the clay and the cooking is slowed down to a gentle simmer.

Soak the base and lid according to the manufacturer's instructions, for about 10–15 minutes. The pots will become very hot during cooking and so are liable to crack if they are subjected to a severe temperature change. For this reason be extra careful about adding new liquids or cold foods to the pot during cooking.

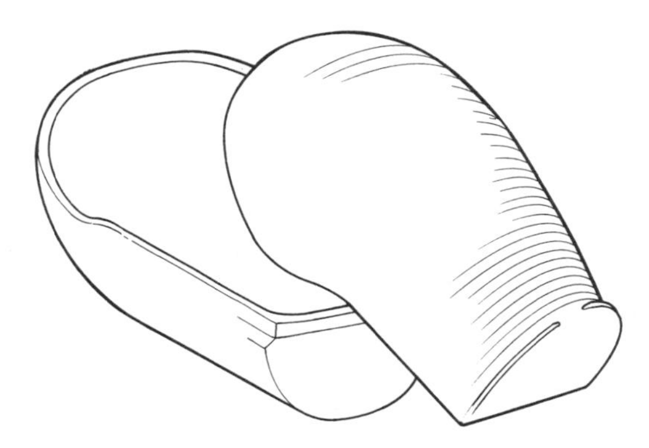

Special microwave utensils There is an ever-widening range of microwave cookware on the market specifically designed for the microwave oven. Some of these products are disposable while others are designed to be re-used a few times, if not permanently. Some can be used, within certain temperature limits, in the conventional oven too and many are safe for use in the dishwasher and freezer. Check the manufacturer's instructions for use and care instructions. The diagram below shows a few examples of microwave cookware.

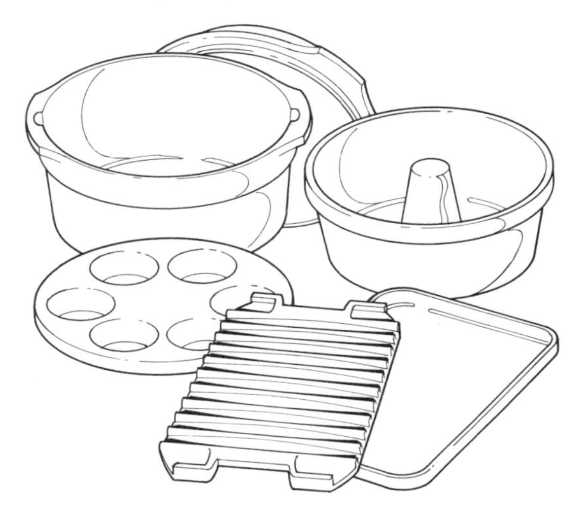

Thermometers specially designed for the microwave are also available. Conventional thermometers cannot be used since the mercury is affected by microwave energy. Insert the thermometer into the thickest part of the food, away from any bone if present, to get accurate readings and results.

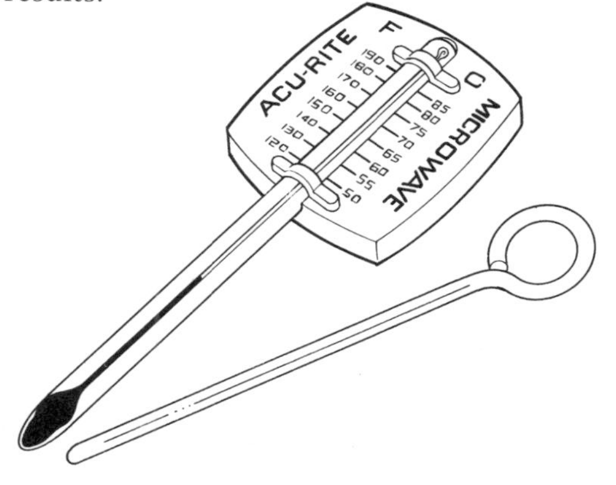

Microwave browning dishes and skillets are ceramic dishes that have a special coating which absorbs microwave energy and so becomes hot when preheated in the microwave according to the manufacturer's instructions – usually about 5 minutes. The food is then placed on the hot surface of the dish to sear and brown the outside as shown in the diagram below. It is very useful for browning steaks, chops, chicken pieces and larger pieces of meat prior to roasting. It can also be used for frying eggs and toasting sandwiches. Always use oven gloves when handling a browning dish and protect kitchen surfaces as the dish does get hot.

Microwave roasting racks are also available. Made of hard plastic or ceramic they lift meats and poultry above their juices while cooking. They can also be used for reheating bread and rolls, giving a crisp texture to the end product.

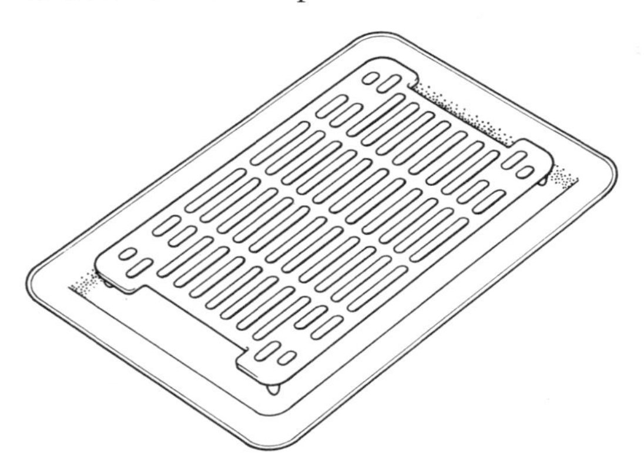

Recipe Guidelines

As with any other new appliance it is important to understand the 'mechanics' of its operation for very best results – it is for this reason that I strongly recommend that you read the introductory section to this book. It will arm you with a wealth of ideas and expertise to get the very best results from the recipes that follow.

All the recipes in this book have been double tested for success on a 700 W variable control microwave oven *without* a turntable. Most recipes, for speed and convenience, require the oven to be used on FULL POWER (that is, working at maximum cooking speed) and are suitable for both on/off control or basic operation microwave ovens as well as those ovens with variable control. It is possible, where a recipe uses another power setting such as LOW, DEFROST, MEDIUM or MEDIUM/HIGH, to make the recipe in a microwave oven without these variable control facilities if you follow the chart on the opposite page. Cook the food for the equivalent FULL POWER time and allow a standing or resting period every few minutes during the cooking time. Familiarity with your own microwave oven will indicate the ideal equivalent times and standing periods, but initially use the chart as a basic guideline.

Microwave ovens differ appreciably from one model to another and slightly from each other even within the same range or brand. For this reason always err on the side of safety and cook foods for the minimum times stated, adding a little extra time after testing. It is always easy to cook a little longer but impossible to take time away.

If your microwave oven has a power wattage which is higher than 700 W, then reduce the times in the book accordingly. If your oven has a power wattage which is lower than 700 W, then increase the times accordingly.

The instructions have been devised for an oven without a turntable and therefore include instructions for turning and rotating dishes to get the very best, even cooking results. If your oven has a turntable then these procedures are not required.

Different manufacturers present the variable control settings on their ovens in different ways. To avoid the risk of offending or dissuading anyone from using the recipes if their controls differ from the ones I have used in this book, I have invented, and used, a set of control settings which should prove compatible with all domestic microwave ovens. They are shown in the chart with the equivalent settings available on popular models and the power ratings. If you are in any doubt about the power output of your model at different levels of operation, then refer to your manufacturer's instruction booklet for guidance.

Guide to Comparative Temperature Settings

Description of settings used in this book	LOW		DEFROST	MEDIUM		MEDIUM/ HIGH	FULL
Descriptions of settings available on popular microwave ovens	1 KEEP WARM LOW 2	2 SIMMER MEDIUM/ 3	3 STEW LOW 4	4 DEFROST MEDIUM 5	5 BAKE MEDIUM 6	6 ROAST HIGH 7–8	7 FULL/HIGH NORMAL 10
Approximate % power input	25%	30%	40%	50%	60%	75%	100%
Approximate power output in watts	150 w	200 w	250 w	300 w	400 w	500–550 w	650–700 w
*Cooking time in minutes**	4	3¼	2½	2	1¾	1¼	1
	8	6¾	5	4	3¼	2¾	2
	12	10	7½	6	5	4	3
	16	13¼	10	8	6¾	5¼	4
	20	16¾	12½	10	8¼	6¾	5
	24	20	15	12	10	8	6
	28	23¼	17½	14	11¾	9¼	7
	32	26¾	20	16	13¼	10¾	8
	36	30	22½	18	15	12	9
	40	33¼	25	20	16½	13¼	10

**For times greater than 10 minutes simply add the figures in the appropriate columns together.*

Soups and Starters

The microwave can prove to be a most helpful friend when you are preparing hot and cold appetisers for meals. A minute or two after your guests arrive, you can offer them tempting hot nibbles to stimulate both appetite and conversation, then follow with a flavoursome soup or starter at just a few minutes' notice. Since all the preparation can be done ahead you can join your guests too, safe in knowing the microwave will take care of any last-minute cooking or reheating. It will also help with that cumbersome chore, the washing up, because you can heat and serve in the same bowl or on the same plate.

Cold starters like pâtés, mousses and potted shellfish can be made well ahead in the microwave with the minimum of fuss and stored in the refrigerator until required. So too, hot dishes that need longer cooking, like pasta bakes, stuffed tomatoes and baked vegetables – prepare them well ahead and simply reheat for a couple of minutes. The microwave won't give your food that dried out 'cooked-again' appearance.

Cook-ahead cold starters have always been the main ally of the busy hostess, but with the microwave you can surprise friends and family alike with some mouthwatering hot beginnings to memorable meals.

Top left: Smoked Haddock Chowder (page 34); *Below:* Red Pepper and Tomato Soup (page 33)
Overleaf *Left:* Spaghetti with Bacon and Pesto Sauce (page 156); *Top right:* Speedy Italian Pizza (page 142); *Bottom right:* Savoury Tomato Rice (page 154)

RED PEPPER AND TOMATO SOUP

(Illustrated on page 29)
Serves 4
Power setting FULL
Total cooking time 12½ minutes

2 tablespoons oil
1 onion, peeled and sliced
2 red peppers, seeds removed and sliced
450 g/1 lb tomatoes, peeled, seeds removed and chopped
600 ml/1 pint hot ham stock
1 teaspoon dried mixed herbs
2 teaspoons granulated sugar
4–5 teaspoons concentrated tomato purée
1 tablespoon lemon juice
salt and freshly ground black pepper
yogurt to serve

Place the oil in a large bowl and cook for ½ minute. Add the onion and sliced pepper and cook for 6 minutes. Add the tomatoes and stir in the stock, herbs, sugar, tomato purée and lemon juice. Cover and cook for a further 6 minutes, then taste and adjust the seasoning.

Remove a few slices of pepper from the bowl and purée the soup. Return the reserved pepper slices to the soup and serve topped with a swirl of yogurt.

CELERY AND STILTON SOUP

Serves 4
Power setting FULL
Total cooking time 13 minutes

40 g/1½ oz butter
175 g/6 oz celery, trimmed and finely chopped
3 tablespoons plain flour
600 ml/1 pint hot chicken stock
225 g/8 oz Stilton cheese, grated
salt and freshly ground black pepper

Place the butter in a bowl and cook for 1 minute to melt. Add the celery, tossing to coat in the butter, then cover and cook for 4 minutes. Add the flour and cook for 1 minute. Gradually add the stock and cook for 6 minutes, stirring every 2 minutes until thickened.

Gradually add the cheese, a little at a time, stirring, until melted. Season to taste and cook for 1 minute to reheat. Serve with warm wholemeal bread.

Top: Bacon Dip with Crudités (page 39); *Below:* Baked Avocados (page 40)

CURRIED BEAN AND APPLE SOUP

Serves 4–6
Power setting FULL
Total cooking time 11 minutes

25 g/1 oz butter or margarine
1 onion, peeled and chopped
450 g/1 lb cooking apples, peeled, cored and chopped
2 (225-g/7.9-oz) cans curried beans with sultanas
600 ml/1 pint boiling chicken stock
salt and freshly ground black pepper
1 dessert apple, cored and thinly sliced to serve

Place the butter or margarine in a large bowl and cook for 1 minute to melt. Add the onion and cook for 2 minutes. Add the apples, three-quarters of the beans and the stock. Cover with cling-film, snipping two holes in the top to allow the steam to escape. Cook for 6 minutes, allow to cool slightly, then purée in a liquidiser until smooth. Alternatively press the soup through a fine sieve. Add the reserved beans to the soup with seasoning to taste and cook for 2 minutes to reheat. Serve topped with thinly sliced apple.

SMOKED HADDOCK CHOWDER

(Illustrated on page 29)
Serves 4
Power setting FULL
Total cooking time 19–20 minutes

225 g/8 oz potatoes, peeled and grated
175 g/6 oz onions, peeled and grated
100 g/4 oz celery, finely chopped
600 ml/1 pint hot fish or chicken stock
600 ml/1 pint milk
450 g/1 lb smoked haddock fillet, skinned
salt and freshly ground black pepper
2 tablespoons chopped parsley
1 tablespoon lemon juice
paprika or chopped parsley to garnish

Place the potato, onion, celery and stock in a bowl. Cover and cook for 10 minutes, stirring twice during cooking. Add the milk and set aside.

Place the fish in a shallow dish and cover with cling film, snipping two holes in the top to let the steam escape. Cook for 4–5 minutes or until cooked. Cut the haddock into chunks, discarding any bones, then add it to the potato mixture together with seasoning to taste, the parsley and lemon juice. Cover and cook for 5 minutes.

Serve hot sprinkled with paprika or chopped parsley.

THREE FISH SOUP

(Illustrated on page 49 and back cover)
Serves 4–6
Power setting FULL
Total cooking time 15½–17½ minutes

25 g/1 oz butter or margarine
1 small onion, peeled and finely chopped
1 medium potato, peeled and cubed
½ small red chilli, seeds removed and finely chopped
½ teaspoon paprika
225 g/8 oz monk fish or haddock fillet, skinned and cut into chunks
1.15 litres/2 pints hot chicken or fish stock
225 g/8 oz tomatoes, peeled, seeds removed and chopped
1 small clove garlic, crushed
1 bay leaf
1 teaspoon anchovy essence
salt and freshly ground black pepper
100 g/4 oz cooked mussels
100 g/4 oz peeled prawns
5 tablespoons single cream
GARNISH
chopped parsley
a few cooked mussels in their shells (optional)

Place the butter or margarine in a large bowl and cook for ½ minute to melt. Add the onion and potato and cook for 4 minutes. Add the chilli, paprika and monkfish or haddock and cook for a further 4 minutes. Stir in the stock, tomatoes, garlic, bay leaf, anchovy essence and seasoning to taste. Cover and cook for 6–8 minutes or until the potato and fish are cooked.

Stir in the mussels and prawns and cook for 1 minute. Finally, stir in the cream and serve at once garnished with chopped parsley and a few mussels in their shells, if liked.

MUSSEL BISQUE

Serves 4
Power setting FULL
Total cooking time 13–14 minutes

40 g/$1\frac{1}{2}$ oz butter
3 tablespoons plain flour
900 ml/$1\frac{1}{2}$ pints milk
150 ml/$\frac{1}{4}$ pint white wine
salt and freshly ground black pepper
4 (113-g/4-oz) cans mussels, drained and liquor reserved
3 tablespoons double cream
2 egg yolks
1 tablespoon chopped parsley

Place the butter in a large jug or basin and cook for 1 minute. Add the flour, mixing well. Gradually add the milk and cook for 6–7 minutes or until the sauce is thick and smooth, stirring every 1 minute.

Transfer to a soup tureen or serving bowl and add the wine. Season to taste and add the mussels, then cover and cook for 4 minutes. Add a little of the drained fish liquor to the cream and egg yolks mixing well. Stir into the soup. Cook for 2 minutes, stirring every $\frac{1}{2}$ minute. *Do not allow the soup to boil.* Sprinkle with parsley and serve.

ANGLER'S TREAT

Serves 4
Power setting MEDIUM or FULL
Total cooking time 4 or $7\frac{1}{2}$ minutes

4 large tomatoes
3 hard-boiled eggs, shelled and very finely chopped
1 (175-g/6-oz) smoked trout
2 teaspoons horseradish sauce
salt and freshly ground black pepper
parsley sprigs to garnish

Using a serrated knife, cut off and reserve the tops of the tomatoes from the stem end. Carefully scoop out the seeds and pulp, using a teaspoon. Discard the pulp from all but one of the tomatoes. Mix the reserved tomato pulp with the chopped egg. Flake the flesh from the trout and add to the egg mixture together with the horseradish sauce and seasoning to taste. Mix well to combine all the ingredients, then spoon equal amounts into the tomato cases and top with the reserved lids.

Stand the tomatoes on a plate and cook on MEDIUM POWER for $7\frac{1}{2}$ minutes or on full power for 4 minutes, giving the dish a half turn once during the cooking time. Garnish each tomato cap with a sprig of parsley before serving. Serve hot or allow to cool and serve with a mixed salad.

COQUILLES ST JACQUES

Serves 4
Power setting FULL, MEDIUM and MEDIUM/HIGH
Total cooking time 17½–22½ minutes

40 g/1½ oz butter
100 g/4 oz button mushrooms, sliced
2 spring onions, trimmed and chopped
1 stick celery, chopped
15 g/½ oz plain flour
½ teaspoon salt
¼ teaspoon dried thyme
½ small canned pimiento, finely chopped
4 tablespoons dry white wine
8–10 scallops, cleaned
3 tablespoons single cream
1 egg yolk, beaten
CRUMB TOPPING
25 g/1 oz butter
25 g/1 oz fine dry breadcrumbs
2 tablespoons Parmesan cheese

Place the butter, mushrooms, onion and celery in a dish and cook on FULL POWER for 2–3 minutes, stirring after 1 minute.

Add the flour, salt, thyme and pimiento, mixing well. Gradually add the wine to blend the ingredients together. Add the scallops and cook on FULL POWER for 5–6 minutes, stirring halfway through the cooking time. Stir in the single cream and egg yolk and cook on MEDIUM POWER for 3–4 minutes, stirring halfway through the cooking time.

To make the topping, place the butter in a small bowl and cook on FULL POWER for ½ minute. Stir in the breadcrumbs and Parmesan cheese.

Divide the fish mixture between 4 scallop shells or small dishes, sprinkle with the crumb mixture and cover with dampened greaseproof paper. Cook for 7–9 minutes on MEDIUM/HIGH POWER until hot, rearranging halfway through the cooking time. Serve hot.

SMOKED MACKEREL MOUSSE

Serves 4–6
Power setting DEFROST and FULL
Total cooking time 12½–13 minutes

300 ml/½ pint milk
½ small onion, peeled
1 small carrot
1 bay leaf
2 tablespoons water
2 teaspoons gelatine
25 g/1 oz butter or margarine
2 tablespoons plain flour
275 g/10 oz smoked mackerel fillet, skinned and flaked
1 large onion, peeled and chopped
1 tablespoon horseradish relish
150 ml/¼ pint natural yogurt
1 tablespoon lemon juice
salt and freshly ground black pepper
2 egg whites

Place the milk in a jug with the onion half, carrot and bay leaf and cook on DEFROST POWER for 10 minutes. Meanwhile, place the water in a bowl and sprinkle over the gelatine. Leave to soak for 10 minutes.

Place the butter or margarine in a bowl and cook on FULL POWER for 1 minute. Add the flour, mixing well. Strain the milk and gradually add it to the flour mixture, stirring continuously. Cook on FULL POWER for 1½–2 minutes, stirring every ½ minute until thick and smooth. Stir in the soaked gelatine until dissolved. Allow to cool.

Place the sauce, fish, onion and horseradish relish in a liquidiser and purée until smooth. Stir in the yogurt, lemon juice and seasoning to taste.

Whisk the egg whites until they stand in firm peaks and fold into the mackerel mixture. Spoon into six ramekin or small soufflé dishes and chill until set. Serve chilled, with warm toast or French bread.

Simple Salmon Mousse

Serves 6
Power setting FULL
Total cooking time 1 minute

1 (439-g/15½-oz) can red salmon, drained and flaked
6 tablespoons mayonnaise
1 tablespoon concentrated tomato purée
salt and freshly ground black pepper
dash of Tabasco sauce
3 tablespoons lemon juice
20 g/¾ oz gelatine
5 egg whites
Garnish
cucumber slices
lemon slices

Mash the salmon with the mayonnaise and tomato purée. Season and flavour to taste with the salt, pepper and Tabasco sauce. Place the lemon juice in a small bowl and sprinkle over the gelatine. Leave for 2–3 minutes to soften, then heat in the microwave for 1 minute. Allow to cool slightly, then stir into the salmon mixture until well blended.

Whisk the egg whites until they stand in stiff peaks. Fold into the salmon mixture then turn into a large, oiled fish mould or terrine and chill until set.

To serve, dip the mould briefly into hot water, then invert it on to a serving dish. Garnish with cucumber and lemon slices. Serve with melba toast or brown bread and butter.

Bacon Dip

(Illustrated on page 32)
Serves 4
Power setting FULL
Total cooking time 5–6 minutes

6 rashers rindless bacon
225 g/8 oz full fat soft cheese
3–4 tablespoons single cream
freshly ground black pepper

Place the bacon on a bacon rack or plate and cover with absorbent kitchen paper. Cook for 5–6 minutes until crisp. Allow to cool.

Beat the cheese to soften, then add the cream to make a soft dropping consistency. Crumble the bacon and fold into the dip. Season to taste with pepper and serve with crisp vegetables or crackers.

CRAB AND RIGATONI GRATINÉ

Serves 4
Power setting FULL
Total cooking time $24\frac{1}{2}$–$28\frac{1}{2}$ minutes

75 g/3 oz butter
1 Spanish onion, peeled and chopped
3 tablespoons plain flour
600 ml/1 pint milk
3 tablespoons capers, roughly chopped
1 teaspoon malt vinegar
1 (184-g/$6\frac{1}{2}$-oz) can crabmeat
salt and freshly ground black pepper
275 g/10 oz rigatoni
750 m/$1\frac{1}{4}$ pints boiling water
100 g/4 oz Lancashire cheese, grated

Place the butter in a bowl and cook for $1\frac{1}{2}$ minutes to melt. Add the onion and cook for 3 minutes, stirring after 2 minutes. Add the flour and cook for 1 minute. Gradually add the milk and cook for 5–6 minutes, stirring every 2 minutes until smooth and thick. Stir in the capers, malt vinegar and flaked crab. Season well to taste.

Place the pasta in a dish with the boiling water. Cover and cook for 12–14 minutes. Allow to stand for 5 minutes, then drain.

Fold the pasta into the crab sauce and place in a deep dish. Sprinkle with the cheese and cook for 3–4 minutes until hot. Brown under a hot grill to serve.

BAKED AVOCADOS

(Illustrated on page 32)
Serves 4
Power setting FULL
Total cooking time 4 minutes

2 large ripe avocado pears
lemon juice to brush
50 g/2 oz fresh brown breadcrumbs
2 teaspoons finely grated onion
4 tablespoons single cream
salt and freshly ground black pepper
15 g/$\frac{1}{2}$ oz butter
sliced stuffed olives, sliced gherkin or lemon twists and parsley sprigs to garnish

Cut the avocados in half lengthways, remove the stones and brush with lemon juice to stop discoloration. Scoop out the flesh and coarsely mash it with the breadcrumbs, onion, cream and seasoning to taste. Return the mixture to the avocado shells and dot with butter. Place on a plate, pointed ends inwards, and cook for 4 minutes.

Garnish with sliced stuffed olives, sliced gherkin or lemon twists and parsley sprigs.

FENNEL ITALIENNE

Serves 4
Power setting FULL
Total cooking time 15–18 minutes

2 heads fennel
4 tablespoons water
salt and freshly ground black pepper
75 g/3 oz full fat soft cheese
50 g/2 oz Double Gloucester cheese, grated
1 tablespoon grated Parmesan cheese
1 egg yolk
1 (227-g/8-oz) can tomatoes
1 onion, peeled and chopped
6 stuffed green olives
3 tablespoons red wine
150 ml/$\frac{1}{4}$ pint hot chicken or vegetable stock
$\frac{1}{2}$ teaspoon dried oregano

Trim the fennel into a neat shape discarding any bruised stems. Place in a deep bowl with the water and a little salt. Cover with cling film, snipping two holes in the top to allow the steam to escape, and cook for 10 minutes. Drain and halve each fennel head.

Scoop out and reserve the triangular core and a few inner leaves to form a hollow. Beat the soft cheese with the Double Gloucester, Parmesan and egg yolk. Season to taste and spoon evenly into the hollows.

Meanwhile, purée the reserved fennel with the tomatoes, onion, olives, red wine, stock and oregano. Pour into one large or four small dishes and top with the stuffed fennel. Cover with cling film, snipping two holes in the top, and cook for 5–8 minutes. Rearrange the dishes halfway through the cooking time if individual dishes have been prepared, or give a large dish a half turn. Remove the cling film and brown quickly under a hot grill until golden. Serve at once.

PASTA HORS D'OEUVRE

Serves 4
Power setting FULL
Total cooking time 12 minutes

75 g/3 oz pasta shells
300 ml/½ pint boiling water
1 teaspoon oil
75 g/3 oz lean cooked ham, finely chopped
2 sticks celery, chopped
2 dessert apples, cored and chopped
6 tablespoons French dressing (below)
1 teaspoon concentrated curry sauce or paste
watercress sprigs to garnish

Place the pasta in a deep bowl with the water and oil, cover with cling film, snipping two holes in the top to allow the steam to escape, and cook for 12 minutes. Allow to stand for 10 minutes, drain and allow to cool.

Mix the ham with the celery, apple, French dressing and curry sauce or paste. Fold into the pasta and serve in individual portions garnished with watercress sprigs.

French Dressing Pour 2 tablespoons vinegar and 6 tablespoons salad oil into a jar which has an airtight lid. Add a generous sprinkling of salt and freshly ground black pepper, a pinch of caster sugar and 2 teaspoons chopped mixed fresh herbs. Shake the jar vigorously until the ingredients are all thoroughly mixed.

FESTIVAL SALAD STARTER

Serves 4
Power setting FULL
Total cooking time 4–4½ minutes

2 Spanish onions, peeled and finely sliced
2 green peppers, seeds removed and coarsely chopped
6 small tomatoes, peeled and chopped
4 rashers rindless streaky bacon
1 tablespoon olive or sunflower oil
3 tablespoons vinegar
1 teaspoon chilli powder
salt
few drops of Tabasco sauce
few drops of Worcestershire sauce
1 lettuce

Separate the onion slices into rings and place them in a salad bowl with the green pepper and tomato.

Place the bacon on a microwave bacon rack or plate and cover with absorbent kitchen paper. Cook for 3½–4 minutes until crisp, reserving the bacon drippings. Place the drippings in a small bowl with the oil, vinegar, chilli powder, salt to taste, Tabasco and Worcestershire sauce. Heat in the microwave for ½ minute. Pour over the salad vegetables and toss lightly.

Wash and dry the lettuce and add to the salad vegetables tossing well to mix. Crumble the cool bacon and sprinkle over the salad to serve.

FRENCH COUNTRY PÂTÉ

(Illustrated on page 150)
Serves 6–8
Power setting FULL and MEDIUM
Total cooking time 18 minutes

15 g/½ oz butter
225 g/8 oz chicken livers
350 g/12 oz boneless rabbit, minced
225 g/8 oz lean bacon, rinds removed and minced
250 g/9 oz boneless lean pork, minced
75 g/3 oz pork fat, minced
2 cloves garlic, peeled and finely chopped
¼ teaspoon ground allspice
salt and freshly ground black pepper
100 ml/4 fl oz brandy
225 g/8 oz rindless streaky bacon
1 bay leaf

Place the butter in a small bowl and heat on FULL POWER for ½ minute. Add the chicken livers and cook on FULL POWER for 1½ minutes. Remove and allow to cool.

Mince the chicken livers and mix with the rabbit, bacon, pork, pork fat, garlic and allspice. Season generously with salt and pepper and moisten thoroughly with the brandy.

Line a 1.15-litre/2-pint terrine with the streaky bacon. Spoon the minced meat mixture into the terrine, packing it down well. Place a bay leaf on top. Cover with absorbent kitchen paper and cook on MEDIUM POWER for 6 minutes. Allow to rest for 5 minutes.

Cook the pâté on MEDIUM POWER for a further 6 minutes. Give the dish a half turn and cook on MEDIUM POWER for a further 4 minutes. Remove and cover with foil. Press down and weight until cold. Chill for 2–4 hours.

To serve, unmould on to a serving dish and cut into thin slices. Accompany with warm toast or melba toast and mixed salad ingredients.

Farmhouse Pâté

Serves 6–8
Power setting FULL
Total cooking time 13–14 minutes

50 g/2 oz butter
2 onions, peeled and chopped
2 cloves garlic, peeled and chopped
225 g/8 oz chicken livers, trimmed and chopped
225 g/8 oz belly of pork, trimmed and chopped
8 rashers streaky bacon, rinds removed and chopped
2 teaspoons chopped fresh sage or 1 teaspoon dried sage
4 tablespoons brandy
4 tablespoons double cream
salt and freshly ground black pepper
50 g/2 oz clarified butter (see below)
bay leaves to garnish

Place the butter in a large bowl and cook for 1 minute. Add the onion and garlic and cook for 5 minutes, stirring halfway through the cooking time. Add the chicken livers, pork, bacon and sage. Cover with greaseproof paper and cook for 7–8 minutes or until the meat is cooked. Place the mixture in a liquidiser with the brandy and cream and blend until smooth. Season to taste and spoon into a terrine or dish. Pour over the clarified butter (melt for 1 minute in the microwave if it is solid). Garnish with bay leaves and chill until set. Serve the pâté with hot toast, melba toast or crisp crackers.

To clarify butter Place the butter in a basin and cook for 3–4 minutes without allowing the butter to brown. Strain through a sieve lined with absorbent kitchen paper.

Fish and Shellfish

Fish and shellfish have naturally delicate tender flesh and which requires minimum cooking. The microwave, with its fast speed cooking, ensures that all seafood is cooked to retain the delicate texture and remain full of flavour and moisture.

It seems remarkable and unbelievable at first that a piece of fish can cook in 2–3 minutes, so it is recommended that many fish and shellfish are cooked just until the outer flesh appears opaque but the centre appears still slightly translucent. The middle will finish cooking on standing. Don't be tempted to cook any longer – overcooking will only dry and toughen the fish.

Whole fish, fillets, steaks and large or small shellfish can be cooked in the microwave in an infinite number of ways. They can be cooked with just a knob of butter and seasoning, in a rich or simple sauce, steamed or poached, or cooked in breadcrumbs, or with cream for a richer dish. I would not recommend cooking fish in batter since the batter does not crisp well – but the texture and appearance can be improved with a quick flash under a hot grill before serving.

Whether cooked conventionally or in the microwave oven, juices of salmon or halibut steaks coagulate on the surface of the fish. To eliminate this, before cooking, line the dish with absorbent kitchen paper to absorb juices, then turn the fish over to serve.

Defrosting Fish in the Microwave Oven

Fish defrosts rapidly so take care not to toughen it by over-defrosting. Always remove fish from the microwave while it is still slightly icy.

Defrosting fish fillets and steaks The shape of the freezer pack, as well as its weight, influences the defrosting time. Thick fillets or bulky packs take longer than thinner packets of the same weight (1).

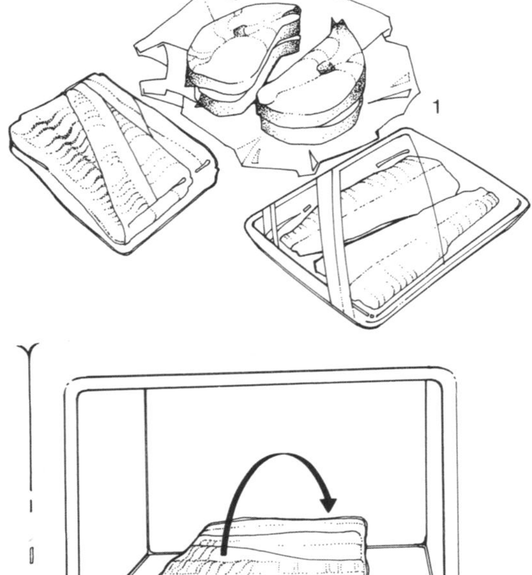

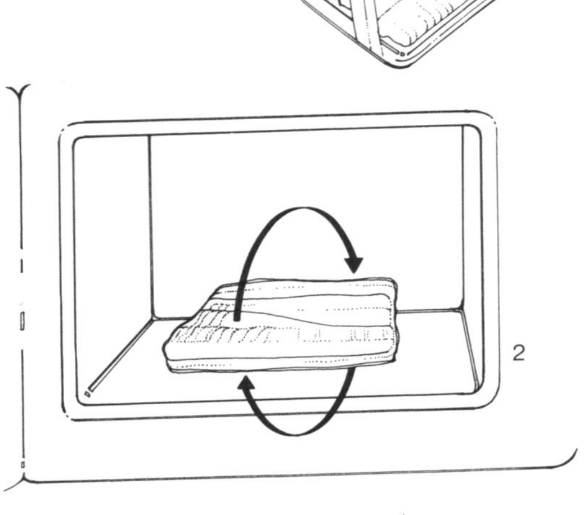

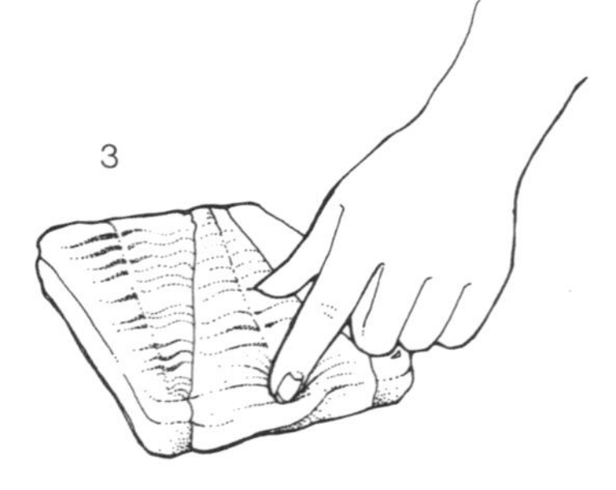

Place the unopened paper or plastic commercial packet or home-frozen package directly on the oven base and cook for half the minimum defrosting time. Turn the package over so that the side which was closest to the back of the oven is brought to the front and give it a quarter turn (2). Cook for remaining minimum defrosting time. Check the fish at this point: the corners should not feel warm but the outer pieces may have started to loosen (3). Cook a little longer – to maximum defrosting time if necessary. Hold under cold running water until the fish can be separated (4).

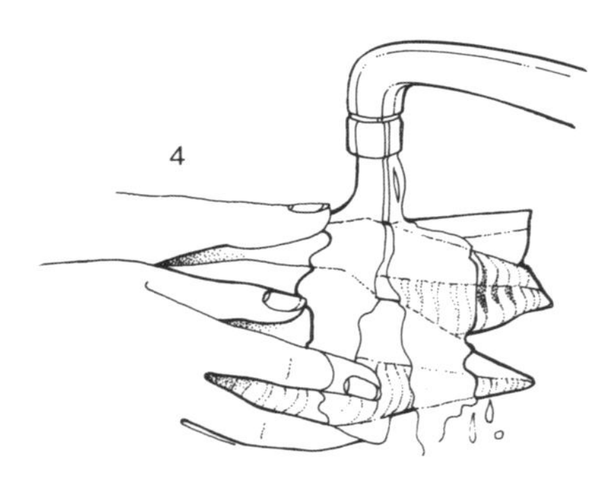

Defrosting whole fish The shape and weight of a whole fish will determine the defrosting time. For example, a short, thick fish may take longer to defrost than a long, thin one of the same weight.

Arrange the fish in a dish large enough to hold it, or them, easily. Cook for half the minimum defrosting time, then turn the fish over and cook for the remaining minimum defrosting time. Test the fish at this point: it

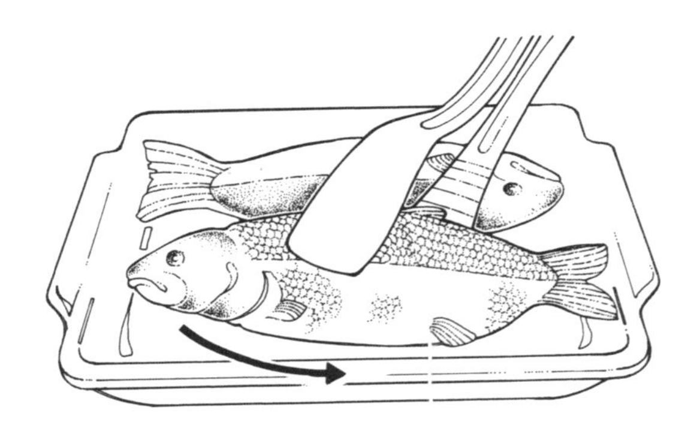

should feel cold and pliable and may still be icy in the cavity. Cook a little longer to the maximum defrost time if necessary. Place under cold running water and rinse the cavity to ensure that it has completely defrosted.

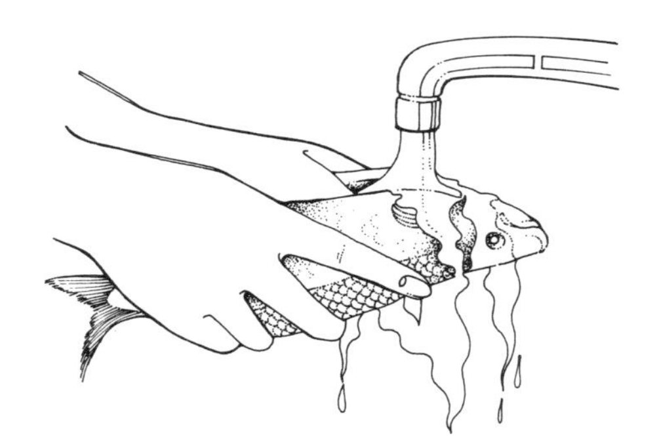

Defrosting shellfish Spread out small pieces of loose-packed shellfish, such as shrimps, prawns or scallops in a single layer in a baking dish. Cook for half the recommended defrosting time, rearrange the pieces and cook for the remaining defrosting time. Test after the minimum defrosting time – the shellfish should feel cool and soft, but still be translucent.

Blocks of shellfish, such as crabmeat and scallops, can be defrosted in the freezer package or without it. Place in a covered dish in the oven (1) and cook for half the minimum recommended defrosting time. Turn the block over and break it up gently with a fork – the centre may still be firm (2). Cook uncovered for the remaining minimum defrosting time, breaking off pieces as they loosen. Test at this point – the pieces should be loose and still feel icy. Leave to stand until completely defrosted.

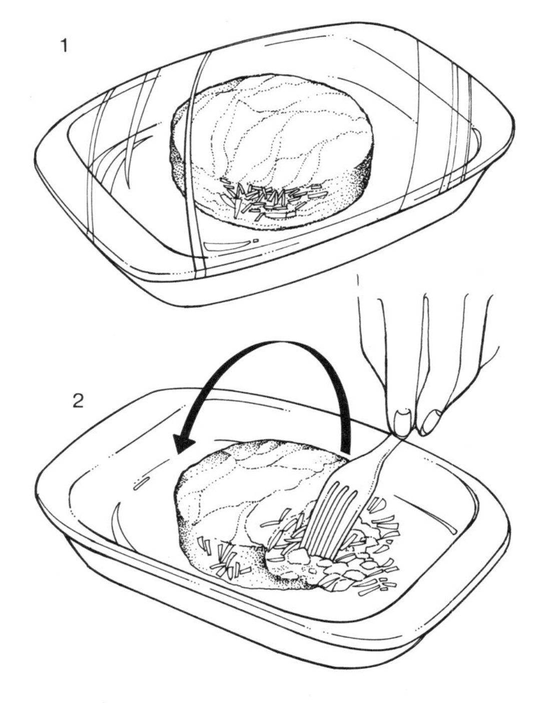

Large pieces of shellfish such as lobster, lobster tails, whole crabs or crab legs and claws should be arranged in a dish with the light underside uppermost. Paper towels should be positioned to hold the tail uppermost (3). Cook for half the recommen-

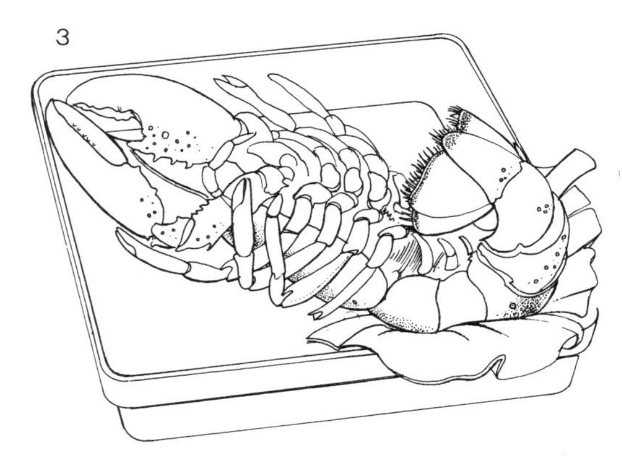

ded defrosting time. Turn over and cook for the remaining defrosting time. Check at this point – the defrosted shellfish should be flexible and transparent and still feel cool (4).

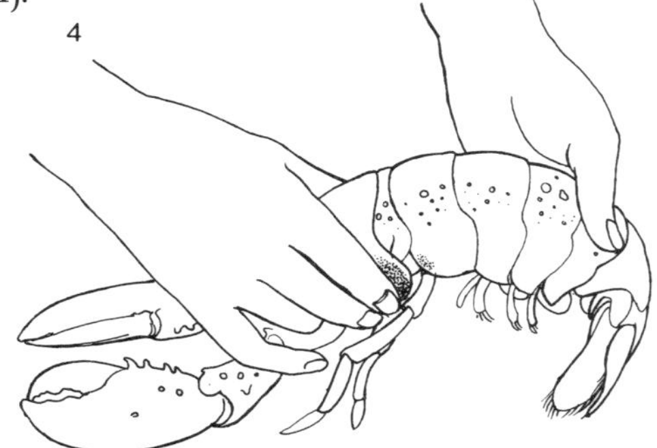

Guide to Defrosting Fish and Shellfish

Fish	*Quantity*	*Heating time in minutes on* DEFROST POWER
Fish fillets	450 g/1 lb	7–8
Fish steaks	1 (175-g/6-oz) steak	2
	2 (175-g/6-oz) steaks	3–4
Whole fish	1 (225–275-g/8–10-oz) whole fish	4–6
	2 (225–265-g/8–10-oz) whole fish	10–12
	1 (1.5–1.75-kg/3–4-lb) whole fish	20–22

Shellfish	*Quantity*	*Heating time in minutes on* DEFROST POWER
Crabmeat	450 g/1 lb	14–16
Lobster whole	450 g/1 lb	12
	675 g/$1\frac{1}{2}$ lb	16–18
Prawns and Scampi	450 g/1 lb	7–8
Scallops	450 g/1 lb	8–10
Shrimps	450 g/1 lb	7–8

Note To defrost fish and shellfish on FULL POWER, cook for $\frac{1}{4}$–$\frac{1}{2}$ minute, allow to stand for 2 minutes, then repeat until evenly thawed throughout, turning and rotating the food and dish occasionally.

Cooking Fish in the Microwave Oven

To cook fish fillets in a sauce Arrange the fish fillets in a cooking dish, thickest parts to the outside of the dish and pour the sauce over them (see diagram below). Cover with greaseproof paper and cook for half the recommended time. Give the dish a half turn and cook for the remaining time, or until the fish flakes easily.

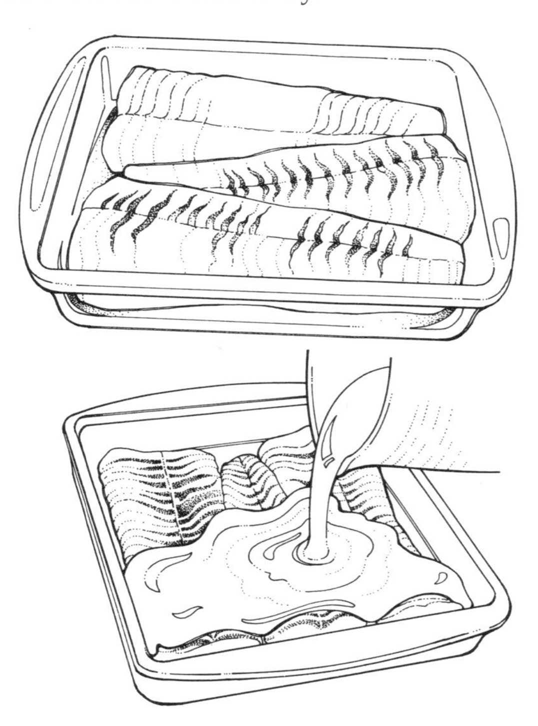

To cook steamed fish Dampen a piece of absorbent kitchen paper with water. Arrange the fish in a dish with the thickest parts to the outside of the dish. Cover with

Top: Three Fish Soup (page 35); *Below:* Stuffed Plaice Swirls (page 36)
Overleaf *Top left:* Jambalaya (page 63); *Top and bottom right:* Red Wine Scallops (page 65); *Below:* Lemon Poached Salmon Steaks with Hollandaise Sauce (pages 59 and 166)

the damp absorbent kitchen paper as shown in the diagram below and cook for half the recommended time. Give the dish a half turn and cook for the remaining time, or until the fish flakes easily.

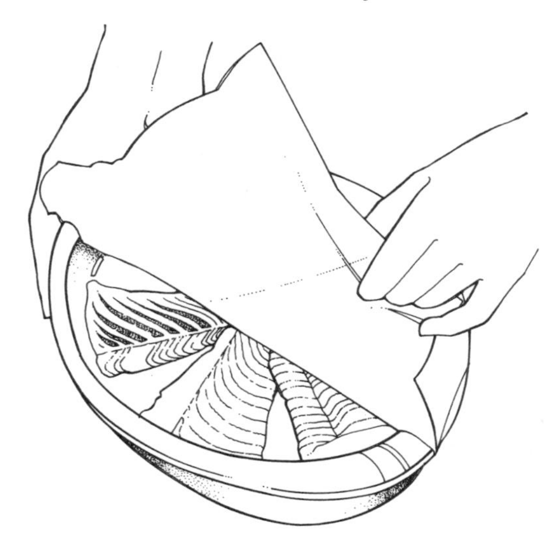

To cook fish steaks Place the fish steaks in a dish, tucking in any flaps to make a neat shape and securing with wooden cocktail sticks if necessary (1). Add water and lemon juice as recommended or brush with a lemon butter mixture. If liked, the dish can be lined with absorbent kitchen paper before cooking the fish. Cover tightly with cling film, then either turn back the corner or snip two holes in the top to allow the steam to escape. Cook for half the recommended time. If the dish is lined with absorbent kitchen paper turn the steaks over and re-cover (2), alternatively if absorbent kitchen paper is not used, give the dish a half turn. Cook for the remaining time, or until the fish flakes easily.

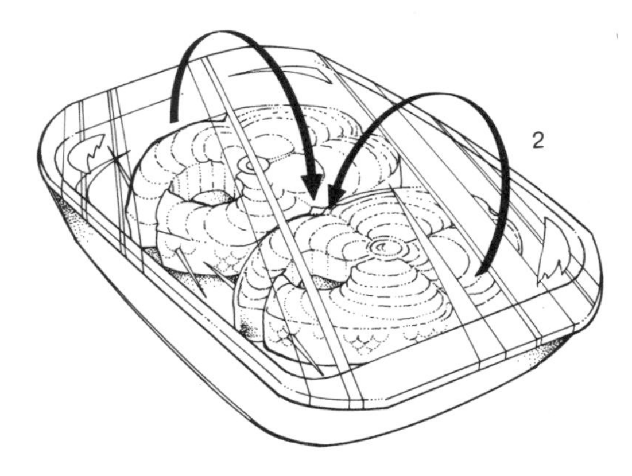

To cook whole fish Place the fish in the dish and brush with a sauce, butter or add water as recommended. Shield and protect the head and the tail area with a little foil. Slash the skin 2–3 times to prevent it from bursting during cooking. Cover lightly with cling film and turn back one corner or snip two holes in the top to allow the steam to escape. Cook for the recommended time.

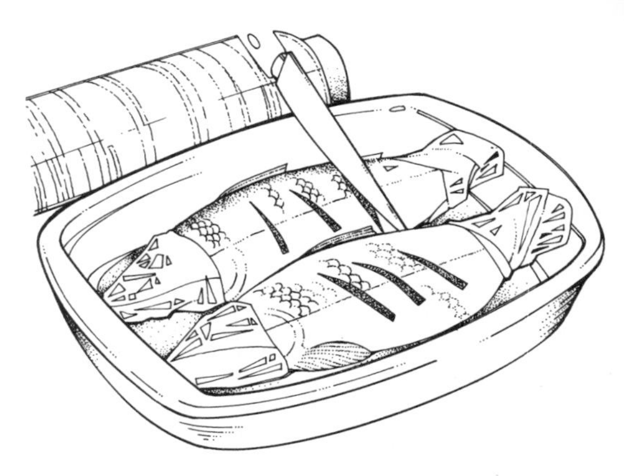

Top right: Chinese-style Carrots with Bean sprouts (page 125); *Below:* Speedy Sweet and Sour Prawns (page 60) with cooked rice

Guide To Cooking Fish

Fish		*Quantity*	*Cooking time in minutes on* FULL POWER	*Preparation*
Bass	whole	450 g/1 lb	5–7	*Shield the head and tail with foil. Cut the skin in two or three places to prevent it from bursting.*
Cod	fillets	450 g/1 lb	5–7	*Place the fillet tails to the centre of the dish or shield with foil. Cut the skin in two or three places to prevent it from bursting.*
	steaks	450 g/1 lb	4–5	*Cover with greaseproof paper before cooking.*
Haddock	fillets	450 g/1 lb	5–7	*Place the fillet tails to the centre of the dish or shield with foil. Cut the skin in two or three places to prevent it from bursting.*
	steaks	450 g/1 lb	4–5	*Cover with greaseproof paper before cooking.*
Halibut	steaks	450 g/1 lb	4–5	*Cover with greaseproof paper before cooking.*
Kippers	whole	1	1–2	*Cover with cling film and snip two holes in the top to allow the steam to escape.*
Red Mullet and Red Snapper	whole	450 g/1 lb	5–7	*Shield the head and tail with foil. Cut the skin in two or three places to prevent it from bursting.*
Salmon	steaks	450 g/1 lb	4–5	*Cover with greaseproof paper before cooking.*
Salmon Trout	whole	450 g/1 lb	7–8	*Shield the head and tail with foil. Cut the skin in two or three places to prevent it from bursting.*
Scallops		450 g/1 lb	5–7	*Cover with dampened absorbent kitchen paper.*
Smoked Haddock	whole	450 g/1 lb	4–5	*Cover with cling film, snipping two holes in the top to allow the steam to escape.*
Trout	whole	450 g/1 lb	8–9	*Shield the head and tail with foil, cut the skin in two or three places to prevent it from bursting.*

Guide to Reheating Boiled Shellfish

Lobster	tails	450 g/1 lb	5–6	*Turn tails over halfway through the cooking time.*
	whole	450 g/1 lb	6–8	*Allow to stand for 5 minutes before serving. Turn over halfway through the cooking time.*
Prawns and Scampi		450 g/1 lb	5–6	*Arrange the peeled shellfish in a ring in a shallow dish and cover with cling film, snipping two holes in the top to allow the steam to escape.*
Shrimps		450 g/1 lb	5–6	*Arrange the peeled shrimps in a ring in a shallow dish and cover with cling film, snipping two holes in the top to allow the steam to escape.*

Haddock with Parsley and Yogurt Sauce

Serves 4
Power setting FULL
Total cooking time 13–14 minutes

4 haddock fillets, skinned
salt and freshly ground black pepper
2 teaspoons English mustard
50 g/2 oz butter
about 250 ml/8 fl oz milk
25 g/1 oz plain flour
150 ml/¼ pint natural yogurt
2 teaspoons cornflour
2 tablespoons chopped parsley

Sprinkle the fish with seasoning to taste. Mix the mustard with half of the butter and spread over the fish. Roll up from the tail end and secure with wooden cocktail sticks. Place in a shallow dish with 2 tablespoons of the milk. Cover with cling film, snipping two holes in the top to allow the steam to escape, and cook for 7 minutes or until the fish is tender. Pour off and reserve any cooking juices.

Place the remaining butter in a bowl and cook for 1 minute to melt, then add the flour, mixing well. Place the cooking juices in a measuring jug and make up to 300 ml/½ pint with the remaining milk. Gradually add this liquid to the flour mixture and cook for 3 minutes, stirring every ½ minute to keep the sauce smooth. Mix the yogurt with the cornflour and parsley and stir into the hot sauce. Cook for 1½–2 minutes, stirring every ½ minute.

Place the fish on a serving dish, coat with the sauce and cook for ½–1 minute to reheat. Serve with creamed potatoes or boiled rice.

STUFFED PLAICE SWIRLS

(Illustrated on page 49 and back cover)
Serves 6
Power setting FULL
Total cooking time 10–12 minutes

3 large plaice fillets, skinned
75 g/3 oz butter
175 g/6 oz leeks, chopped
100 g/4 oz mushrooms, sliced
1 teaspoon lemon juice
1 tablespoon snipped chives
50 g/2 oz long-grain rice, cooked
salt and freshly ground black pepper

Cut each piece of plaice into two long fillets. Grease six ramekin dishes and place a fish fillet round the inside of each dish.

Place 25 g/1 oz of the butter in a bowl and cook for 1 minute to melt. Add the leeks, cover with cling film, snipping two holes in the top to allow the steam to escape, and cook for 3 minutes. Add the mushrooms and cook for a further 2 minutes. Meanwhile mix the remaining butter with the lemon juice, form into a roll and wrap in cling film or foil. Chill until firm, then cut into six slices.

Add the chives and cooked rice to the leeks and mix well to blend. Season generously, then spoon into the centre of each ramekin. Cover with cling film, snipping two holes in the top. Cook for 4–6 minutes, re-arranging the ramekins halfway through the cooking time. The fish fillets are cooked when the flesh flakes easily. Pour away any excess liquid then invert the ramekins on to serving dishes. Serve the sliced lemon butter with the fish.

PLAICE AND MUSHROOM SUPREME

Serves 4
Power setting FULL
Total cooking time 12–13½ minutes

4 large plaice fillets, skinned
1 tablespoon white wine or chicken stock
salt and freshly ground black pepper
40 g/1½ oz butter
1 small onion, peeled and finely chopped
75 g/3 oz button mushrooms, sliced
25 g/1 oz plain flour
150 ml/¼ pint milk
150 ml/¼ pint hot chicken stock
2 teaspoons snipped chives
2 tablespoons single cream

Cut the fish fillets in half lengthways and roll up. Secure with wooden cocktail sticks and place in a shallow dish. Pour over the wine or stock and season to taste. Cover with cling film, snipping two holes in the top to allow the steam to escape, and cook for 5–6 minutes until tender. Pour off and reserve any cooking juices.

Place the butter in a bowl with the onion and mushrooms and cook for 4 minutes, stirring halfway through the cooking time. Stir in the flour, mixing well. Gradually add the milk and the stock, then cook for 2 minutes, stirring every ½ minute to keep the sauce smooth. Add the chives and cream and cook for ½ minute.

Place the fish on a serving dish, cover with the sauce and cook for ½–1 minute to reheat. Serve with creamed potatoes or boiled rice.

PRAWN-STUFFED TROUT

(Illustrated on page 61)
Serves 4
Power setting FULL
Total cooking time 14 minutes

50 g/2 oz butter
75 g/3 oz dry white breadcrumbs
100 g/4 oz peeled prawns, coarsely chopped
grated rind and juice of 1 large lemon
2 teaspoons finely chopped parsley or snipped chives
salt and freshly ground black pepper
1 egg, beaten
4 (275-g/10-oz) trout, gutted
GARNISH
2 lemon slices
parsley sprigs

Place the butter in a bowl and heat for 1 minute to melt. Stir in the breadcrumbs, prawns, lemon rind, parsley or chives and seasoning to taste. Add the egg and mix well. Divide the stuffing into four portions and use one portion to stuff the body cavity of each trout.

Place the trout on a plate and sprinkle with the lemon juice. Cover with cling film, snipping two holes in the top to allow the steam to escape, and cook for 6 minutes. Give the dish a half turn and cook for a further 7 minutes. Allow to stand for 3 minutes. Serve garnished with twists of lemon and parsley sprigs.

SOUSED HERRINGS

Serves 4
Power setting FULL
Total cooking time 6–8 minutes

4 herrings, gutted and boned
salt and freshly ground black pepper
150 ml/$\frac{1}{4}$ pint vinegar
150 ml/$\frac{1}{4}$ pint water
4 peppercorns
1 onion, peeled and sliced

Trim the heads, tails and fins from the fish and season generously. Roll up, skin-side out, from the tail ends and secure with wooden cocktail sticks. Place in a shallow dish with the vinegar, water and peppercorns. Top with the onion. Cover with cling film, snipping two holes in the top to allow the steam to escape, and cook for 6–8 minutes. Give the dish a half turn after 3 minutes. Leave the fish to cool, covered, in the cooking liquid.

Chill and drain before serving with a crisp salad.

LEMON POACHED SALMON STEAKS

(Illustrated on pages 50/51)
Serves 4
Power setting FULL
Total cooking time 7 minutes

4 salmon steaks, cut 2.5 cm/1 in thick
2 tablespoons lemon juice
7 tablespoons water
1 teaspoon salt
1 teaspoon grated lemon rind
GARNISH
4 lemon slices, halved
parsley sprigs

Place the salmon steaks in a shallow dish, tucking in any flaps of skin to make a good neat shape and securing with wooden cocktail sticks if necessary. Sprinkle with the lemon juice and leave to marinate for 10–15 minutes.

Pour over the water and sprinkle with the salt and lemon rind. Cover the dish with cling film, snipping two holes in the top to allow the steam to escape. Cook in the microwave for 7 minutes, giving the dish a half turn twice during cooking. Remove from the oven and leave to stand for 5 minutes. Garnish with halved lemon slices and parsley sprigs.

Serve the salmon hot with Hollandaise sauce (page 166) or cold with mayonnaise.

POACHED SALMON TROUT

Serves 8
Power setting FULL
Total cooking time 28 minutes

1 (1.75-kg/4-lb) salmon trout, gutted
2 tablespoons lemon juice
4 tablespoons boiling water
GARNISH
150 ml/¼ pint mayonnaise
1 lemon, thinly sliced
¼ cucumber, thinly sliced

Place the salmon in a shallow dish with the lemon juice and boiling water. Prick the salmon skin in several places to prevent it from bursting during cooking. Cover with cling film, snipping two holes in the top to allow the steam to escape. Cook for 28 minutes, giving the dish a quarter turn every 7 minutes.

Remove the cling film and allow to cool. Remove and discard the skin from the salmon, then place the fish on a serving plate. To serve, pipe swirls of mayonnaise down the backbone of the salmon and garnish with lemon and cucumber slices.

SPEEDY SWEET AND SOUR PRAWNS

(Illustrated on page 52)
Serves 4
Power setting FULL
Total cooking time 6–8 minutes

1 recipe Sweet and Sour Sauce (see page 168)
450 g/1 lb peeled prawns
1 (227-g/8-oz) can pineapple pieces in natural juice, drained
spring onion curls (below) to garnish

Place the sauce, prawns and pineapple in a dish. Cover and cook for 6–8 minutes, stirring gently after 3 minutes. Serve poured over cooked rice and garnish with spring onion curls.
Note To make spring onion curls, trim the onions and cut the green portion into fine strips. Place the onions in a bowl of cold water and allow to stand for about 30 minutes. Drain on absorbent kitchen paper.

PRAWN GUMBO

Serves 6
Power setting FULL and MEDIUM/HIGH
Total cooking time 32–34 minutes

1 onion, peeled and sliced
50 g/2 oz butter
2 tablespoons cornflour
250 ml/8 fl oz warm water
2 (398-g/14-oz) cans peeled tomatoes
1 large green pepper, seeds removed and chopped
2 cloves garlic, crushed
2 teaspoons salt
1 teaspoon ground nutmeg
$\frac{1}{4}$ teaspoon freshly ground black pepper
450 g/1 lb peeled prawns
450 g/1 lb okra or ladies fingers, trimmed and cut into 2.5-cm/1-in pieces

Place the onion and butter in a large dish. Cook on FULL POWER for 3 minutes, stirring after 2 minutes.

Mix the cornflour with the water and add to the onion with the remaining ingredients, stirring well. Cover and cook on MEDIUM/HIGH POWER for 29–31 minutes, stirring halfway through the cooking time. Serve with cooked rice.

Top: Prawn Gumbo; *Below:* Prawn-stuffed trout (page 58)

JAMBALAYA

(Illustrated on pages 50/51)
Serves 4
Power setting FULL
Total cooking time 14–17 minutes

450 g/1 lb cooked ham, cubed
1 green pepper, seeds removed and chopped
1 small onion, peeled and chopped
1 clove garlic, peeled and finely chopped
25 g/1 oz butter
1 (298-g/10½-oz) can condensed tomato soup
4 tablespoons hot water
100 g/4 oz peeled prawns
1 dried bay leaf, crushed
pinch of dried oregano
salt and freshly ground black pepper
175 g/6 oz cooked long-grain rice

Place the ham, pepper, onion, garlic and butter in a 1.75-litre/3-pint casserole. Cook for 6–7 minutes until the onion and pepper are soft.

Stir in the soup, water, prawns, bay leaf, oregano and seasoning to taste. Cook for 4 minutes.

Add the rice, stirring well, and cook for a further 4–6 minutes until bubbling hot.

Top: Rabbit Stew with Dumplings (page 83); *Below:* Chicken Véronique (page 72)

LOBSTER THERMIDOR

Serves 4
Power setting FULL and MEDIUM
Total cooking time 15–19 minutes

25 g/1 oz butter
100 g/4 oz button mushrooms, sliced
½ small onion, peeled and chopped
15 g/½ oz plain flour
salt and freshly ground black pepper
pinch of paprika
3 tablespoons chicken stock
6 tablespoons whipping cream
1 egg yolk, beaten
2 tablespoons sherry
2 medium lobsters, cooked and halved
2 tablespoons grated Cheddar or Parmesan cheese

Place the butter, mushrooms and onion in a 1.4-litre/2½-pint dish. Cook on FULL POWER for 3 minutes, stirring after 2 minutes.

Stir in the flour, seasoning to taste and paprika until smooth. Cook on FULL POWER for 1 minute. Gradually add the stock and cream. Cook on MEDIUM POWER for 3–4 minutes, stirring after 2 minutes, until thickened. Stir part of the hot mixture into the egg yolk, then return the mixture to the rest of the sauce. Add the sherry and cook on MEDIUM POWER for 3–4 minutes. Remove and flake the flesh from the lobsters, reserving the shells. Stir the lobster into the sauce.

Divide the mixture evenly between the lobster shells and cover with dampened greaseproof paper. Cook on FULL POWER for 5–7 minutes, re-arranging after 3 minutes, until heated through. Sprinkle with grated cheese, brown under a hot grill and serve.

RED WINE SCALLOPS

(Illustrated on pages 50/51)
Serves 4
Power setting FULL
Total cooking time 28–31 minutes

675 g/1½ lb potatoes, peeled and diced
350 ml/12 fl oz cold water
salt and freshly ground black pepper
50 g/2 oz butter
2 tablespoons milk
8–10 scallops, cleaned
1 teaspoon lemon juice
1 onion, peeled and finely chopped
1 clove garlic, peeled and finely chopped
100 g/4 oz button mushrooms, sliced
20 g/¾ oz plain flour
150 ml/¼ pint dry red wine
2 tomatoes, peeled and chopped
snipped chives or chopped parsley to garnish

Place the potatoes in a dish with 200 ml/7 fl oz of the water and salt to taste. Cover with cling film, snipping two holes in the top to allow the steam to escape, and cook for 14 minutes, stirring halfway through the cooking time. Drain well and mash with seasoning to taste, half of the butter and the milk.

Place the scallops in a dish with the remaining 150 ml/¼ pint water and the lemon juice. Cover with cling film, snipping two holes in the top to allow the steam to escape, and cook for 3–6 minutes. Drain and halve the scallops, then set aside, reserving the stock.

Place the remaining butter in a bowl with the onion and garlic. Cook for 2 minutes. Add the mushrooms, stirring to coat them in the juices and cook for 1 minute. Add the flour and cook for 2 minutes, stirring halfway through the cooking time. Gradually add the reserved stock and wine. Cook for 4 minutes, stirring every 1 minute. Stir in the tomatoes and scallops and cook for 2 minutes.

Place the potato in a piping bag fitted with a large star nozzle and pipe a border around the outside of four scallop shells or small serving dishes. Spoon in the scallop mixture and place under a hot grill until golden. Serve at once, sprinkled with snipped chives or chopped parsley.

Poultry and Game

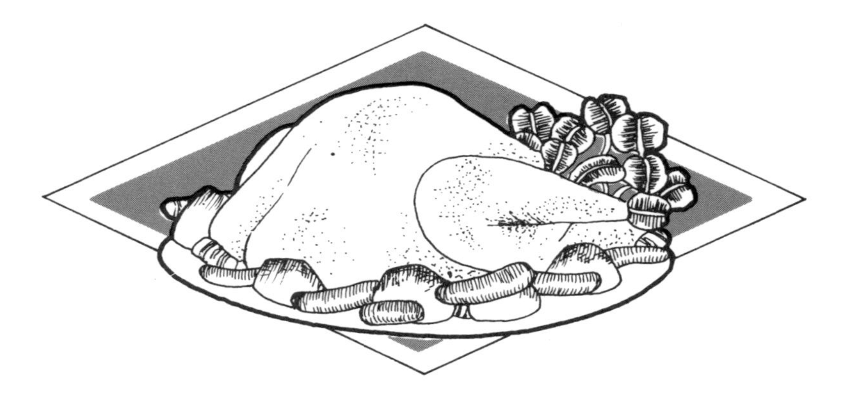

There seems to be a bird for all seasons, all tastes, all pockets and all occasions. Poultry has the popular vote for weekday eating all year round and game is grander; but between them they inspire a huge range of splendid, tempting dishes to please delicate digestions, slimming diets, robust appetites and gourmet tastes.

Cooking poultry or game is one of the best uses of the microwave oven – it helps to keep the meat juicy and tender. It will not, however, brown and crisp the skin as well as the conventional oven. If you like a crisp brown skin then cook on the slower MEDIUM POWER rather than FULL since this gives the skin longer to dry out and colour. A quick flash under a hot grill will also do the trick, or alternatively, brush the skin with a brown sauce or gravy, brown seasonings or spices, tomato purée or ketchup.

Cook poultry and game for the times recommended, then observe a 10–15 minute standing time, wrapped in foil. This allows time for the inside to finish cooking without toughening the delicate breast meat.

Defrosting Poultry and Game in the Microwave Oven

To defrost chicken pieces If the chicken pieces are in a block, then wrap them in plastic or greaseproof paper and place them on the base of the microwave oven (1). If they are in pieces, then arrange them in a dish, meatier parts to the outside of the dish (2). Cook for half the recommended defrosting time. Unwrap, turn the block over or rearrange the individual pieces (3) and cook for the remaining defrosting time. Separate the pieces if necessary and let them stand until defrosted, or place in a cooking dish and cook for 1–2 minutes more. The defrosted chicken should be soft to the touch, very moist and cold.

To defrost a whole chicken, game bird or duck Whole chickens, ducks and game birds are usually frozen in plastic bags. Leave the bird in the bag, remove the twist tie and place on the oven base (1). Cook for half the recommended defrosting time, unwrap and place in a dish. Shield the wing tips, tail and legs (and any other areas which feel warm or have begun to change colour) with foil, then cook for the remaining defrosting time (2).

The giblets can generally be loosened now but not removed. Run under cold water to free the giblets and rinse the icy but not frozen cavity (3).

To defrost a turkey Place the turkey in its plastic wrapper, breast side down on the base of the oven (see diagram). Cook for a quarter of the recommended defrosting time. Give the turkey a half turn and cook for a quarter of the defrosting time. Unwrap the turkey and stand it in a cooking dish. Shield the legs, wing tips and any warm or brown areas with foil and secure with wooden cocktail sticks to prevent the foil blowing away. Turn the turkey breast side up and cook for a quarter of the defrosting time. Check the breast meat for warm spots and shield it if necessary. Give the dish a half turn and cook for the final quarter of the defrosting time. Rinse the inside of the turkey with cold water and remove the giblets.

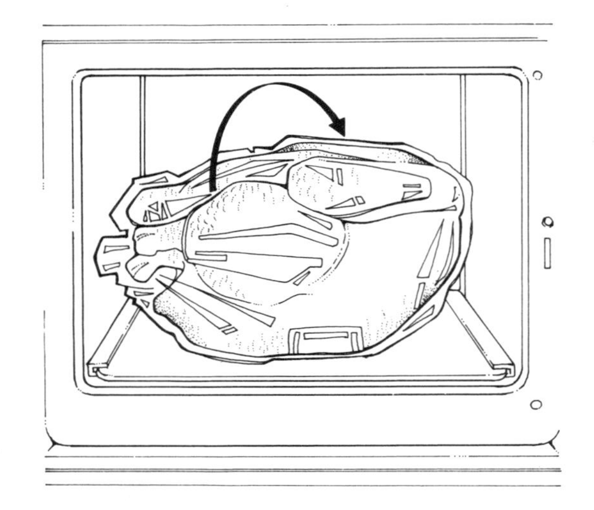

Guide to Defrosting Poultry and Game

Poultry/Game		*Cooking time in minutes on* DEFROST POWER *per 450 g/1 lb*	*Preparation*
Chicken	whole	6	*Shield the wing tips with foil. Give the dish a quarter turn every $1\frac{1}{2}$ minutes. Remove the giblets at the end of the defrosting time.*
	pieces	5	*Place the meatiest part of the chicken pieces to the outside of the dish. Turn over halfway through the defrosting time.*
Duck		4–6	*Shield the wings, tail end and legs with foil. Give the dish a quarter turn every $1\frac{1}{2}$ minutes. Remove the giblets at the end of the defrosting time.*
Grouse, guinea fowl, partridge, pheasant, pigeon, poussin, quail and woodcock		5–6	*Shield the tips of the wings and legs with foil. Turn over halfway through the defrosting time and give the dish a quarter turn every $1\frac{1}{2}$ minutes.*
Turkey		10–12	*Shield the tips of the wings and legs with foil. Turn over twice during the defrosting time and give the dish a quarter turn every 6 minutes. Shield any warm spots with foil during defrosting. Remove the giblets at the end of the defrosting time.*

To defrost poultry and game on FULL POWER, cook for 1 minute per 450 g/1 lb, allow to stand for 10 minutes, then continue cooking in bursts of 1 minute per 450 g/1 lb until the poultry or game is thawed.

Cooking Poultry and Game in the Microwave Oven

To cook chicken pieces Chicken pieces cook extremely fast in the microwave and for this reason they do not become brown or crisp. Unless cooked in a sauce, they will be more attractive if brushed with a browning agent, coated with browned crumbs or cooked in a browning dish to sear and brown them first. However, plain cooked chicken is ideal for making sandwiches and salads.

To cook chicken pieces, arrange them in a baking dish or on a plate with the meatiest portions to the outside of the dish. Brush the portions with a browning agent, if desired, or add any sauce ingredients.

Cover with greaseproof paper for the first half of the cooking time. For crisp, dryer chicken, uncover during the second half of the cooking time. Give the dish a half turn midway through the cooking time when cooking more than four pieces.

Check to see that the meat is cooked: the chicken should be tender with no pink flesh next to the bone. For chickens cooked in a sauce, remove the greaseproof paper after cooking and allow to stand for 5 minutes to blend the flavours.

To cook a whole chicken or game bird Whole chickens should, ideally, be cooked on MEDIUM POWER. This ensures a well-cooked chicken without the necessity to shield the protruding bones or handle the bird a great deal during cooking. They can, however, be cooked quite well on FULL POWER if the tips of the wings and legs are shielded with a little foil prior to cooking.

Place the chicken on a roasting rack or in a dish and brush it with a browning agent if used. Place in a roasting bag or cover with greaseproof paper. If using a roasting bag secure the end loosely with a piece of string or an elastic band. Place in the oven, breast side down, and cook for half the recommended time (1). Turn the chicken breast side up, re-cover, if liked, and cook for the remainder of the recommended time.

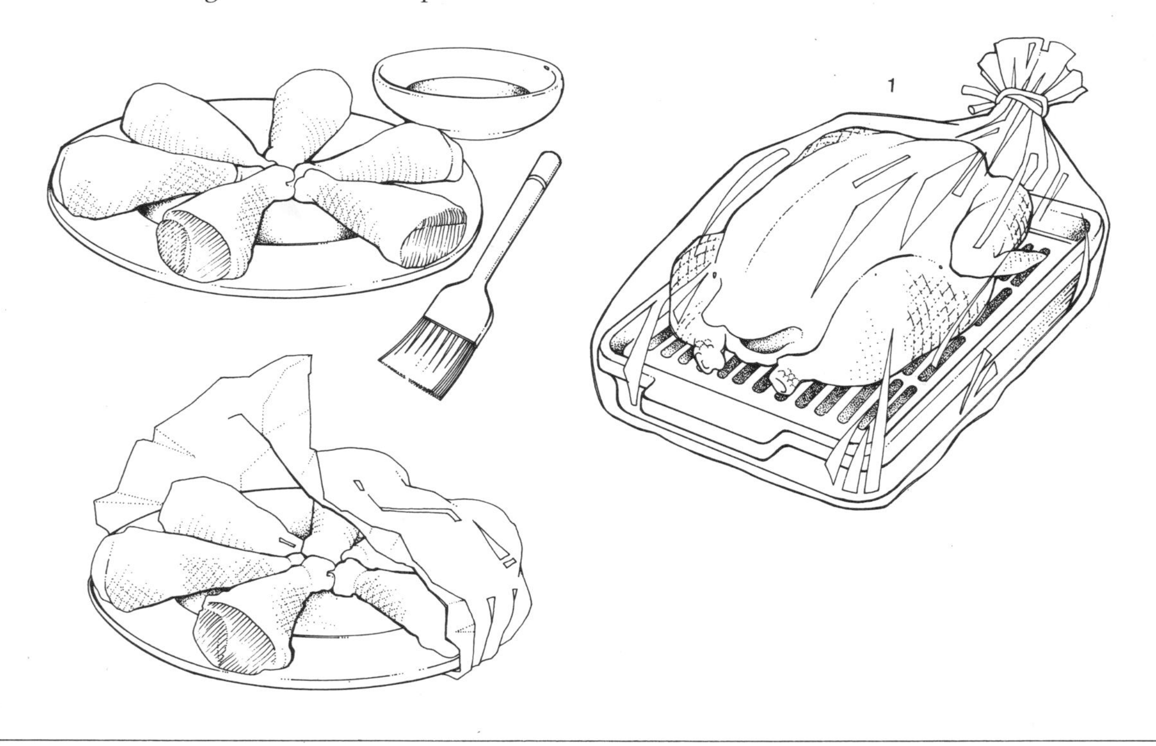

Check to see that the meat is cooked by cutting the skin between the inner thigh and breast: there should be no traces of pink flesh and the juice should run clear (2).

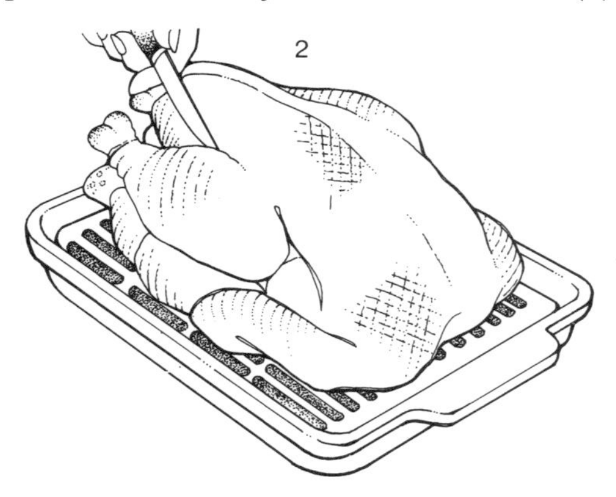

To cook chicken livers and giblets Chicken livers may be sautéed in a browning dish, or cooked in a little liquid on MEDIUM POWER before they are used in other dishes. Cook 450 g/1 lb chicken or poultry livers for about 18–22 minutes.

Prick giblets with a fork before cooking, as they do tend to pop. Giblets from a 1.5-kg/3-lb chicken, cooked with 250 ml/8 fl oz water will take 16–20 minutes to cook on MEDIUM POWER.

To cook a whole duck Shield the wings, tail and leg ends of a duck with foil prior to cooking, then place the bird breast side down on a trivet or plate first in a roasting

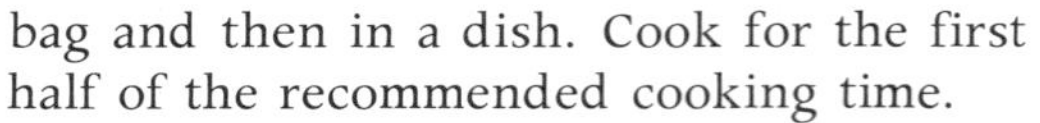

bag and then in a dish. Cook for the first half of the recommended cooking time.

Turn the duck so that the breast is facing up, remove the foil and prick the skin. Brush with a browning agent if liked.

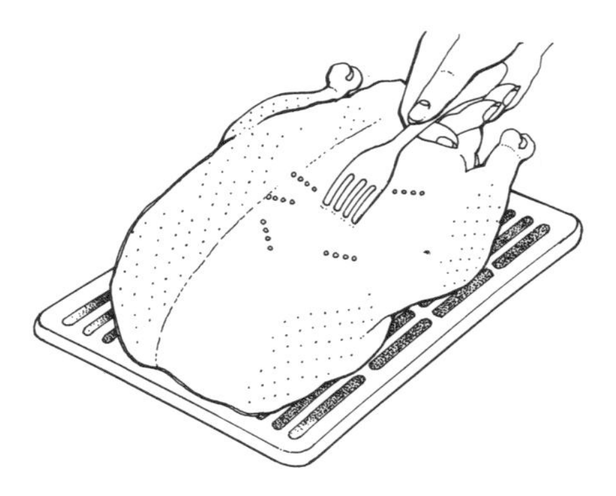

Cook for the remaining time. The duck is cooked when the juices run clear without any trace of pink. For a crisp skin, brown under a hot grill.

To cook a whole turkey Shield the tips of the wings and legs with foil before cooking a turkey.

Place on a roasting rack or in a dish and brush with a browning agent if used. Place in a roasting bag or cover with greaseproof paper. If using a roasting bag, secure the end loosely with a piece of string or an elastic band. Place breast side down and cook for a quarter of the recommended

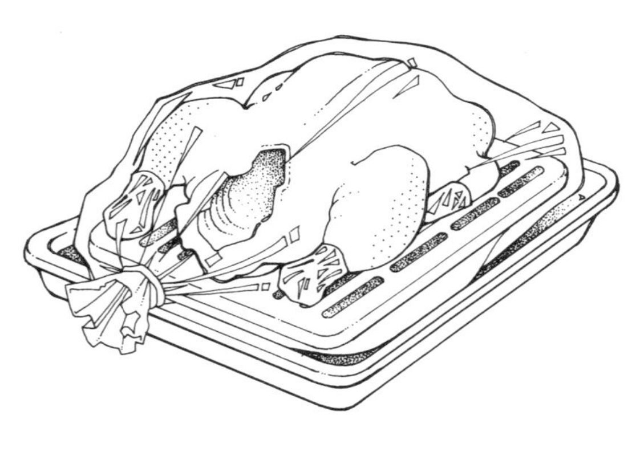

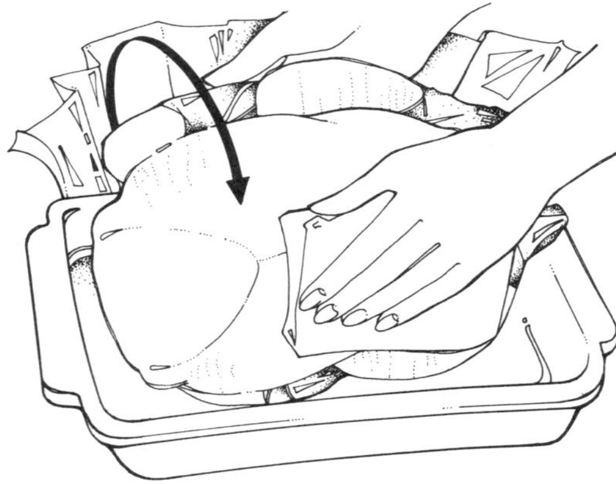

time. Turn the turkey on its side and cook for a further quarter of the recommended time. Turn the bird over on to the other side and cook for a third quarter of the cooking time.

Finally turn the turkey breast side up. Remove the foil and cook for the remaining cooking time. Allow to stand for 15–20 minutes, wrapped in foil, before carving.

Guide to Roasting Poultry and Game

Poultry/Game	*Cooking time in minutes on* FULL POWER *per 450g/1 lb*	*Cooking time in minutes on* MEDIUM POWER *per 450g/1 lb*	*Preparation*
Chicken whole	6–8	9–10	*Shield the tips of the wings and legs with foil. Place in a roasting bag in a dish with 2–3 tablespoons stock. Give the dish a half turn halfway through the cooking time.*
pieces 1	2–4		*Place the meatiest part of the chicken piece to the outside of the dish. Cover with greaseproof paper. Give the dish a half turn halfway through the cooking time.*
2	4–6		
3	5–7		
4	$6\frac{1}{2}$–10		
5	$7\frac{1}{2}$–12		
6	8–14		
Duck whole	7–8	9–11	*Shield the tips of the wings, tail end and legs with foil. Prick the skin thoroughly to help release the fat. Place in a dish in a roasting bag on a trivet or upturned saucer and turn over halfway through the cooking time.*
Grouse, guinea fowl, partridge, pheasant, pigeon, poussin, quail and woodcock	6–8	9–11	*Shield the tips of the wings and legs with foil. Smear the breast with a little butter and place in a roasting bag in a dish. Turn the dish halfway through the cooking time.*
Turkey	9–11	11–13	*Shield the tips of the wings and legs with foil. Place in a roasting bag in a dish with 2–3 tablespoons stock. Turn over at least once during the cooking time and give the dish a quarter turn every 15 minutes.*

COQ AU VIN

Serves 4
Power setting FULL
Total cooking time 26½–30½ minutes

4 rashers rindless bacon
40 g/1½ oz plain flour
100 ml/4 fl oz dry red wine
100 ml/4 fl oz hot chicken stock
2 tablespoons brandy
2 teaspoons chopped parsley
1 teaspoon salt
1 clove garlic, crushed
1 bay leaf
¼ teaspoon dried thyme
freshly ground black pepper
225 g/8 oz mushrooms, sliced
1 large onion, peeled and sliced
1 (1.5-kg/3-lb) oven-ready chicken, cut into 8 pieces

Place the bacon in a medium-sized casserole and cook for 3½–4 minutes until crisp. Remove with a slotted spoon. Add the flour to the bacon drippings, blending well. Gradually add the wine, stock and brandy, mixing well. Stir in the parsley, salt, garlic, bay leaf, thyme and pepper to taste. Add the cooked bacon, mushrooms, onion and chicken. Cover and cook for 15 minutes.

Stir and rearrange the chicken pieces. Cook, uncovered, for 8–11 minutes until the chicken is cooked. Leave to stand for 5–10 minutes before serving.

CHICKEN VÉRONIQUE

(Illustrated on page 62)
Serves 4
Power setting FULL and LOW
Total cooking time 9–10 minutes

50 g/2 oz butter
50 g/2 oz plain flour
450 ml/¾ pint hot chicken stock
150 ml/¼ pint dry white wine or dry cider
450 g/1 lb cooked chicken, cut into bite-sized pieces
150 ml/¼ pint single cream
100 g/4 oz seedless green grapes
salt and freshly ground black pepper

Place the butter in a large bowl and heat on FULL POWER for 1 minute. Add the flour, chicken stock, wine or cider and stir until smooth. Cook on FULL POWER for 4 minutes, stirring twice during the cooking time. Add the chicken, cream, grapes and seasoning to taste. Cover the bowl with cling film, snipping two holes in the top to allow the steam to escape, and cook on LOW POWER for 4–5 minutes or until the mixture is heated through, stirring halfway through the cooking time. Do not allow to boil or the sauce may curdle. Leave to stand for 5 minutes before serving on a bed of cooked rice.

CHICKEN KEBABS

(Illustrated on page 79)
Serves 4
Power setting FULL
Total cooking time 12 minutes

4 chicken breasts, skinned and boned
4 tablespoons lemon juice
4 tablespoons oil
1 teaspoon dried oregano
1 teaspoon salt
freshly ground black pepper
1 small aubergine, cut into bite-sized pieces
8 baby courgettes or 2 medium courgettes, trimmed and cut into chunks
8 large button mushrooms
1 tomato, quartered
chopped parsley to garnish

Cut the chicken into bite-sized pieces. Mix the lemon juice with the oil, oregano, salt and pepper to taste. Place in a shallow bowl, add the chicken and leave to marinate for 1–2 hours. Add the aubergine, courgettes, mushrooms and tomatoes to the marinade and toss lightly.

Divide the ingredients between four or six wooden kebab skewers and brush with the marinade. Arrange in a large shallow dish and cook for 12 minutes. Baste the kebabs with any remaining marinade and give the dish a half turn halfway through the cooking time. Serve hot on a bed of cooked rice or shredded lettuce. Sprinkle with chopped parsley before serving.

ORIENTAL CHICKEN

Serves 4
Power setting FULL
Total cooking time 10½–13 minutes

150 ml/¼ pint light soy sauce
1½ tablespoons oil
1 tablespoon dry sherry
2 boneless chicken breasts, cut into 1-cm/½-in strips
1 green pepper, seeds removed and cut into 1-cm/½-in strips
50 g/2 oz flaked almonds
1 onion, peeled and sliced into rings

Place the soy sauce, oil and sherry in a bowl. Add the chicken and leave to marinate for 30 minutes.

Preheat a browning dish for 5 minutes. Quickly add the chicken in its marinade, the green pepper and almonds. Stir briskly until the sizzling slows. Add the onion and cook for 5½–8 minutes, stirring every 2 minutes until the chicken is cooked.

Serve with cooked rice.

WALDORF CHICKEN SALAD

(Illustrated on page 79)
Serves 4
Power setting FULL
Total cooking time 18–24 minutes

1 (1.5-kg/3-lb) oven-ready chicken
25 g/1 oz butter
3 sticks celery, sliced
4 dessert apples, cored and diced
50 g/2 oz walnuts, coarsely chopped
150 ml/¼ pint mayonnaise
150 ml/¼ pint single or soured cream
2 teaspoons lemon juice
1 crisp lettuce heart
watercress sprigs to garnish (optional)

Dot the chicken with the butter, cover the wings with a little foil and place it in a roasting bag. Secure the end loosely with string or an elastic band. Cook for 18–24 minutes, giving the chicken a half turn halfway through the cooking time. Remove and allow to cool.

Remove and discard the skin from the chicken. Cut the flesh into cubes and mix with the celery, apples and walnuts. Blend the mayonnaise with the single or soured cream and add the lemon juice, mixing well. Fold this dressing into the chicken mixture.

Arrange crisp lettuce leaves on the base of a serving dish. Spoon the chicken mixture on top and garnish with watercress sprigs, if liked.

TRADITIONAL CHRISTMAS TURKEY

Serves 8–10
Power setting FULL or MEDIUM
Total cooking time about 2 hours or 2 hours 10 minutes

175 g/6 oz fresh cranberries
1 tablespoon soft brown sugar
1 tablespoon dry cider
40 g/1½ oz butter or margarine
1 onion, peeled and finely chopped
100 g/4 oz mushrooms, chopped
225 g/8 oz pork sausagemeat
4 tablespoons chopped parsley
100 g/4 oz fresh breadcrumbs
salt and freshly ground black pepper
1 egg, beaten
1 (4.5-kg/10-lb) oven-ready turkey
15 g/½ oz butter

Place the cranberries in a dish with the sugar and cider. Cover and cook on FULL POWER for 3–4 minutes until the fruit is soft.

Place 25 g/1 oz of the butter or margarine in a bowl and cook on FULL POWER for 1 minute to melt. Add the onion and mushrooms and cook on FULL POWER for 4 minutes, stirring halfway through the cooking time.

Mix the cranberries with the onion and mushroom mixture, the sausagemeat, parsley, breadcrumbs and seasoning to taste. Bind together with the egg and use to stuff the neck of the turkey. Weigh, and calculate the cooking time at 12 minutes per 450 g/1 lb on MEDIUM POWER or 10 minutes per 450 g/1 lb if using FULL POWER. Rub the skin with the remaining butter and protect the turkey wings with a little foil. Place in a roasting bag on a roasting rack or upturned plate, securing the end of the bag with string or an elastic band. Cook for the calculated time, turning at least once during cooking.

Leave to stand for 10–15 minutes before carving.

CIDER-GLAZED HARVEST TURKEY

Serves 8
Power setting FULL or MEDIUM
Total cooking time about 1½ hours or 1 hour 50 minutes

225 g/8 oz cooking apples, peeled, cored and finely chopped
50 g/2 oz shredded beef suet
50 g/2 oz hazelnuts, coarsely chopped
50 g/2 oz fresh breadcrumbs
finely grated rind of ½ orange
1 tablespoon brown sugar
salt and freshly ground black pepper
about 150 ml/¼ pint strong, medium dry cider
1 (3.5-kg/8-lb) oven-ready turkey
25 g/1 oz butter
¼ teaspoon cinnamon
watercress sprigs to garnish

Place the apples in a bowl and mix in the suet, hazelnuts, breadcrumbs, orange rind and sugar. Season to taste and moisten with enough of the cider to bind the ingredients together. Use to stuff the neck of the turkey. Weigh and calculate the cooking time at 12 minutes per 450 g/1 lb on MEDIUM POWER or 10 minutes per 450 g/1 lb if using FULL POWER. Rub the skin of the turkey with the butter and cinnamon, and protect the turkey wings with a little foil. Place on a roasting rack or upturned plate in a roasting bag, securing the end with string or an elastic band. Cook for the calculated time, turning at least once during cooking. Leave to stand for 10–15 minutes before carving. Serve garnished with watercress sprigs.

TURKEY TETRAZZINI

Serves 4–6
Power setting FULL
Total cooking time 24–28 minutes

600 ml/1 pint boiling water
200 g/7 oz spaghetti
50 g/2 oz butter
100 g/4 oz mushrooms, sliced
1 small onion, peeled and chopped
1½ teaspoons lemon juice
40 g/1½ oz plain flour
salt to taste
½ teaspoon paprika
pinch of nutmeg
475 ml/16 fl oz hot chicken stock
100 ml/4 fl oz whipping cream
675 g/1½ lb cooked turkey, cubed
50 g/2 oz Parmesan cheese, grated
a little paprika

Place the boiling water in a bowl and gradually lower the spaghetti in as it softens. Cover and cook for 9 minutes. Allow to stand for 5–10 minutes, drain and place in a greased shallow dish.

Place the butter in a bowl with the mushrooms, onion and lemon juice. Cook for 2–3 minutes, stirring after 1 minute. Stir in the flour, salt to taste, paprika and nutmeg, blending well. Cook for 1 minute. Gradually add the stock, mixing well, and cook for 5–6 minutes, stirring after 3 minutes, until thickened.

Add the whipping cream and turkey. Pour this mixture over the spaghetti and sprinkle with cheese and paprika. Cook for 7–9 minutes, giving the dish a half turn halfway through the cooking time.

DUCK IN MUSTARD SAUCE

Serves 4
Power setting FULL or MEDIUM
Total cooking time 33½ or 45½ minutes

1 (1.8-kg/4-lb) oven-ready duckling
salt and freshly ground black pepper
25 g/1 oz butter
1 onion, peeled and chopped
100 ml/4 fl oz dry red wine
juice of ½ lemon
grated rind of 1 lemon
2 teaspoons Dijon mustard
watercress sprigs to garnish

Remove and reserve the giblets from the duckling. Rinse and pat dry with absorbent kitchen paper, then season generously and place the duckling, breast side down, in a roasting bag on a roasting rack or on an upturned saucer. Secure the end loosely with string or an elastic band. Cook on FULL POWER for 28 minutes, turning breast side up halfway through the cooking time. Alternatively cook on MEDIUM POWER for 40 minutes, again turning the breast side up halfway through the cooking time. Remove the duck from the roasting bag and wrap it in foil. Allow to stand while preparing the sauce.

Place the butter in a small bowl and cook on FULL POWER for 1 minute. Add the reserved duck liver and cook for 1½ minutes, turning halfway through the cooking time. Remove and mash to a smooth paste. Add the onion to the cooking juices and cook on FULL POWER for 2 minutes. Add the wine, lemon juice, lemon rind, mustard and duck liver, stirring well. Cook for 1 minute.

To serve, carve or cut the duck into portions and pour over a little of the hot sauce. Garnish with watercress sprigs and serve the remaining sauce separately.

Top: Chicken Kebabs (page 73); *Below:* Waldorf Chicken Salad (page 74)

DUCK À L'ORANGE

Serves 4
Power setting MEDIUM or FULL
Total cooking time 34–36 or 42–51 minutes

1 (2-kg/4½-lb) oven-ready duck, trussed
salt and freshly ground black pepper
1 orange, peeled, pith removed and cut into segments
SAUCE
grated rind of 1 orange
juice of 3 oranges
15 g/½ oz cornflour
1 tablespoon honey
GARNISH
orange slices
watercress sprigs

Shield the tips of the wings, tail end and legs of the duck with foil. Prick the skin thoroughly, then season, and stuff the neck cavity with the orange segments. Place the duck in a roasting bag and stand it on a trivet or upturned saucer. Cook on FULL POWER for 17 minutes or MEDIUM POWER for 25 minutes. Drain and reserve the juices from the bag. Turn the duck over and cook on FULL POWER for a further 15–17 minutes or on MEDIUM POWER for a further 15–24 minutes, until cooked. Remove the bird from the oven and leave to stand, covered in foil, for 10 minutes.

Mix the orange rind, orange juice, cornflour and honey together, then make up to 300 ml/ ½ pint with the duck juices. Place in a jug and cook on FULL POWER for 2 minutes, stirring every ½ minute.

If you prefer crisp skin place the duck under a hot grill for a few minutes. Serve the orange sauce separately. Garnish the duck with orange slices and watercress sprigs.

Top: Duck a l'Orange; *Below:* Casseroled Pigeons in Port Wine (page 82)

CASSEROLED PIGEONS IN PORT WINE

(Illustrated on page 80)
Serves 4
Power setting FULL
Total cooking time 27 minutes

2 pigeons, cleaned and trussed
4 rashers rindless streaky bacon
25 g/1 oz butter
1 tablespoon oil
1 onion, peeled and finely chopped
1 tablespoon plain flour
2 tablespoons redcurrant jelly
150 ml/$\frac{1}{4}$ pint port
150 ml/$\frac{1}{4}$ pint hot chicken stock
1 tablespoon concentrated tomato purée
salt and freshly ground black pepper
100 g/4 oz button mushrooms
50 g/2 oz celery, chopped
2 tablespoons chopped parsley
celery leaves to garnish

Wrap each of the pigeons in streaky bacon and secure with wooden cocktail sticks. Preheat a browning dish according to the manufacturer's instructions – about 5 minutes. Add the butter, oil and the pigeons, then cook for 4 minutes, turning to brown on all sides. Remove from the dish and reserve. Add the onion to the dish juices, cover and cook for 2 minutes. Add the flour, stirring well. Gradually add the redcurrant jelly, port, stock, tomato purée and seasoning to taste. Cook for 2 minutes, stirring after 1 minute. Return the pigeons to the dish and spoon the sauce over them. Cover and cook for 8 minutes, stirring and giving the dish a half turn after 4 minutes.

Add the mushrooms, celery and parsley and cook for 6 minutes. Allow to stand for 10 minutes before serving garnished with celery leaves.

RABBIT STEW WITH DUMPLINGS

(Illustrated on page 62)
Serves 4
Power setting FULL and MEDIUM
Total cooking time 1 hour

675 g/1½ lb boned rabbit or 4 large rabbit portions
2 tablespoons plain flour
salt and freshly ground black pepper
1 onion, peeled and sliced
1 clove garlic, crushed
2 carrots, peeled and sliced
2 medium potatoes, peeled and cubed
1 (398-g/14-oz) can peeled tomatoes, drained
300 ml/½ pint hot chicken stock
1 bouquet garni
SAGE DUMPLINGS
50 g/2 oz self-raising flour
25 g/1 oz shredded beef suet
1 tablespoon chopped fresh sage or 2 teaspoons dried sage
salt and freshly ground black pepper
a little cold water to mix

Place the meat in a bowl with the flour and a generous sprinkling of seasoning. Toss to coat. Add the onion, garlic, carrots, potatoes, tomatoes, stock and bouquet garni and mix well. Cover and cook on FULL POWER for 10 minutes. Give the dish a half turn. Reduce the power to MEDIUM and cook for 10 minutes. Give the dish a half turn, stir, re-cover and cook on MEDIUM POWER for a further 20 minutes.

Meanwhile place all the ingredients for the dumplings in a bowl and mix to a soft dough with water. Turn on to a floured surface and form into four dumplings.

Stir the stew and add the dumplings. Cook on MEDIUM POWER for 20 minutes. Allow to stand for 5 minutes and remove the bouquet garni before serving.

Meat

Almost every family has meat on the menu at least once a week whether it is the traditional Sunday roast, a mid-week 'meat-stretching' dish like spaghetti bolognese, outdoor or indoor fare such as barbecued spareribs, or a hearty and satisfying hotpot or casserole.

The microwave will cope magnificently with cooking all these meat dishes – and some dinner party specials too – in about a quarter to half the expected conventional cooking time. It is important when buying meat for microwave cooking to choose lean, tender cuts wherever possible. Because of the speed of microwave cooking, less tender cuts do not have the same opportunity to tenderise as they would have over long slow conventional cooking times. You can, however, cook less tender cuts on a lower power setting such as MEDIUM, LOW or DEFROST, if your microwave oven has these facilities, and achieve the same results as conventional cooking. If your microwave oven has only FULL POWER, then allow the meat to rest at regular intervals for about 5 minutes during the cooking time for tender results.

A browning dish is perhaps the most valuable aid to cooking meat in the microwave – especially small cuts like steaks, chops, sausages and meat pieces for casseroles. Unlike a larger roasting cut, because of the very fast cooking times, these do not have the opportunity to brown.

Browning sauces or browning aids will undoubtedly prove useful too. Experiment by brushing meats with soy sauce, tomato ketchup, gravy browning, special microwave browning seasonings and spices, or brown sauce and a paprika or chilli sauce mixture to get good, golden brown results.

Defrosting Meat in the Microwave Oven

Defrosting roasting joints Place the joint on a trivet set over a cooking dish and cook for half the recommended defrosting time. Turn over and feel the roast for warm spots – especially on the edges, thinner and warmer areas. Shield warm areas with small pieces of foil. Cook for the remaining defrosting time.

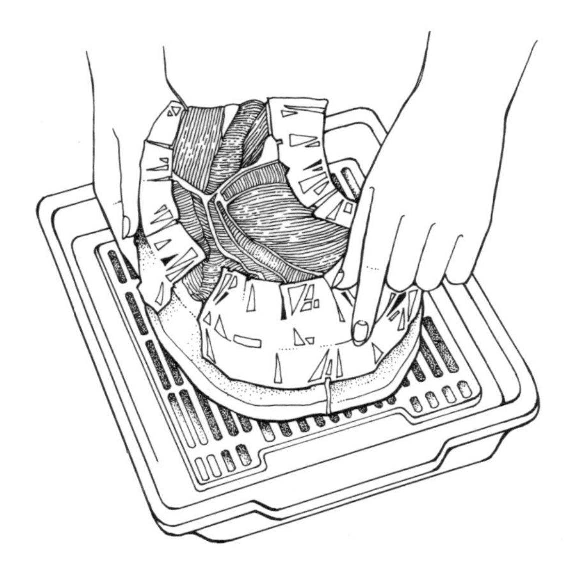

Defrosting meat steaks Remove as much wrapping as possible from steaks and separate with a knife if they are stacked (1).

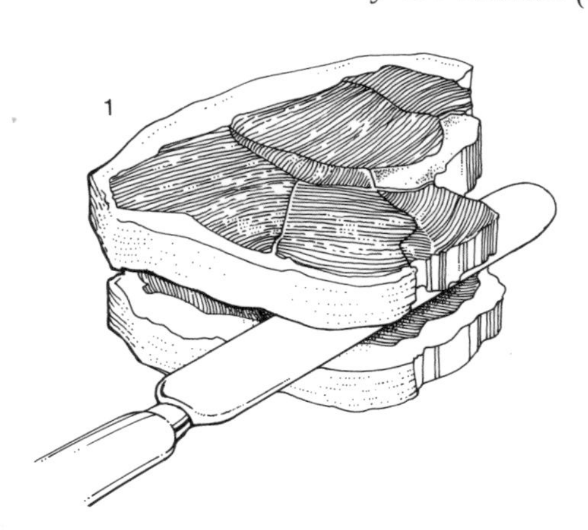

Place in a dish, thinner ends to the centre, and cook for half the defrosting time. Turn over and cook for the remaining defrosting time (2).

Defrosting minced meat Place the paper or plastic pack in the oven and cook for a third of the recommended defrosting time. Turn over and cook for a further third of the defrosting time (1). Open the pack,

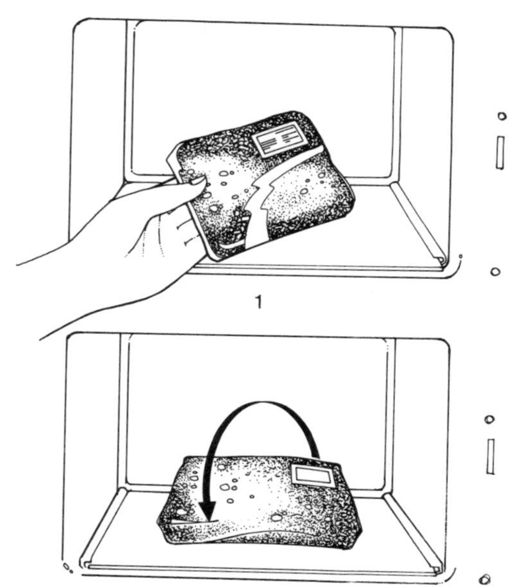

scrape away and reserve any soft meat. Place the remaining meat block in a dish and break it up with a fork (2). Cook for the remaining defrosting time.

Defrosting cubes or small pieces of meat Place the packaged beef cubes in the oven and cook for half the recommended defrosting time. Separate the pieces and place them in a dish in a single layer as shown in the diagram below. Cook for the remaining defrosting time.

Guide to Defrosting Meat

Meat		*Defrosting time in minutes on* DEFROST POWER *450 g/1 lb*	
Beef	joints	9	*Turn over at least once during the defrosting time.*
	steaks (large)	8	
	steaks (small)	4	
	minced beef	10	*Break up with a fork during the defrosting time.*
Lamb	joints	10	*Turn over at least once during the defrosting time.*
	chops	5	
Pork	joints	8½	*Turn over at least once during the defrosting time.*
	chops	5	
Veal	joints	9	*Turn over at least once during the defrosting time.*
Kidney		4	*Turn over at least once during the defrosting time.*
Liver		4	*Turn over at least once during the defrosting time.*

Note If your microwave does not have DEFROST POWER, then cook meat on FULL POWER for 1 minute for every 450 g/1 lb and leave to stand for 10 minutes to defrost. Repeat until the meat is thoroughly thawed.

Cooking Meat in the Microwave

Wherever possible use a MEDIUM POWER setting, where given, if not use FULL.
Weigh the raw meat carefully to calculate the cooking time. This is particularly important if the meat is stuffed.
Season the meat before cooking and place it on a roasting rack or an upturned saucer in a roasting bag, or cover with greaseproof paper (see diagram below).

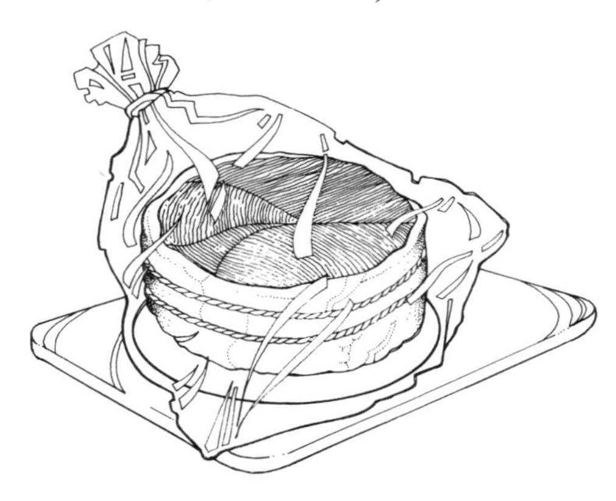

There are special thermometers for use in the microwave. If you have one, mark the distance from the outside of the meat to the centre of the thickest muscle with your finger on the thermometer. Mark the point where the sensor touches the edge of the meat.

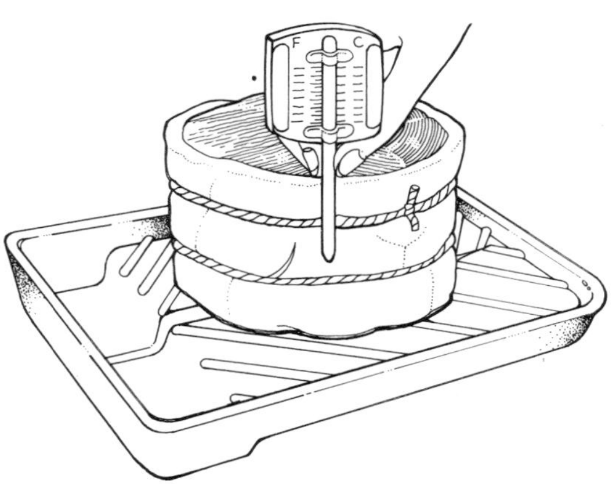

Insert the thermometer to the depth marked by your finger. Choose an angle where the sensor is in the centre of a meaty section, not touching fat or bone.

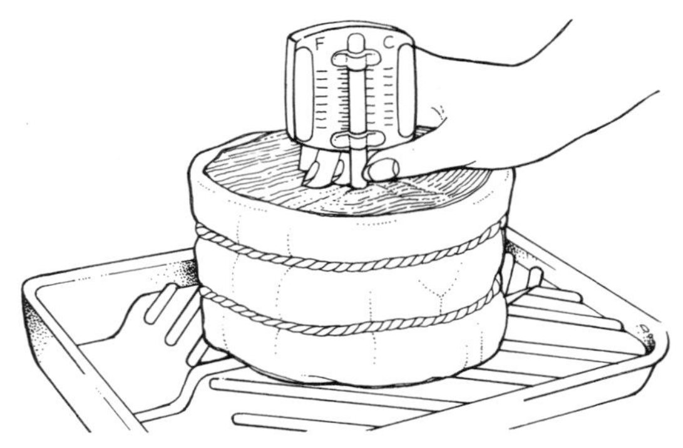

Regular-shaped roasts cook more evenly than irregular shapes. Shield thin ends of roasts with foil to prevent overcooking in these areas.

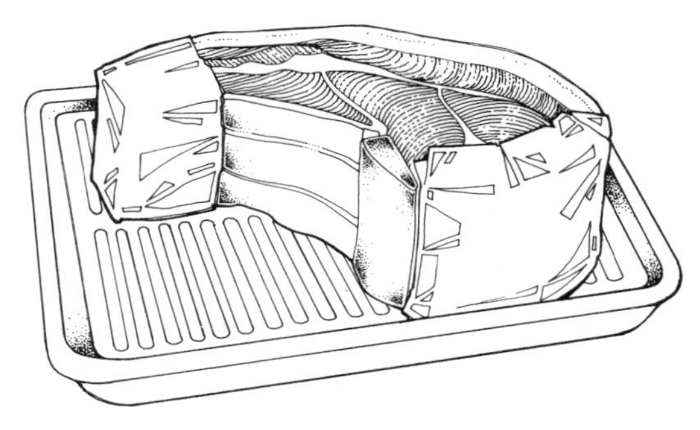

In most cases divide the cooking time into quarters and turn the meat over four times during cooking. A piece of absorbent kitchen paper can help with this operation.

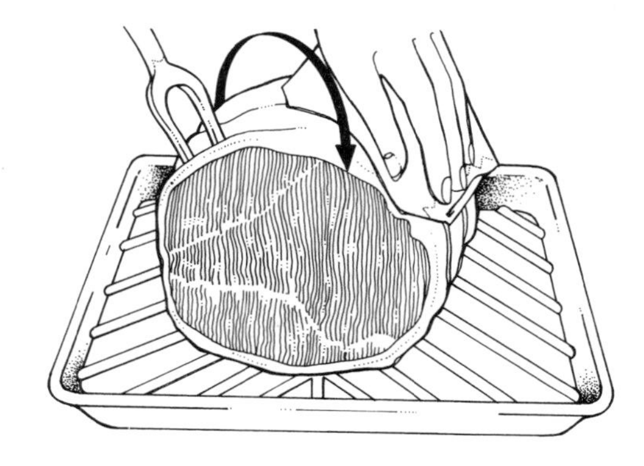

Drippings and juices attract microwave energy away from the meat: when cooking a roast, drain the drippings at intervals to speed up cooking and prevent spattering.

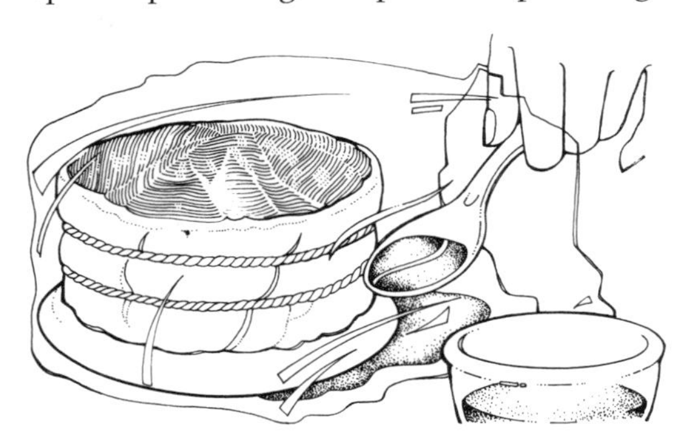

Always observe the standing times at the end of cooking to use up the residual heat in the meat.

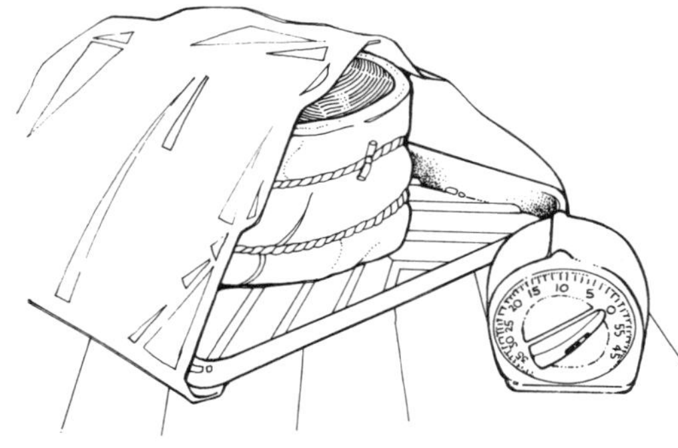

Meat can be cooked in a clay pot. Soak the pot and lid in water for 30 minutes; drain but do not dry. Place the meat in the pot, fat side down, and add any other ingredients. Cook for the recommended time, turning the meat once or twice during cooking.

Rotate meatloaves and whole, shaped meat dishes during the cooking time. Give the dish a half turn halfway through cooking.

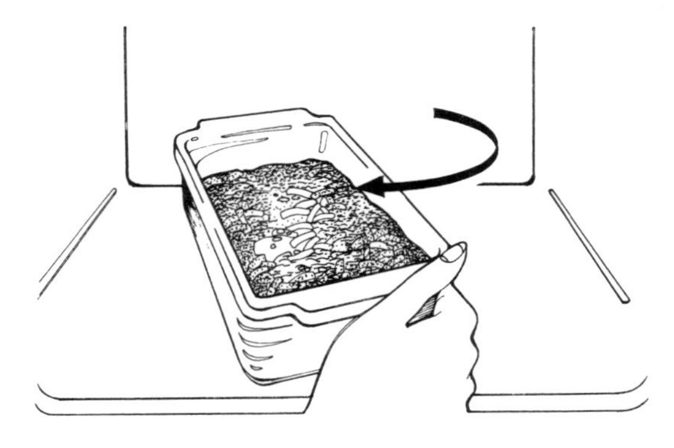

When cooking chops, spareribs or burgers, turn over and rearrange them halfway through the cooking time.

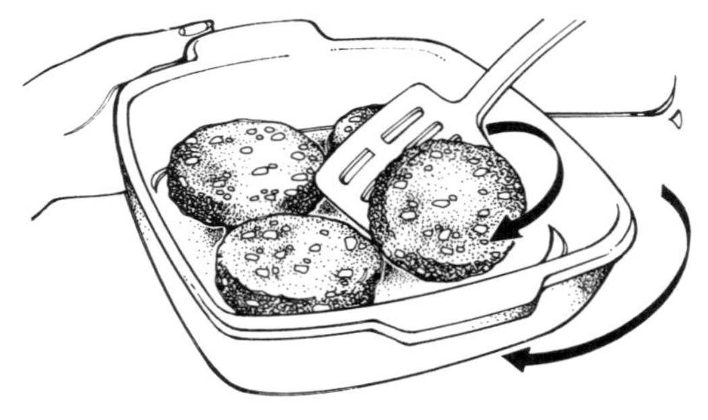

When cooking meatballs turn or rearrange halfway through the cooking time.

Top: Stuffed Bacon Chop (page 107); *Below:* Bacon and Onion Suet Pudding (page 108)
Overleaf *Top:* Barbecued Spareribs (page 106); *Below left:* Honey-glazed Pork Chops (page 103); *Right:* Somerset Pork with Cider Cream (page 105)

STAINLESS STEEL
MADE IN JAPAN

Cook bacon on a bacon or roasting rack covered with a single sheet of absorbent kitchen paper, or place between two layers of absorbent kitchen paper to cook.

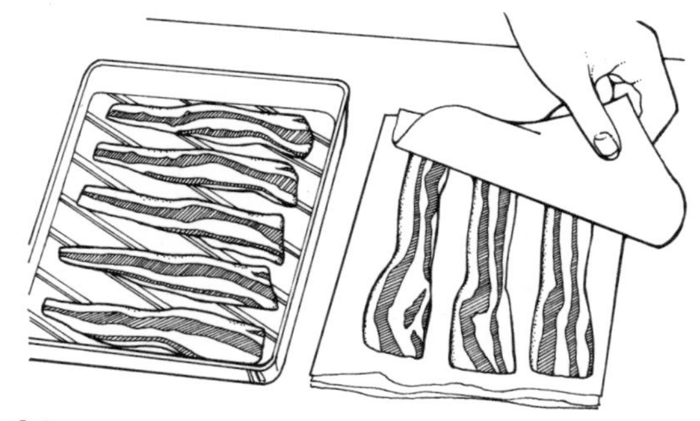

Guide to Cooking Meat

Type and cut of meat		*Cooking time in minutes on* **MEDIUM POWER** *per 450 g/1 lb or for quantity given*	*Cooking time in minutes on* **FULL POWER** *per 450 g/1 lb or for quantity given*	*Preparation*
Beef				
topside	rare	12	5–6	*Choose a good quality joint with an even covering of fat and a neat shape. Allow to stand for 15–20 minutes, wrapped in foil, before carving.*
	medium	14	6½–7½	
	well done	16	8½–9½	
sirloin	rare	12	5–6	
	medium	14	6½–7½	
	well done	16	8½–9½	
rib	rare	12–13	5½–6½	*Ideally, bone and roll the joint before cooking. Allow to stand for 15–30 minutes, wrapped in foil, before cooking.*
	medium	14–15	7–8	
	well done	16–17	8–10	
minced beef		14–16	10–12	
rump steak	rare		2	*Preheat a browning dish according to the manufacturer's instructions. Add the meat and brown. Turn over and cook for the recommended time.*
	medium	—	3–4	
	well-done		4	
fillet steak	rare		2	
	medium	—	2–3	
	well done		3	
braising steak		16–17	10	*Ideally, cook on* **MEDIUM POWER**. *If using* **FULL POWER**, *leave to rest for 10 minutes halfway through the cooking time.*
hamburgers	1 (100-g/4-oz)		2–3	*Preheat a browning dish according to the manufacturer's instructions. Add the hamburgers and cook for the recommended time, turning the 100-g/4-oz burgers over halfway through the cooking time, and turning 225-g/8-oz burgers over twice during the cooking time.*
	2 (100-g/4-oz)	—	3–4	
	3 (100-g/4-oz)		4–5	
	4 (100-g/4-oz)		5–6	
	1 (225-g/8-oz)		2½–3½	
	2 (225-g/8-oz)		6–7	

Top: Meatballs in Chilli Sauce (page 99); *Below:* Spicy Mid-Winter Pie (page 97)

Type and cut of meat		*Cooking time in minutes on* MEDIUM POWER *per 450g/1 lb or for quantity given*	*Cooking time in minutes on* FULL POWER *per 450g/1 lb or for quantity given*	*Preparation*
Lamb				
leg	on bone	11–13	8–10	*Choose a good quality joint. Roll the meat into a neat shape if it is off the bone. Cover the pointed end with foil to protect it if on the bone. Allow to stand for 25–30 minutes, wrapped in foil, before carving.*
	off bone	12–13	9–10	
breast		14–16	12	*Roll and stuff, if liked, before cooking. Allow to stand for 30 minutes, wrapped in foil, before cooking.*
crown roast		—	5	*Cover tips of bone with foil during cooking.*
loin of lamb		11–13	8–10	*Choose a good quality joint. Roll into a neat shape if off the bone. Allow to stand for 25–30 minutes, wrapped in foil, before carving.*
chops	loin or 2		6–7	*Preheat the browning dish according to the manufacturer's instructions. Add the chops and cook for the recommended time, turning over halfway through the cooking time.*
	chump 4	—	7–9	
	6		15–17	
Pork				
leg		13–15	10	*Choose a good quality joint. Cover the pointed end with foil to protect from over cooking. Score fat with a sharp knife and sprinkle liberally with salt to get a crisp crackling. Allow to stand for 20 minutes, wrapped in foil, before carving. Brown under a hot grill if liked.*
loin		14–16	10–13	*Roll into a neat shape before cooking. Allow to stand for 20 minutes, wrapped in foil, before carving.*
fillet		—	7	
chops	loin or 2	14–18	—	*Preheat the browning dish according to the manufacturer's instructions. Add the chops and cook for the recommended time, turning over halfway through the cooking time.*
	chump 3	19–24		
	4	26–32		
	6	33–37		
Veal *leg or shoulder joint*		11–12	8½–9	*Secure into a neat shape before cooking. Allow to stand for 20 minutes, wrapped in foil, before carving.*

Type and cut of meat		*Cooking time in minutes on* MEDIUM POWER *per 450 g/1 lb or for quantity given*	*Cooking time in minutes on* FULL POWER *per 450 g/1 lb or for quantity given*	*Preparation*
Bacon or Gammon				
joint		11–12	—	
gammon steaks (each)			14	*Cook in a browning dish if liked (observing preheating times) or cover with cling film. Turn halfway through the cooking time.*
Bacon	4 slices	—	3½–4	*Place on a plate or bacon rack and cover with absorbent kitchen paper. Turn rashers over halfway through cooking.*
	450 g/1 lb		12–14	
Liver		—	5–6	
Kidney		—	7–8	
Sausages	2	—	1½–2	*Prick thoroughly and arrange on a rack or plate. Cover with absorbent kitchen paper and turn halfway through the cooking time.*
	4	—	3–3½	

FILLET OF BEEF WITH MUSTARD BUTTER

Serves 8
Power setting FULL
Total cooking time 20–28 minutes

1 (1.25-kg/2½-lb) beef fillet
salt and freshly ground black pepper
2 tablespoons oil
MUSTARD BUTTER
100 g/4 oz butter
1 tablespoon wholegrain mustard
1 tablespoon chopped parsley
½ teaspoon lemon juice

Tie the joint into a neat, even shape with string. Season to taste and rub with the oil. Cream the butter with the mustard and beat in the chopped parsley and lemon juice. Form into a roll, wrap in foil and chill until firm.

Preheat a large browning dish for 5 minutes, or according to the manufacturer's instructions. Add the beef and roll it quickly to brown on all sides. Cook for 15 minutes for rare beef, 18–19 minutes for medium beef and 22–23 minutes for well-done beef, turning over halfway through the cooking time. Wrap in foil and leave to stand for 10–15 minutes.

Carve the beef thinly and arrange on a serving dish, placing a slice of chilled mustard butter between each slice of beef. Serve hot.

FLANK OF BEEF WITH HORSERADISH

Serves 6
Power setting FULL and MEDIUM
Total cooking time 51–59 minutes

1 (1.25-kg/2½-lb) thick flank of beef
65 g/2½ oz butter
1 large onion, peeled and chopped
100 g/4 oz fresh white breadcrumbs
100 g/4 oz Cheddar cheese, finely chopped
3 tablespoons horseradish relish
salt and freshly ground black pepper
1 egg, beaten
6 tablespoons hot water

Slice the meat almost through and open it out like a book. Beat the meat well to flatten it out, then carefully score a diamond pattern on the newly-cut surface.

Place 40 g/1½ oz of the butter in a bowl and cook on FULL POWER for 1 minute to melt. Add the onion, breadcrumbs, cheese, horseradish relish and seasoning to taste and mix well. Bind the ingredients together with the beaten egg.

Place this stuffing neatly down the length of the meat on the unscored side. Roll up and secure with string, then dot lightly with the remaining butter.

Preheat a browning dish for 5 minutes. Add the beef and quickly turn it to brown on all sides. Stir in the water and cook on MEDIUM POWER for 23 minutes. Turn over and give the dish a half turn. Cook on MEDIUM POWER for 22–30 minutes until cooked. Allow to stand for 10–15 minutes, covered in foil, before serving thickly sliced with any juices from the dish.

BEEF SPICE HOTPOT

(Illustrated on pages 110/111)
Serves 4
Power setting FULL and MEDIUM
Total cooking time 61 minutes

1 kg/2 lb lean braising steak
50 g/2 oz plain flour
2 teaspoons mustard powder
½ teaspoon salt
2 tablespoons oil
2 large onions, peeled and chopped
2 tablespoons concentrated tomato purée
2 tablespoons paprika
pinch of cayenne pepper
1 teaspoon dried thyme
600 ml/1 pint pale ale
100 g/4 oz button mushrooms

Cut the meat into 3.5-cm/1½-in cubes. Mix the flour, mustard and salt together and toss the meat in this mixture. Preheat a browning dish on FULL POWER for 5 minutes, or according to the manufacturer's instructions. Add the oil and cook on FULL POWER for 1 minute. Add the beef, turning quickly on all sides to brown evenly and cook on FULL POWER for a further 5 minutes.

Transfer to a large casserole and add the onion, tomato purée, paprika, cayenne, thyme and pale ale. Cover and cook on MEDIUM POWER for 35 minutes. Add the mushrooms and continue to cook on MEDIUM POWER for a further 15 minutes. Leave to stand for 5 minutes before serving.

SPICY MID-WINTER PIE

(Illustrated on page 92)
Serves 6–8
Power setting FULL and LOW
Total cooking time 51–52 minutes

3 tablespoons oil
2 tablespoons plain flour
1 tablespoon mustard powder
2 teaspoons salt
½ teaspoon freshly ground black pepper
1.25 kg/2½ lb stewing steak, cut into 2.5-cm/1-in pieces
10 pickling or very small onions, peeled
1 small turnip, peeled and diced
4 sticks celery, diced
6 carrots, peeled and sliced
2 teaspoons dried mixed herbs
300 ml/½ pint hot beef stock
dash of Worcestershire sauce
1 (370-g/13-oz) packet frozen puff pastry, thawed
beaten egg to glaze

Blend the oil, flour, mustard powder, salt and pepper in a large deep dish and cook on FULL POWER for 3 minutes until the colour of the mixture is slightly darkened. Add the stewing steak and cook on FULL POWER for 5 minutes. Add the onions, turnip, celery, carrots, herbs, stock and Worcestershire sauce. Cover and cook on LOW POWER for 35 minutes, stirring occasionally. Place in a large pie dish.

Roll out the pastry on a lightly floured surface to make a pie lid, 2.5 cm/1 in larger than the dish. Brush the edges of the pie dish with beaten egg. Place the pastry over the dish, folding the edges under to form a double thickness around the rim. Flute the edges, then make three cuts in the pie crust to allow the steam to escape. Decorate the pie with any remaining pastry cut into leaves. Brush with beaten egg. Cook on FULL POWER for 8–9 minutes until the pastry puffs up, holds its shape and is no longer raw. Immediately place under a hot grill to brown. Serve steaming hot.

STEAK AND KIDNEY HOTPOT

Serves 4
Power setting FULL and LOW
Total cooking time 1 hour 3 minutes

2 tablespoons oil
25 g/1 oz plain flour
2 teaspoons mustard powder
2 teaspoons salt
½ teaspoon freshly ground black pepper
450 g/1 lb braising steak, cut into 2.5-cm/1-in cubes
8 lamb's kidneys, skinned, halved and cored
2 small swedes, peeled and quartered
4 small onions, peeled and quartered
1 large onion, peeled and chopped
300 ml/½ pint beer or beef stock
100 g/4 oz mushrooms
chopped parsley to garnish

Blend the oil, flour, mustard powder, salt and pepper in a large deep dish and cook on FULL POWER for 3 minutes until beige in colour. Add the beef and kidney, stir and cook on FULL POWER for 5 minutes. Add the swede, onion and beer or stock. Cover and cook on LOW POWER for 50 minutes, stirring occassionally. Add the mushrooms and cook on FULL POWER for a further 5 minutes.

Leave the dish to stand, covered, for 15 minutes before serving garnished with chopped parsley.

BEEF STROGANOFF

Serves 4
Power setting FULL
Total cooking time 10½ minutes

50 g/2 oz butter
675 g/1½ lb beef fillet, trimmed and cut into thin strips
1 large onion, peeled and finely sliced
225 g/8 oz mushrooms, sliced
25 g/1 oz plain flour
150 ml/¼ pint dry white wine
salt and freshly ground black pepper
150 ml/¼ pint soured cream

Place the butter in a bowl and cook for 1 minute to melt. Add the beef and cook for 4 minutes, stirring after 2 minutes. Remove the meat with a slotted spoon and reserve.

Add the onion and mushrooms to the beef juices. Cover and cook for 4 minutes. Stir in the flour, blending well, then add the wine and the reserved meat. Cook for 1½ minutes. Add seasoning to taste and gently stir in the soured cream. Serve with noodles and a salad.

MEATBALLS IN CHILLI SAUCE

(Illustrated on page 92)
Serves 4
Power setting FULL
Total cooking time 18½ minutes

2 tablespoons oil
1 onion, peeled and finely chopped
450 g/1 lb lean minced beef
50 g/2 oz breadcrumbs
1 tablespoon finely chopped parsley
½ teaspoon dried oregano
salt and freshly ground black pepper
about ½ beaten egg
SAUCE
1 (398-g/14-oz) can peeled tomatoes
1 teaspoon chilli seasoning
1 onion, peeled and chopped
1 green pepper, seeds removed and chopped
1 teaspoon sugar
3 tablespoons dry red wine
1 tablespoon cornflour

Heat the oil in a large dish for ½ minute. Add the onion and cook for a further 3 minutes, until lightly browned.

Meanwhile, mix the beef, breadcrumbs, parsley, oregano, seasoning to taste and enough egg to bind the mixture. Divide into eight portions and form into meatballs. Place the meatballs in a single layer on top of the onion. Cook in the microwave for 5 minutes, turning the meatballs once and giving the dish a half turn halfway through cooking.

Place the tomatoes, chilli seasoning, onion, pepper, sugar and wine in a large jug and cook in the microwave for 5 minutes, stirring halfway through the cooking time. Blend the cornflour with a little water and stir into the sauce. Pour the sauce over the meatballs and return to the microwave. Cook for a further 5 minutes, turning the dish halfway through the cooking time. Serve hot with boiled rice or jacket potatoes.

SPAGHETTI BOLOGNESE

Serves 4
Power setting FULL
Total cooking time 42–44 minutes

450 g/1 lb lean minced beef
1 clove garlic, crushed
1 onion, peeled and finely chopped
100 g/4 oz button mushrooms, thinly sliced
2 tablespoons plain flour
1 (398-g/14-oz) can peeled tomatoes
salt and freshly ground black pepper
1 teaspoon chopped parsley
¼ teaspoon dried mixed herbs
2 teaspoons concentrated tomato purée
150 ml/¼ pint dry red wine
150 ml/¼ pint beef stock
275 g/10 oz spaghetti
1.5 litres/2¾ pints boiling water
½ teaspoon oil
15 g/½ oz butter
75 g/3 oz Parmesan cheese, grated

Preheat a browning dish for 5 minutes or according to the manufacturer's instructions. Quickly stir in the beef, garlic and onion. Cook for 8 minutes, stirring and breaking up the meat occasionally during cooking. Transfer to a large bowl, add the mushrooms and flour, then cook for a further 1 minute. Add the tomatoes, seasoning to taste, parsley, herbs, tomato purée, wine and beef stock. Cover and cook for 15 minutes, stirring halfway through the cooking time. Leave to stand while cooking the spaghetti.

Place the spaghetti in a deep bowl and pour over the boiling water. Add a little salt to taste and the oil. Cook, uncovered, for 8–10 minutes until just beginning to soften. Cover tightly with cling film and leave to stand for 10 minutes. Meanwhile cook the sauce, uncovered, for a further 5 minutes, stirring occasionally.

Drain the spaghetti and toss in the butter. Season to taste and pile on to a warmed serving dish. Top with the meat sauce and Parmesan cheese.

MEATLOAF WITH PEPPER SAUCE

(Illustrated on page 112)
Serves 4
Power setting FULL
Total cooking time 22 minutes

1 tablespoon oil
1 onion, peeled and chopped
225 g/8 oz minced beef
225 g/8 oz minced pork
6 tablespoons fresh brown breadcrumbs
1 clove garlic, peeled and crushed
1 tablespoon concentrated tomato purée
salt and freshly ground black pepper
1 egg, beaten
PEPPER SAUCE
25 g/1 oz butter
1 large green pepper, seeds removed and chopped
1 tablespoon plain flour
300 ml/$\frac{1}{2}$ pint boiling beef stock
1 tablespoon concentrated tomato purée
50 g/2 oz button mushrooms, sliced
GARNISH
tomato slices or
watercress sprigs

Place the oil in a bowl and cook for 2 minutes. Add the onion, mixing well, and cook for a further 3 minutes, stirring after 2 minutes. Add the beef, pork, breadcrumbs, garlic, tomato purée and seasoning to taste, then mix well. Bind the ingredients together with the beaten egg, then press the mixture into a 1.2-litre/2-pint oval pie dish and cook for 5 minutes. Remove from the oven, wrap the dish in foil and leave to stand for 15 minutes. Remove the foil and cook for a further 5 minutes. Re-wrap in foil and leave to stand while preparing the sauce.

Place the butter in a jug and cook for 1 minute to melt. Add the pepper, stir well and cook for 3 minutes. Stir in the flour and cook for 1 minute. Gradually add the stock, tomato purée and mushrooms. Cook for 2 minutes, stirring after 1 minute. Season to taste and serve with the meatloaf – either poured over it or poured into a warmed sauce boat. Garnish the turned-out meatloaf with tomato slices or watercress sprigs.

LOIN OF LAMB FLORENTINE

(Illustrated on pages 110/111 and front cover)
Serves 4
Power setting FULL or MEDIUM
Total cooking time about 51 or 39 minutes

25 g/1 oz butter or margarine
1 onion, peeled and chopped
1 (300-g/10.6-oz) packet frozen cut leaf spinach, thawed
6 tablespoons fresh breadcrumbs
salt and freshly ground black pepper
finely grated rind of ½ orange
1 tablespoon orange juice
1 (1.5-kg/3-lb) loin of lamb, boned
2 tablespoons redcurrant jelly

Place the butter or margarine in a bowl and cook on FULL POWER for 1 minute. Add the onion and cook on FULL POWER for 2 minutes. Drain and discard all the excess liquid from the spinach, then add to the onion with the breadcrumbs, seasoning to taste, orange rind and orange juice. Mix all these stuffing ingredients together thoroughly.

Place the meat, skin-side down on a clean surface or board and spread with the stuffing. Fold over to enclose the stuffing and sew the edges together with fine string to form a neat and even shape.

Weigh the roast calculating the cooking time at 12 minutes per 450 g/1 lb on MEDIUM POWER or 9 minutes per 450 g/1 lb if using FULL POWER. Place on a roasting rack or an upturned saucer in a roasting bag, securing the end with string or an elastic band, and cook for half the calculated cooking time. Remove from the oven and remove the meat from the roasting bag.

Place the redcurrant jelly in a small bowl and heat for ½ minute, then brush it over the lamb. Return to the microwave, uncovered, and cook for the remaining time. If a crisp golden skin is liked, place the joint under a hot grill to brown before serving. Leave to stand, wrapped in foil, for 10–15 minutes.

To serve, remove the string and carve the lamb into thick slices.

CUCUMBER-STUFFED LOIN OF LAMB

Serves 4
Power setting FULL
Total cooking time 23 minutes

1 (1-kg/2-lb) loin of lamb, boned
STUFFING
½ cucumber, grated
1 small onion, peeled and grated
1 tablespoon chopped fresh mint
100 g/4 oz fresh breadcrumbs
1 teaspoon salt
1 teaspoon freshly ground black pepper
1 egg, beaten
1 tablespoon oil for brushing

Lay the lamb flat on a surface, skin side down. Mix all the stuffing ingredients together blending well, then arrange the mixture down the centre of the meat, roll up neatly and secure with string. Score the skin in a triangular pattern and brush with the oil.

Preheat a browning dish for 5 minutes, or according to the manufacturer's instructions. Add the roast, turning it quickly to brown evenly on all sides. Cook for 18 minutes, turning the meat over and giving the dish a half turn after 9 minutes. Leave to rest for 5 minutes before serving sliced, with fresh green vegetables and buttered new potatoes.

HONEY-GLAZED PORK CHOPS

(Illustrated on pages 90/91)
Serves 2
Power setting FULL
Total cooking time 10–10½ minutes

2 large pork chops
salt and freshly ground black pepper
1 tablespoon clear honey
5 tablespoons dry cider
2 teaspoons chopped fresh sage or 1 teaspoon dried sage

Place the chops in a shallow dish and season generously. Pour over the honey and cider and sprinkle the sage on top. Leave to marinate for 20–30 minutes.

Preheat a large browning dish for 5 minutes, or according to the manufacturer's instructions. Add the chops, moving them round quickly and turning them over so that they brown evenly. Cook for 2½ minutes.

Turn the chops over, pointing the thin ends to the centre of the dish. Spoon over a little of the remaining marinade and cook for a further 2½–3 minutes or until the meat flesh is cooked and no longer pink. Allow to stand for 3 minutes, then serve with the remaining juices poured over the chops. Serve with the vegetables of your choice or a mixed salad.

ROAST PORK WITH SAGE AND ONION STUFFING

Serves 6
Power setting FULL or MEDIUM
Total cooking time about 55 minutes or $1\frac{1}{4}$ hours

225 g/8 oz onions, peeled and chopped
25 g/1 oz butter or margarine
125 g/$4\frac{1}{2}$ oz fresh white breadcrumbs
1 tablespoon finely chopped fresh sage or 1 teaspoon dried sage
salt and freshly ground black pepper
beaten egg to bind
1 (1.8-kg/4-lb) loin of pork, boned and skin scored finely
2 tablespoons oil
sage sprigs to garnish (optional)

Place the onion in a bowl with the butter or margarine and cook on FULL POWER for 5 minutes. Add the breadcrumbs, sage and seasoning to taste. Stir in sufficient beaten egg to bind the ingredients together.

Lay the pork, skin-side down, on a surface and make a deep slit down the thick meaty part. Open out and spread with the stuffing. Bring the edges of the pork together to make a neat roll and sew together with fine string.

Weigh the roast calculating the cooking time at 14 minutes per 450 g/1 lb on MEDIUM POWER or 10 minutes per 450 g/1 lb if using FULL POWER. Rub the scored skin with the oil and about 1 teaspoon of salt, then place the joint on a roasting rack or an upturned saucer in a roasting bag, securing the end with string or an elastic band. Cook for the calculated cooking time, giving the dish a half turn three times during cooking. If the crackling is not crisp enough for your liking, place the pork under a hot grill. Wrap in foil and leave to stand for 10–15 minutes before serving. Remove the string and carve as usual. Serve garnished with small sage sprigs, if liked.

GRAVY

Makes 300 ml/$\frac{1}{2}$ pint
Power setting FULL
Total cooking time 5–6 minutes

2 tablespoons pan juices or dripping from roast meat
1–2 tablespoons plain flour
300 ml/$\frac{1}{2}$ pint hot beef or chicken stock
salt and freshly ground black pepper

Place the pan juices or dripping in the microwave roasting dish or in a bowl and stir in the flour – the quantity varies slightly according to how thick you want the gravy. Cook for 3 minutes until the flour turns golden. Gradually add the stock, mixing well, then cook for 2–3 minutes until smooth and boiling. Season to taste and serve.

SPICY PORK STROGANOFF

(Illustrated on pages 110/111)
Serves 4–6
Power setting FULL
Total cooking time 16 minutes

1 kg/2 lb pork fillet
50 g/2 oz butter
1 large onion, peeled and chopped
2 tablespoons paprika
2 teaspoons mustard powder
150 ml/$\frac{1}{4}$ pint hot chicken stock
2 tablespoons concentrated tomato purée
salt and freshly ground black pepper
150 ml/$\frac{1}{4}$ pint soured cream

Cut the pork fillet into thin strips. Place the butter in a large bowl and cook for 1 minute to melt. Add the meat and onion and cook for 10 minutes, stirring after 5 minutes. Sprinkle over the paprika and mustard and mix well. Add the stock, tomato purée and seasoning to taste and blend well. Cover with cling film, snipping two holes in the top to allow the steam to escape, and cook for a further 4 minutes. Stir in the soured cream, cook for 1 minute then leave to stand for 3 minutes. Serve with buttered pasta or boiled rice.

SOMERSET PORK WITH CIDER CREAM

(Illustrated on pages 90/91)
Serves 4
Power setting FULL
Total cooking time 23 minutes

25 g/1 oz butter
2 medium onions, peeled and sliced
675 g/1$\frac{1}{2}$ lb pork fillet, cubed
100 g/4 oz button mushrooms
300 ml/$\frac{1}{2}$ pint dry cider
salt and freshly ground black pepper
2 tablespoons cornflour
3 tablespoons double cream
finely chopped parsley to garnish

Place the butter in a medium-sized casserole dish and cook for 1 minute to melt, then add the onion and continue to cook for 5 minutes. Add the pork fillet and cook for a further 7 minutes, stirring halfway through the cooking time.

Stir in the mushrooms, cider and seasoning to taste, then cook for 8 minutes. Blend the cornflour with a little water and stir into the pork mixture. Cook for a further 2 minutes, stirring occasionally, remove from the oven and stir in the cream. Sprinkle with chopped parsley and serve immediately, with boiled rice and a green salad.

BARBECUED SPARERIBS

(Illustrated on pages 90/91)
Serves 4–6
Power setting FULL and MEDIUM or LOW
Total cooking time 45–50 minutes or 1 hour 15 minutes – 1 hour 25 minutes

1.5 kg/3-lb meaty spareribs, cut into 7.5-cm/3-in lengths
150 ml/$\frac{1}{4}$ pint tomato ketchup
1 small onion, peeled and chopped
2 tablespoons lemon juice
15 g/$\frac{1}{2}$ oz melted butter
1 small clove garlic, crushed
1$\frac{1}{2}$ teaspoons sugar
salt and freshly ground black pepper

Place the spareribs in a shallow rectangular dish. Mix all the remaining ingredients together and pour half of this sauce over the spareribs. Cover with cling film, snipping two holes in the top to allow the steam to escape. Cook on FULL POWER for 5 minutes. Reduce the power to MEDIUM or LOW: cooking on LOW POWER is recommended for less tender spareribs. Cook on MEDIUM POWER for 20 minutes or on LOW POWER for 35 minutes.

Turn the ribs over and discard about 175 ml/6 fl oz of the cooking juices. If all the juices are retained, the finished dish will be too wet and weak in flavour. Pour in the remaining sauce, re-cover and cook on MEDIUM POWER for 20–25 minutes or until the meat is tender. Leave to stand, covered, for 10 minutes before serving.

PORK AND MANGO CURRY

(Illustrated on page 109)
Serves 6
Power setting FULL
Total cooking time 40 minutes

1 tablespoon oil
2 small green or red peppers, seeds removed and finely sliced
1 Spanish onion, peeled and thickly sliced
1 teaspoon turmeric
2 teaspoons salt
1 tablespoon garam masala or curry powder
1 teaspoon ground cumin
1 teaspoon ginger
$\frac{1}{2}$ teaspoon chilli seasoning
800 g/1$\frac{3}{4}$ lb pork fillet, cubed
25 g/1 oz plain flour
5 medium tomatoes, peeled and chopped
2 teaspoons concentrated tomato purée
450 ml/$\frac{3}{4}$ pint hot water
1 (425-g/15-oz) can mango slices, drained *or* 2 large mangoes, peeled, stoned and sliced

Place the oil, pepper, onion, turmeric, salt, garam masala or curry powder, cumin, ginger and chilli seasoning in a large bowl and cook, uncovered, for 6 minutes, stirring halfway through the cooking time.

Meanwhile, toss the pork in the flour. Add to the onion mixture, cover with cling film, snipping two holes in the top to allow the steam to escape, and cook for 24 minutes, stirring halfway through the cooking time. Add the tomatoes, tomato purée, water and mango slices, cover with cling film, again snipping two holes in the top, and cook for 10 minutes. Allow to stand for 5 minutes before serving with a selection of accompaniments; for example boiled rice, poppadums, desiccated coconut, sliced bananas and apples dipped in lemon juice, mango chutney or a tomato and onion salad.

STUFFED BACON CHOPS

(Illustrated on page 89)
Serves 4
Power setting FULL and MEDIUM
Total cooking time 33–38 minutes

4 bacon chops, cut 2.5 cm/1 in thick
50 g/2 oz butter
3 sticks celery, chopped
1 onion, peeled and chopped
50 g/2 oz fresh white breadcrumbs
1 egg, beaten
salt and freshly ground black pepper
1 tablespoon snipped chives

Carefully make a split into each chop, cutting through almost to the edge to form a pocket.

Place half the butter in a bowl with the celery and onion, then cook on FULL POWER for 3 minutes, stirring halfway through the cooking time. Add the breadcrumbs, egg and seasoning to taste. Spoon the stuffing into the pockets in the bacon chops. Cream the remaining butter with the chives and spread on all sides of the chops.

Preheat a browning dish according to the manufacturer's instructions – about 5 minutes on FULL POWER. Lay the chops in the dish and place in the microwave. Reduce the power to MEDIUM and cook, covered with greaseproof paper, for 15 minutes.

Turn the chops over, re-cover and cook on MEDIUM POWER for 10–15 minutes, until the bacon is cooked.

BACON AND ONION SUET PUDDING

(Illustrated on page 89)
Serves 4
Power setting FULL and DEFROST
Total cooking time 38 minutes

450 g/1 lb collar bacon, cubed
1 ham or chicken stock cube
5 teaspoons plain flour
1 tablespoon chopped parsley
1 small onion, peeled and finely sliced
1 small green pepper, seeds removed and chopped
1 small cooking apple, peeled, cored and sliced
75 ml/3 fl oz water
SUET PASTRY
100 g/4 oz self-raising flour
generous pinch of salt
50 g/2 oz shredded beef suet
4 tablespoons cold water

Place the bacon in a bowl with the crumbled stock cube, flour and parsley and toss to coat the cubes of meat. Add the onion, pepper and apple and mix well. Transfer this mixture to a 1.2-litre/2-pint pudding basin, add the water and stir to mix.

Cook on FULL POWER for 5 minutes; stir, then cover with cling film, snipping two holes in the top to allow the steam to escape. Cook on DEFROST POWER for 10 minutes, then stir the mixture, re-cover and cook on DEFROST POWER for a further 10 minutes.

Mix all the ingredients for the pastry with a round-bladed knife, then knead lightly to form a soft dough. Roll out the pastry on a lightly floured surface, to a round large enough to cover the top of the basin. Lift the pastry over the meat and cook on DEFROST POWER for 13 minutes, giving the basin a half turn every 3 minutes. Cover with foil and allow to stand for 10 minutes before serving.

Bottom: Pork and Mango Curry (page 106) with accompaniments – mango chutney (top), sliced bananas with desiccated coconut (right), sliced tomatoes with spring onions (left) and poppadums;
Centre: Pilaf with Bacon and Peas (page 154)
Overleaf *Top:* Loin of Lamb Florentine (page 102); *Bottom right:* Pork Stroganoff (page 105); *Left:* Beef Spice Hotpot (page 96)

WINTER WARMING STUFFED CABBAGE

Serves 4
Power setting FULL
Total cooking time 38–40 minutes

1 (1-kg/2-lb) winter cabbage
100 ml/4 fl oz water
75 g/3 oz butter
1 onion, peeled and chopped
2 sticks celery, chopped
2 teaspoons ground coriander
1 (240-g/8½-oz) smoked pork sausage, finely chopped
50 g/2 oz fresh breadcrumbs
2 tablespoons chopped parsley
2 teaspoons lemon juice
1 egg, beaten
salt and freshly ground black pepper
5 tablespoons hot chicken stock

Remove the coarse outer leaves from the cabbage. Trim the base and remove some of the thick stem with a potato peeler. Using a sharp knife remove a 1.5-cm/¾-in slice from the top of the cabbage. Secure the cabbage into a good neat shape by tying with string around the middle. Place in a dish with the water. Cover with cling film, snipping two holes in the top to allow the steam to escape, and cook for 15 minutes, giving the dish a half turn halfway through the cooking time. Drain and allow to cool enough to handle.

Meanwhile, place 50 g/2 oz of the butter in a bowl and cook for 1 minute. Add the onion, celery and coriander and cook for 3 minutes. Add the sausage, breadcrumbs, parsley, lemon juice and egg. Season to taste and blend well.

Using a sharp knife, scoop out and reserve the centre of the cabbage leaving a 1-cm/½-in shell. Pack the prepared stuffing into the cabbage and place in a shallow dish. Add the stock and cover with cling film, snipping two holes in the top. Cook for 13–15 minutes, giving the dish a half turn halfway through the cooking time. Cut into wedges to serve.

Shred the reserved cabbage and place in a bowl with 4 tablespoons water. Cover and cook for 6 minutes. Drain and toss in the remaining butter. Serve the stuffed cabbage wedges with the buttered cabbage.

Top: Winter Warming Stuffed Cabbage; *Below:* Meatloaf with Pepper Sauce (page 101)

Vegetables and Salads

With microwave cooking, vegetables are not only an essential part of a good meal, but they become one of the best parts. Quick cooking in little additional water ensures that fresh, frozen, or even canned vegetables retain their colour, fresh taste and texture. And there is less draining away of flavour and nutrients.

Vegetables should be tightly covered before cooking. If they are covered with cling film, two holes should be snipped in the top to allow the steam to escape. When vegetables are cooked in their skins, potatoes for example, their own skins form a tight covering, so prick them with a fork before cooking to release excess steam. Add salt to the vegetables after cooking, or put the salt in the dish with the water before adding the vegetables. Salting the top of the vegetables before microwave cooking causes darkened, dried-out spots to appear on the cooked food.

Vegetables, like other foods, continue to cook after they are removed from the microwave oven, so take care to allow a little standing time before deciding whether the vegetables are cooked to your taste, or if you would like to cook them a little longer. Add 2–3 minutes standing time to the times quoted on the cooking chart, then drain and serve the vegetables. The times given in the cooking chart allow for a just-tender texture. Reduce the time by 1–2 minutes for a crisp texture and increase it by 1–2 minutes for a soft texture. If you cook more, or less, vegetables than stated in the chart, remember to adjust the cooking times accordingly.

Cooking Vegetables in the Microwave Oven

Small, even-sized pieces of vegetables cook faster than larger ones. Cut vegetables, wherever possible, to a uniform size.

Large or uneven pieces should be arranged with the thinner or more tender portions to the centre of the dish (1). Give the dish a half turn midway through the cooking time.

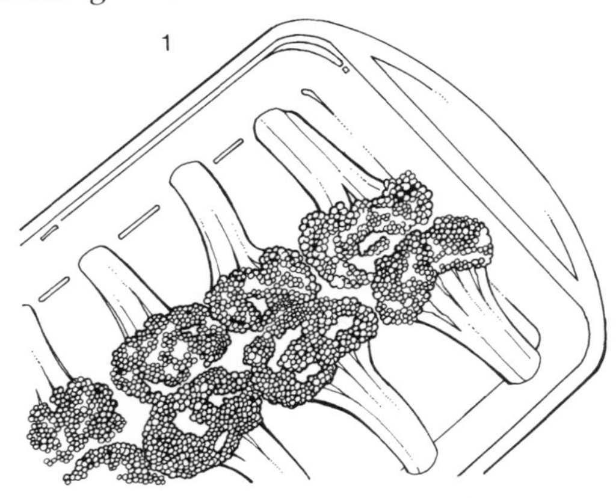

Stir fresh, canned or frozen vegetables halfway through the cooking time – this helps to distribute the heat evenly. Rotate the dish for those vegetables that are too large to stir (2).

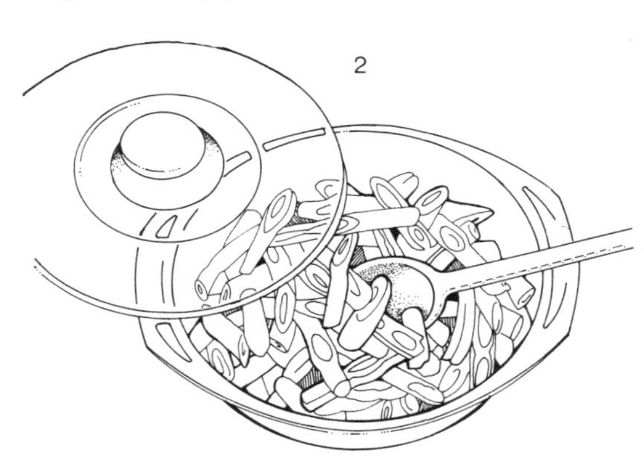

Whole or chunky vegetables should be turned over halfway through the cooking time to ensure even cooking (3).

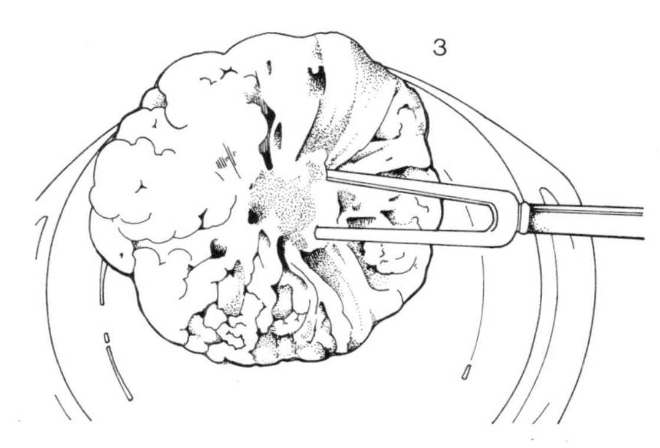

Frozen vegetables can be cooked in their packet, freezer container (if suitable) or plastic pouch. Puncture or pierce the packet before cooking and flex or shake it halfway through the cooking time to distribute the heat.

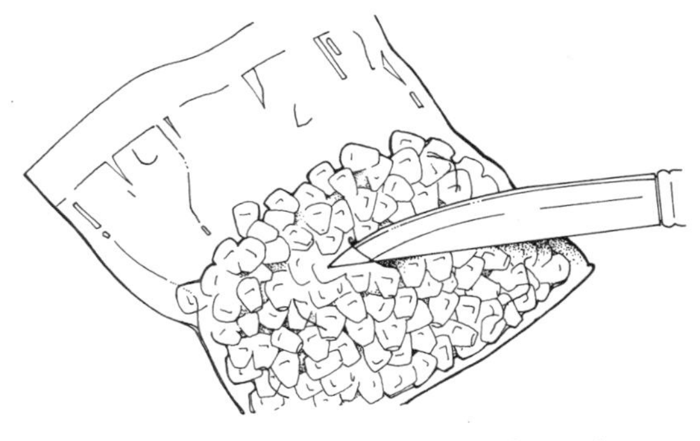

Pierce any vegetables cooked in their skins – like potatoes, aubergines or marrow – to prevent bursting.

Arrange large, whole vegetables in a ring so that all sides will be exposed to the microwave energy.

If the vegetables are cooked in a plastic bag or roasting bag, the bag should be tied loosely with a piece of string or an elastic band to allow the steam to escape.

Guide to Cooking Frozen Vegetables

All frozen vegetables can be successfully defrosted and cooked or reheated in the microwave oven in one simple operation. Generally, no extra water is necessary, but 2–3 tablespoons of water may be added if liked. Make sure the packaging or wrapping is suitable for the microwave and remove any metal or wire tags and ties. Cover during defrosting and heating and gently shake or stir the contents to ensure even heat distribution. The times below are approximate – should you like your vegetables a little crisper, then reduce the times slightly; if you should like them a little softer then increase the times slightly.

Guide to Cooking Frozen Vegetables

Vegetable	*Quantity*	*Cooking time in minutes on* FULL POWER
Asparagus	225 g/8 oz 450 g/1 lb	6–7 11
Beans, broad	225 g/8 oz 450 g/1 lb	8 10
Beans, French or runner	225 g/8 oz 450 g/1 lb	7 10
Broccoli	225 g/8 oz 450 g/1 lb	6–8 8–10
Cabbage	225 g/8 oz 450 g/1 lb	6–7 10–11
Carrots	225 g/8 oz 450 g/1 lb	7 10
Cauliflower florets	225 g/8 oz 450 g/1 lb	5 8
Corn kernels	225 g/8 oz 450 g/1 lb	4 7–8
Corn on the cob	1 2	4–5 7–8
Courgettes	225 g/8 oz 450 g/1 lb	4 7
Diced mixed vegetables	225 g/8 oz 450 g/1 lb	5–6 7–9
Peas	225 g/8 oz 450 g/1 lb	4 8
Spinach, chopped, or leaf	225 g/8 oz 450 g/1 lb	7–8 10–11
Root vegetable stewpack (mixed)	225 g/8 oz 450 g/1 lb	7 10
Swedes	225 g/8 oz 450 g/1 lb	7 11
Turnips	225 g/8 oz 450 g/1 lb	8 12

Guide to Cooking Fresh Vegetables

Vegetable	*Quantity*	*Water/salt*	*Preparation*	*Cooking time in minutes on* FULL POWER	*Cooking notes*
Artichokes, globe	1 2 4	8 tablespoons/ ½ teaspoon 8 tablespoons/ ½ teaspoon 250 ml/8 fl oz/ 1 teaspoon	*Discard the tough, outer leaves. Snip the tips and off the remaining leaves and cut off the stems. Cover to cook.*	5–6 7–8 14–15	*To test if cooked, at the minimum time, try to pull a leaf from the whole artichoke. If it comes away freely, the artichoke is cooked. Drain upside down before serving.*
Asparagus	450 g/1 lb	6 tablespoons/ ½ teaspoon	*Place in a dish, arranging any thicker stems to the outside of the dish and tender tips to the centre. Cover to cook.*	12–14	*Give the dish a half turn after 6 minutes cooking time.*
Aubergines	2 medium, halved	2 tablespoons/ —	*Cover to cook.*	7–9	*Scoop out the cooked flesh from the halved aubergines and use as required.*
	1 whole, peeled and cubed	2 tablespoons/ ¼ teaspoon		5–6	*Stir the cubed aubergine after 3 minutes cooking time.*
Beans, all except thin French beans	450 g/1 lb	8 tablespoons/ ½ teaspoon	*Cover to cook.*	14–16	*Stir the beans twice during cooking. Test after the minimum time to see if cooked.*
French beans	450 g/1 lb	8 tablespoons/ ½ teaspoon	*Cover to cook.*	5–7	
Beetroot	2 medium 5 medium	8 tablespoons/ ½ teaspoon 8 tablespoons/ ½ teaspoon	*Cover to cook.*	12–16 22–25	*Stir or rearrange halfway through the cooking time. Allow to stand for 10 minutes before peeling.*
Broccoli	450 g/1 lb	8 tablespoons/ ½ teaspoon	*Place in a dish arranging the stalks to the outside and florets in the centre. Cover to cook.*	10–12	*Stir or give the dish a half turn after 6 minutes.*

Vegetable	*Quantity*	*Water/salt*	*Preparation*	*Cooking time in minutes on* FULL POWER	*Cooking notes*
Brussels sprouts	450 g/1 lb	4 tablespoons/ ½ teaspoon	*Trim away any damaged or coarse leaves and cut large sprouts in half. Cover to cook.*	7–9	*Stir the sprouts after 4 minutes cooking time.*
Cabbage, shredded	450 g/1 lb	8 tablespoons/ ½ teaspoon	*Use a large dish and ensure that the cabbage fits loosely. Cover to cook.*	8–9	*Stir or rearrange halfway through the cooking time.*
	450 g/1 lb	8 tablespoons/ ½ teaspoon		10–12	
Carrots, whole	450 g/1 lb	8 tablespoons/ ½ teaspoon		12–14	*Stir or rearrange halfway through the cooking time.*
	1 kg/2 lb			18–20	
sliced	450 g/1 lb	8 tablespoons/ ½ teaspoon	*Cut carrots into 1-cm/½-in thick slices. Slicing carrots diagonally reduces the cooking time by 2 minutes. Cover to cook.*	12–14	
Cauliflower, whole	1 medium about 675 g/1½ lb	8 tablespoons/ ½ teaspoon	*Cook whole cauliflower on* MEDIUM HIGH *power. Cover to cook.*	13–17	*Turn a whole cauliflower or florets halfway through the cooking time. Allow whole cauliflower to stand for 5 minutes after cooking.*
florets	450 g/1 lb	8 tablespoons/ ½ teaspoon		10–12	
Celery, whole or sliced	450 g/1 lb	4 tablespoons/ ¼ teaspoon	*Cover to cook.*	14–16	*Turn or stir halfway through the cooking time.*
Chicory, whole	4 medium	4 tablespoons/ —	*Cover to cook and add salt after cooking.*	5–8	*Rearrange halfway through the cooking time.*
Corn on the cob	1	3 tablespoons/ —	*Cover to cook.*	4–5	*Cook the corn in the husk, if liked, with no extra water. Rearrange halfway through the cooking time if cooking 4–6 cobs.*
	2	3 tablespoons/ —		7–8	
	4	5 tablespoons/ —		13–15	
	6	5 tablespoons/ —		17–20	

Vegetable	*Quantity*	*Water/salt*	*Preparation*	*Cooking time in minutes on* FULL POWER	*Cooking notes*
Courgettes, sliced whole	 450 g/1 lb 6 small	 — —	*Cover to cook.*	 5–6 7	*Dot lightly with 25 g/1 oz butter before cooking. Stir or rearrange halfway through the cooking time.*
Leeks, sliced	450 g/1 lb	4 tablespoons/ ½ teaspoon	*Cover to cook.*	10–12	*Stir halfway through the cooking time.*
Marrow, sliced	450 g/1 lb	—	*Cover with greaseproof paper before cooking. Add salt after cooking.*	8–10	*Stir halfway through the cooking time.*
Mushrooms, whole or sliced	225 g/8 oz 450 g/1 lb	2 tablespoons water or butter	*Cover to cook. Add salt, if liked, after cooking.*	2–4 4–6	*Stir halfway through the cooking time.*
Onions, whole or quartered	4 medium 8 medium	4 tablespoons/ ½ teaspoon	*Cover to cook.*	10–12 14–16	*Stir halfway through the cooking time.*
Parsnips, cubed	450 g/1 lb	8 tablespoons/ ½ teaspoon	*Cover to cook.*	8–10	*Stir halfway through the cooking time.*
Peas, shelled	450 g/1 lb 1 kg/2 lb	8 tablespoons/ ½ teaspoon	*Cover to cook.*	9–11 12–14	*Stir halfway through the cooking time. Add 15–25 g/½–1 oz butter after cooking and allow to stand for 5 minutes before serving.*
Potatoes, peeled and quartered	450 g/1 lb	8 tablespoons/ ½ teaspoon	*Cover to cook.*	10–14	*Stir twice during cooking.*
baked in skins	1 2 3 4	— — — —	*Prick thoroughly and cook on absorbent kitchen paper.*	4–6 6–8 8–12 12–16	*Potatoes may still feel firm when cooked. Leave to stand for 3–4 minutes to soften.*

Vegetable	*Quantity*	*Water/salt*	*Preparation*	*Cooking time in minutes on* **FULL POWER**	*Cooking notes*
Spinach	450 g/1 lb	—	*Wash but do not dry before cooking. Place in a roasting bag and secure loosely with string or an elastic band. Add salt after cooking.*	6–8	*Drain if necessary before serving.*
Tomatoes, halved	2	salt to taste	*Add a knob of butter and a little pepper to each half before cooking. Cover to cook.*	1–1½	
Turnips, cubed	450 g/1 lb (2–3 medium turnips)	8 tablespoons/ ¼ teaspoon	*Cover to cook.*	12–14	*Stir twice during cooking.*

Blanching Vegetables for the Freezer

The chances are, if you're a keen gardener, pick-your-own fanatic, or simply someone who likes to enjoy fresh vegetables while they are low in price and high in quality, then you probably like to freeze vegetables for all-year-round eating.

The beauty of the microwave is that minutes after the vegetables are picked you can have them blanched and ready to freeze, without spending all day in the kitchen with a bubbling saucepan and a stop watch. Blanching in the microwave is so much easier.

Prepare the vegetables as you would for normal cooking and place them in a covered dish, then add water as given in the chart. Cook for half the time given in the chart and stir, re-cover and cook for the remaining time, then stir again. Plunge the vegetables into iced water immediately to prevent further cooking. Drain and spread on absorbent kitchen paper to absorb excess moisture. Pack in freezer containers or boil in the bag pouches, seal and label, then freeze. To pack vegetables for free-flow use, spread them on baking sheets or freezer trays and freeze until solid. Pack the frozen vegetables in bags, seal and label.

Alternatively, for extra convenience and speed, the vegetables may be blanched in boil-in-the-bags and then, still in their bags, plunged into iced water up to their necks to cool. This chills the vegetables and expels the air in the bag at the same time, automatically creating a vacuum pack ready for freezing. Seal and label in the usual way.

Guide to Blanching Vegetables

Vegetable	*Quantity*	*Water (table-spoons)*	*Time in minutes on* FULL POWER
Asparagus	450 g/1 lb	3	3–4
Beans	450 g/1 lb	6	5–6
Broccoli	450 g/1 lb	6	5–6
Brussels sprouts	450 g/1 lb	6	5–6
Cabbage, shredded	450 g/1 lb	3	4–4½
Carrots,			
sliced	450 g/1 lb	3	3–4
whole	450 g/1 lb	3	6–7
Cauliflower florets	450 g/1 lb	6	4½–5
Corn on the cob	4	3	5–6
Courgettes, sliced	450 g/1 lb	3	3–3½
Leeks, sliced	450 g/1 lb	3	5–6
Marrow, sliced or cubed	450 g/1 lb	3	4–4½
Onions, quartered	4 medium	6	4–4½
Parsnips, cubed	450 g/1 lb	3	3–4
Peas	450 g/1 lb	3	4–4½
	1 kg/2 lb	3	6–7
Spinach	450 g/1 lb	—	3–3½
Turnips, cubed	450 g/1 lb	3	3–4

Guide to Cooking Dried Beans and Peas

Beans	*Quantity*	*Preparation and cooking time*
Kidney, Flageolet, Butter or Haricot beans and Chick peas	350 g/12 oz	*Place the beans in a large dish with a little chopped onion, celery and carrot. Add 2 teaspoons salt and pepper to taste. Cover with 1.4 litres/2½ pints cold stock and cook on* FULL POWER *for 20 minutes. Stir, re-cover and cook on* MEDIUM POWER *for 1 hour 30 minutes–1 hour 40 minutes, until tender*
Split peas or Lentils	225 g/8 oz	*Place the split peas or lentils in a large dish with a little chopped onion, celery and 1 tablespoon lemon juice. Add a little salt and pepper to taste. Cover with 900 ml/1½ pints cold stock or water. Cover and cook on* FULL POWER *for 15 minutes. Stir and cook on* MEDIUM POWER *for 60–70 minutes, stirring every 30 minutes, until tender.*

Drying Herbs

It is possible to dry herbs in the microwave oven. Lay them between layers of absorbent kitchen paper and cook until the herbs can be crumbled. Allow to cool before storing in airtight jars. Store green herbs in green-coloured bottles to retain the fresh green colour, or store them in a dark cupboard away from sunlight.

SAUSAGE-STUFFED POTATOES

(Illustrated on page 19)
Serves 4
Power setting FULL
Total cooking time 17–18½ minutes

4 (175-g/6-oz) potatoes
4 pork sausages
50 g/2 oz butter
1 tablespoon snipped chives
1 tablespoon mild mustard pickle
salt and freshly ground black pepper
50 g/2 oz cheese, grated

Scrub, dry and prick the potatoes with a fork. Arrange on a double sheet of absorbent kitchen paper, spaced well apart. Cook for 6 minutes, turn over and rearrange, then cook for a further 6–7 minutes. Split in half and scoop out the flesh, reserving the potato skins.

Meanwhile, prick the sausages thoroughly and arrange in a circle on a plate. Cover with a piece of absorbent kitchen paper and cook for 3–3½ minutes. Allow to stand for 1 minute before slicing into bite-sized pieces.

Mash the potato flesh with the butter, then add the chives, mustard pickle and seasoning to taste. Add three-quarters of the sliced sausages and the cheese, mixing well. Return the mixture to the potato skins and garnish with the remaining sausage slices. Cook for a further 2 minutes until hot.

VARIATIONS

Seafood-stuffed Potatoes *(Illustrated on page 19)* Prepare and cook the potatoes as above, but mix the potato flesh with 100 g/4 oz peeled prawns, 4 tablespoons finely chopped spring onions, ½ teaspoon finely grated lemon rind, 1 teaspoon finely chopped parsley, 50 g/2 oz butter and a pinch of cayenne pepper. Return the mixture to the potato skins and cook for a further 2 minutes until hot. Garnish each potato half with a whole unpeeled prawn if liked. *Total cooking time* 14–15 minutes.

Crispy Bacon-stuffed Potatoes *(Illustrated on page 19)* Prepare and cook the potatoes as above. Meanwhile, chop 100 g/4 oz mushrooms and place in a bowl with 15 g/½ oz butter and cook for 2 minutes, stirring halfway through the cooking time. Place 4 rashers rindless bacon on a bacon rack or plate, cover with absorbent kitchen paper and cook for 3½ minutes, giving the plate a half turn halfway through the cooking time. Allow to cool, then crumble. Mix the potato flesh with the drained mushrooms, crumbled bacon, 25 g/1 oz butter and seasoning to taste. Return the mixture to the potato skins and cook for a further 2 minutes until hot. *Total cooking time* 19½–20½ minutes

Stuffed Potatoes with Blue Cheese *(Illustrated on page 19)* Prepare and cook the potatoes as above but mix the potato flesh with 50 g/2 oz blue cheese, 1 tablespoon snipped chives, 1 egg yolk, 50 g/2 oz butter and seasoning to taste. Return the mixture to the potato skins and cook for a further 2 minutes until hot. *Total cooking time* 14–15 minutes

BAKED JACKET POTATOES

Serves 4
Power setting FULL
Total cooking time 12–13 minutes

4 (175-g/6-oz) potatoes
salt and freshly ground black pepper
50 g/2 oz butter

Scrub, dry and prick the potatoes with a fork. Arrange them on a double sheet of absorbent kitchen paper, spaced well apart. Cook for 6 minutes, turn over and rearrange, then cook for a further 6–7 minutes. Allow to stand for 2–3 minutes, split in half and season to taste. Top each half with a little of the butter. Serve at once.

MUSTARD POTATO MAYONNAISE

Serves 4
Power setting FULL
Total cooking time 8 minutes

450 g/1 lb new potatoes, scraped and diced
1 small onion, peeled and chopped
4 tablespoons water
$\frac{1}{2}$ teaspoon salt
4 tablespoons mayonnaise
1 tablespoon double or soured cream
2 teaspoons wholegrain mustard
1 tablespoon finely chopped parsley

Place the potatoes, onion, water and salt in a large shallow dish. Cover with cling film and snip two holes in the top to allow the steam to escape. Cook for 8 minutes, shaking the dish vigorously twice during the cooking time. Leave to stand for 3 minutes, then drain through a fine sieve.

Meanwhile, combine the mayonnaise, double or soured cream and mustard. Stir into the potato mixture and toss gently to coat. Sprinkle with chopped parsley and serve hot or cold.

VARIATION

Horseradish potato mayonnaise Prepare the potato mayonnaise as above but use 2 teaspoons horseradish sauce or relish instead of the wholegrain mustard.

POTATOES WITH PARSLEY AND CELERY SEEDS

Serves 4–6
Power setting FULL
Total cooking time $33\frac{1}{2}$–$36\frac{1}{2}$ minutes

1.5 kg/3 lb medium-sized new potatoes
8 tablespoons water
salt and freshly ground black pepper
50 g/2 oz butter
2 teaspoons celery seeds
3 tablespoons chopped parsley

Scrub the potatoes and place in a bowl with the water and a little salt. Cover with cling film, snipping two holes in the top to allow the steam to escape and cook for 32–35 minutes or until tender, stirring twice during the cooking time. Drain well, then cut into thick slices and arrange in a serving dish.

Place the butter in a bowl with seasoning to taste, the celery seeds and parsley, then cook for $1\frac{1}{2}$ minutes. Spoon over the potatoes and serve at once.

POTATOES DAUPHINOIS

(Illustrated on page 132)
Serves 4
Power setting FULL
Total cooking time 17 minutes

25 g/1 oz butter
1 Spanish onion, peeled and chopped
675 g/$1\frac{1}{2}$ lb potatoes, peeled and thinly sliced
salt and freshly ground black pepper
150 ml/$\frac{1}{4}$ pint milk
finely chopped parsley to garnish

Place the butter and onion in a small bowl and cook for 3 minutes, stirring halfway through the cooking time.

Place a layer of potatoes in the base of a shallow dish, season generously and top with a layer of onion. Continue to layer, seasoning generously between each, finishing with a layer of potato. Pour in the milk, then cover with cling film, snipping two holes in the top to allow the steam to escape. Cook for 7 minutes. Remove the cling film, give the dish a half turn and cook for a further 7 minutes. Allow to stand for 5 minutes before serving garnished with chopped parsley. If you prefer it browned, place under a hot grill prior to garnishing.

VARIATION

Potatoes Savoyard Prepare and cook as above but use 150 ml/$\frac{1}{4}$ pint hot brown stock instead of the milk.

BRAISED CELERY AND PEAS

(Illustrated on page 129)
Serves 4–6
Power setting FULL
Total cooking time 13–15 minutes

1 head celery, trimmed and sliced
1 small onion, peeled and chopped
25 g/1 oz butter
5 teaspoons water
$\frac{1}{2}$ teaspoon salt
350 g/12 oz frozen peas

Place the celery, onion, butter, water and salt in a large dish. Cover and cook for 6 minutes.

Add the peas, cover and cook for 7–8 minutes, stirring after 4 minutes. Allow to stand for 2–3 minutes, then serve.

CHINESE-STYLE CARROTS AND BEAN SPROUTS

(Illustrated on page 52)
Serves 4
Power setting FULL
Total cooking time $20\frac{1}{2}$–21 minutes

1 kg/2 lb young carrots, peeled
50 g/2 oz butter or margarine
1 (432-g/$15\frac{1}{4}$-oz) can pineapple chunks
4 tablespoons vinegar
3 tablespoons soy sauce
100 g/4 oz leeks, very thinly sliced
2 tablespoons sugar
1 tablespoon cornflour
salt and freshly ground black pepper
150 g/5 oz bean sprouts
25 g/1 oz toasted pine nuts or flaked almonds

Cut the carrots diagonally into thin slices. Alternatively, pare strips down the length of each carrot, then cut into fluted slices. Place in a large bowl with the butter. Cover with cling film, snipping two holes in the top to allow the steam to escape and cook for 16 minutes until cooked but still crisp, shaking the dish twice during cooking.

Meanwhile, drain the pineapple juice into a bowl and mix with the vinegar, soy sauce, leeks and sugar. Mix the cornflour with a little water to form a thick paste and blend with the pineapple juice mixture. Add to the carrots, stirring quickly to blend. Cook for $2\frac{1}{2}$–3 minutes until the sauce thickens and clears, stirring occasionally.

Add seasoning to taste, the bean sprouts, nuts and halved pineapple chunks. Cook for 2 minutes and serve.

GLAZED CARROTS

(Illustrated on pages 129 and front cover)
Serves 3–4
Power setting FULL
Total cooking time 11–15 minutes

450 g/1 lb carrots, peeled or scraped and cut into diagonal slices
25 g/1 oz butter
50 g/2 oz brown sugar
1½ teaspoons cornflour
2 tablespoons cold water

Place the carrots, butter and sugar in a bowl. Cover and cook for 9–11 minutes, stirring halfway through the cooking time, until tender.

Mix the cornflour with the water and stir into the carrots. Cover and cook for 2–4 minutes until thickened. Stir before serving.

VARIATION

The carrots can be cooked whole. Choose young carrots, peel or scrape and trim them. Cook as above for the same length of time.

MINTED TOMATO RATATOUILLE

(Illustrated on page 132 and front cover)
Serves 4
Power setting FULL
Total cooking time 17 minutes

4 tablespoons oil
225 g/8 oz onions, peeled and chopped
1 green pepper, seeds removed and sliced
225 g/8 oz courgettes, sliced
225 g/8 oz aubergines, sliced
450 g/1 lb tomatoes, peeled, seeds removed and quartered
100 g/4 oz button mushrooms
2 tablespoons chopped fresh mint
salt and freshly ground black pepper
grated Parmesan cheese to serve

Place the oil, onion and green pepper in a large bowl. Cover with cling film, snipping two holes in the top to allow the steam to escape, and cook for 4 minutes. Add the courgettes and aubergine and cook for 7 minutes, then stir in the tomatoes, mushrooms, mint and seasoning to taste. Cover with cling film, snipping two holes in the top, and cook for a further 6 minutes. Serve hot or cold, dusted with Parmesan cheese.

WILTED LETTUCE SALAD

(Illustrated on page 19)
Serves 4–6
Power setting FULL
Total cooking time 5–6 minutes

3 rashers rindless bacon, cut into 2.5-cm/1-in pieces
3 tablespoons vinegar
2 teaspoons sugar
salt and freshly ground black pepper
pinch of dried tarragon
1 stick celery, chopped
½ bunch spring onions, trimmed and finely chopped
1 lettuce, washed and coarsely torn or shredded
2 oranges, peeled, pith removed and diced

Place the bacon in a large bowl and cook for 3 minutes until crisp. Remove with a slotted spoon and reserve.

Add the vinegar to the bacon juices together with the sugar, seasoning to taste and tarragon. Cook for 2–3 minutes until boiling. Stir in the celery and spring onions.

Gradually add the lettuce to the hot dressing, tossing to coat each piece, until just slightly wilted. Add the orange pieces and reserved bacon and toss lightly. Serve at once.

CHINESE SPICY CUCUMBER SALAD

(Illustrated on pages 130/131)
Serves 4
Power setting FULL
Total cooking time 2½–3½ minutes

1 large cucumber
1 tablespoon salt
2 tablespoons sugar
2 red peppers, seeds removed
2 tablespoons sesame oil
4 thin slices fresh root ginger
4 tablespoons white wine vinegar
1 tablespoon soy sauce

Cut the cucumber in half lengthways and scoop out the seeds with a teaspoon. Cut into 3.5-cm/1½-in lengths, then slice into thin julienne strips. Sprinkle with the salt and half the sugar, then leave to stand for 15 minutes. Cut the red peppers into similar sized strips. Rinse the cucumber under cold running water and pat dry with absorbent kitchen paper.

Place the oil in a large bowl and heat for ½ minute. Add the cucumber, pepper and root ginger. Cook for 2–3 minutes until the vegetables have softened but are still crisp. Add the vinegar, soy sauce and remaining sugar. Toss to coat, then chill and serve with cold cooked meats.

MACKEREL SALAD WITH GOOSEBERRY MAYONNAISE

Serves 6
Power setting FULL
Total cooking time 12 minutes

6 mackerel, cleaned and boned, with heads removed
450 g/1 lb gooseberries, topped and tailed
salt and freshly ground black pepper
150 ml/¼ pint vinegar
150 ml/¼ pint cold water
1 bay leaf
1 small onion, peeled and sliced
6 tablespoons mayonnaise
1 small lettuce, separated into leaves

Lay the fish out flat, skin side down and top each with 2 well-pricked gooseberries. Season to taste and roll up from the tail end, skin side out. Secure the rolls with a wooden cocktail stick and arrange them in a shallow dish. Add the vinegar, water and bay leaf. Top with the sliced onion. Cover with cling film, snipping two holes in the top to allow the steam to escape, and cook for 8 minutes, giving the dish a half turn after 3 minutes. Allow to cool, then chill the fish in the cooking juices.

Meanwhile, place the remaining gooseberries in a bowl. Cover with cling film, snipping two holes in the top, and cook for 4 minutes or until tender, giving the dish a vigorous shake halfway through the cooking time. Cool slightly, then press the fruit through a sieve. Allow to cool completely and mix with the mayonnaise.

Arrange the lettuce leaves on a serving dish. Using a slotted spoon, remove the fish from the cooking liquor and place on the lettuce. Top with a little gooseberry mayonnaise and serve the remainder separately.

From the top: Glazed Carrots (page 126), Braised Celery and Peas (page 125), Macaroni Cheese (page 159)
Overleaf *Left:* Gingered Melon and Chicken Salad (page 134); *Top right:* Rice and Seafood Salad Bowl (page 133); *Bottom right:* Chinese Spicy Cucumber Salad (page 127)

RICE AND SEAFOOD SALAD BOWL

(Illustrated on previous page)
Serves 4
Power setting FULL
Total cooking time 16–18 minutes

175 g/6 oz long-grain rice
1 teaspoon turmeric
450 ml/$\frac{3}{4}$ pint boiling water
salt and freshly ground black pepper
225 g/8 oz haddock fillet
2 tablespoons cold water
1 green pepper, seeds removed and sliced
2 canned pimientos, sliced
2 sticks celery, diced
12 black olives, halved and stoned
1 (170-ml/6-fl oz) jar mussels, drained
100 g/4 oz peeled prawns
50 g/2 oz canned smoked oysters (optional)
3 tablespoons salad oil
1 tablespoon lemon juice
1 clove garlic, crushed
celery leaves to garnish (optional)

Place the rice in a large deep bowl with the turmeric and the boiling water. Add a little salt to taste, cover with cling film, snipping two holes in the top to allow the steam to escape, and cook for 13–14 minutes, stirring halfway through the cooking time. Allow to stand for 5 minutes before removing the cling film and leaving to cool.

Meanwhile, place the haddock fillet in a shallow dish with the cold water. Cover with cling film, snipping two holes in the top and cook for 3–4 minutes or until the fish flakes easily. Divide the fish into bite-sized pieces discarding the skin and any bones.

Mix the rice with the haddock, green pepper, pimiento, celery, olives, mussels, prawns and oysters if used.

Whisk the oil with the lemon juice, garlic and seasoning to taste. Add to the salad and toss to coat. Cover and chill before serving garnished with celery leaves.

Top: Minted Tomato Ratatouille (page 126); *Below:* Potatoes Dauphinois (page 124)

GINGERED MELON AND CHICKEN SALAD

(Illustrated on pages 130/131)
Serves 4
Power setting MEDIUM or FULL
Total cooking time 29–32 minutes *or* 22–26 minutes

1 (1.5-kg/3-lb) oven-ready chicken
2–3 tablespoons hot chicken stock
4 tablespoons salad dressing (see next recipe)
1 small onion, peeled and finely chopped
15 g/½ oz butter
½ teaspoon ginger
¼ teaspoon paprika
2 sticks celery, diced
25 g/1 oz preserved ginger, finely chopped
4 tablespoons mayonnaise
2 tablespoons soured cream
2 tablespoons natural yogurt
salt and freshly ground black pepper
1 ripe honeydew melon
watercress sprigs or celery leaves to garnish

Place the chicken in a roasting bag with the stock, securing the end with a piece of string or elastic band, and place on a roasting rack or on an upturned plate in a larger dish. Cook on MEDIUM POWER for 27–30 minutes or on FULL POWER for 20–24 minutes. Leave to stand for 10–15 minutes, then remove the skin and cut the flesh into bite-sized pieces. Place the chicken in a bowl and add the French dressing. Leave to marinate for 2–4 hours.

Place the onion in a small bowl with the butter, ginger and paprika and cook on FULL POWER for 2 minutes. Allow to cool.

Combine the onion mixture with the celery, preserved ginger, mayonnaise, soured cream, yogurt and seasoning to taste.

Halve the melon and remove the seeds. Cut the flesh into bite-sized pieces and add to the onion mixture together with the drained chicken. Toss gently to mix. Serve in a salad bowl or in the scooped-out melon skins. Chill lightly before serving garnished with watercress sprigs or celery leaves.

MEXICAN SALAMI MEDLEY

(Illustrated on page 20)
Serves 6
Power setting FULL
Total cooking time 4 minutes

3 tablespoons oil
1 clove garlic, peeled and halved
3 slices white bread, crusts removed and cut into cubes
2 (425-g/15-oz) cans red kidney beans, drained
225 g/8 oz salami, cubed
2 small onions, peeled and sliced
1 bunch radishes, trimmed and sliced
1 red pepper, seeds removed and cut into strips
3 small courgettes, trimmed and sliced
SALAD DRESSING
6 tablespoons salad or olive oil
2 tablespoons vinegar
1 teaspoon caster sugar
salt and freshly ground black pepper

Place the oil in a bowl with the garlic and cook for 1 minute. Stir well, then remove the garlic, add the bread cubes and toss well to coat. Cook for 2 minutes, stir and cook for a further 1 minute. Cover with foil, then allow these croûtons to stand for 2 minutes.

Place the beans, salami, onion, radishes, pepper and courgettes in a serving dish. Shake the dressing ingredients together in a screw-top jar and add to the salad. Toss well to coat. Scatter the croûtons over the salad just before serving.

SILVERSIDE SUMMER SALAD

(Illustrated on page 20)
Serves 4
Power setting FULL
Total cooking time 12 minutes

225 g/8 oz long-grain rice
600 ml/1 pint boiling water
salt and freshly ground black pepper
1 large red dessert apple, cored and cubed
1 small green pepper, seeds removed and chopped
2 shallots, peeled and finely chopped
2 tablespoons raisins
3 tablespoons mayonnaise
2 tablespoons French mustard
4 slices silverside of beef
watercress sprigs to garnish

Place the rice in a large bowl with the boiling water and a pinch of salt, cover and cook for 12 minutes. Leave to stand, covered, for 5–10 minutes, then allow to cool.

Place the apple, pepper, shallots and raisins in a bowl, add the rice and mix well. Mix the mayonnaise with the mustard and seasoning to taste. Fold through the rice mixture.

Arrange the rolled beef on a serving platter, with the rice neatly piled between the slices. Garnish with watercress sprigs.

Eggs and Cheese

Both eggs and cheese are remarkably versatile and conjure up many speedy main courses and snacks in the very minimum of time. All the basic ways of cooking eggs and cheese – like scrambling, poaching, baking, frying, making omelettes, soufflés or toasted toppings and fondues – work very well in the microwave oven with the exception of hard-boiled eggs. Never attempt to cook an egg in its shell or reheat a hard-boiled egg in its shell as it will explode with the high pressure which builds up inside and causes expansion.

Eggs cook amazingly fast and, since they are a delicate food, they toughen when overcooked. The yolks, which have a higher fat content, cook faster than the whites. Poach eggs on MEDIUM POWER if you have the facility, to allow the whites time to set without toughening the edges or overcooking the yolks.

When the yolks and whites are mixed together, eggs can sometimes be cooked at higher power settings. Scrambled eggs can be cooked on FULL POWER. Omelettes, however, need time to set and are cooked on MEDIUM POWER.

To cook scrambled eggs Allow 1 teaspoon butter for each egg. Place the butter in a glass measuring jug or bowl and cook on FULL POWER until melted – about $\frac{1}{2}$–1 minute, depending on the quantity. Add the beaten eggs and milk according to the quantities given in the table. Cook on FULL POWER for half the recommended cooking time. Stir the set pieces of egg from the outside to the centre, then cook for the remaining recommended cooking time, stirring twice. When cooked, the eggs should be just beginning to set. Allow to stand for 1–2 minutes to finish cooking from the residual heat until lightly set.

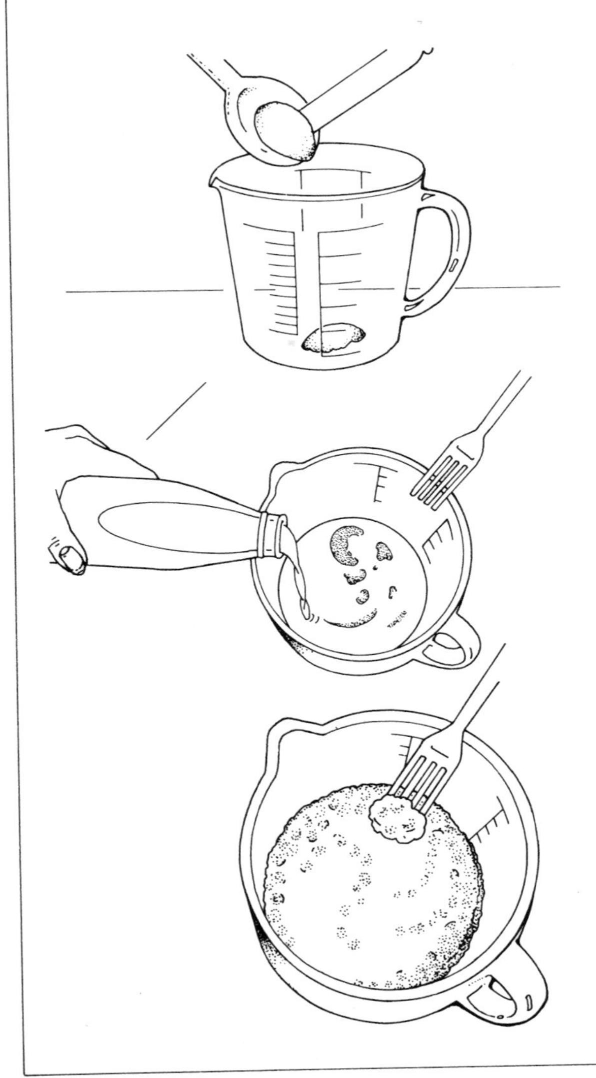

Guide to Cooking Scrambled Eggs

Eggs	*Butter*	*Milk*	*Cooking time in minutes on* FULL POWER
1	1 teaspoon	1 tablespoon	$\frac{3}{4}$–1
2	2 teaspoons	2 tablespoons	$1\frac{3}{4}$–2
4	4 teaspoons	4 tablespoons	$3\frac{3}{4}$–4
6	2 tablespoons	6 tablespoons	$5\frac{1}{2}$–6

To cook baked eggs Place the eggs in either a buttered microwave bun tray or buttered small glass cup, custard cup or shallow dish. Puncture the egg yolk carefully to prevent it from bursting during cooking. Cover with cling film, snipping two holes in the top to allow the steam to escape. Cook on MEDIUM POWER for half the recommended cooking time, give the dish a half turn and cook for the remaining time.

Guide to Cooking Baked Eggs

Eggs	*Cooking time in minutes on* MEDIUM POWER
1	1–$1\frac{1}{4}$
2	2–$2\frac{1}{4}$
4	$3\frac{1}{2}$–4
6	$5\frac{1}{2}$–6

To poach eggs Use either small dishes or cocottes, or a large dish. If you are using small dishes, pour 6 tablespoons hot water into each with a little vinegar. Bring to the boil on FULL POWER for about $1\frac{1}{2}$ minutes. Carefully break the egg into the dish and puncture the yolk quickly with the tip of a pointed knife, then cook for the times recommended in the table.

Alternatively, place 475 ml/16 fl oz hot water in a bowl and bring to the boil by cooking on FULL POWER for 5–6 minutes. Break the eggs on to a plate and quickly puncture the yolk with the tip of a pointed knife. Swirl the boiling water with a spoon and slip the eggs gently into it as shown in the diagram. Cook on MEDIUM POWER for the times given in the table. Allow to stand in the cooking water for $\frac{1}{2}$–1 minute before removing with a slotted spoon.

Guide to Cooking Poached Eggs

Eggs	*Cooking time in minutes on* FULL POWER	*Cooking time in minutes on* MEDIUM POWER
1	$\frac{3}{4}$–1	1
2	1–$1\frac{1}{2}$	$1\frac{3}{4}$
3	$1\frac{1}{2}$–$2\frac{1}{2}$	$2\frac{1}{2}$
4	$2\frac{1}{2}$–3	$3\frac{1}{4}$

To fry eggs in the microwave Fry eggs in a flat-based microwave browning dish. Preheat the dish according to the manufacturer's instructions – approximately 1 minute for each egg on FULL POWER. Allow 1 teaspoon butter to each egg, place it in the dish, then break the eggs into the dish. Cover and cook for the times given in the table.

Guide to Cooking Fried Eggs

Eggs	*Cooking time in minutes on* MEDIUM POWER	*Cooking time in seconds/minutes on* FULL POWER
1	$\frac{3}{4}$–1	40–50 seconds
2	$1\frac{1}{2}$–2	$1\frac{1}{2}$–$1\frac{3}{4}$ minutes
4	2–$2\frac{1}{2}$	2–$2\frac{1}{4}$ minutes

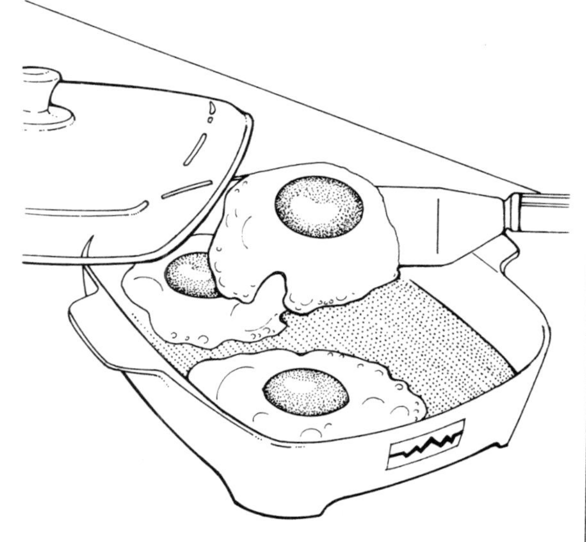

To cook a soufflé It is possible to cook a soufflé in the microwave oven but because of the speed of cooking it is necessary to stabilise the mixture. For success use evaporated milk in the base sauce. For this reason, it is not easy to adapt conventional soufflé recipes.

A microwave-cooked soufflé does not form a crust, rises very high and so requires a larger dish than a similar sized, conventionally baked soufflé. A 2.25-litre/4-pint soufflé dish is the minimum size you can use for a soufflé made from 6 eggs. It is only possible to cook soufflés in the microwave if you have LOW and MEDIUM POWER facilities. The soufflé should be rotated frequently during cooking. When cooked, the soufflé will be dry on top with a creamy centre.

Cooking cheese Cheese reacts in much the same way to microwave cooking as it does to conventional cooking, but faster. For this reason it is important not to overcook cheese or it may become stringy. If possible cook on MEDIUM POWER if your oven has this facility. Stirring, in the case of cheese dips, sauces or fondues, is important to ensure that the dish is smooth and not stringy. Processed cheese tends to melt evenly and is more tolerant to high temperatures.

CHEESE SOUFFLÉ

Serves 6
Power setting FULL, LOW and MEDIUM
Total cooking time 27–32 minutes

25 g/1 oz plain flour
¾ teaspoon salt
½ teaspoon mustard powder
pinch of paprika
2 (170-g/6-oz) cans evaporated milk
225 g/8 oz strong Cheddar cheese, grated
6 eggs, separated
1 teaspoon cream of tartar

Place the flour, salt, mustard and paprika in a bowl. Stir in the evaporated milk and cook on FULL POWER for 4–6 minutes, stirring every 2 minutes until thickened. Add the cheese and stir to mix. Cook on FULL POWER for 1–2 minutes until melted and well blended.

Whisk the egg whites with the cream of tartar until they stand in stiff peaks. Beat the egg yolks separately until thick and creamy. Pour the cheese sauce over the egg yolks and beat well until thoroughly blended. Add the egg whites and fold in gently until well combined.

Pour the mixture into an ungreased 2.25-litre/4-pint soufflé dish. Cook on LOW POWER for 10 minutes, then on MEDIUM POWER for 12–14 minutes, giving the dish a quarter turn every 5 minutes, or until the top edges appear dry and the soufflé has a set appearance. Serve at once.

VARIATIONS

Spinach and Cheese Soufflé *(Illustrated on page 149)* Cook 275 g/10 oz frozen or fresh chopped spinach until cooked (see vegetable cooking charts, pages 116 and 120). Stir into the soufflé mixture with the cheese, then continue as above. Pour into the dish and cook the soufflé on MEDIUM POWER for 20–33 minutes, giving the dish a quarter turn every 5 minutes. *Total cooking time* 25–31 minutes (including cooking time for spinach)

PLAIN OMELETTE

Serves 2
Power setting FULL
Total cooking time 3¾–4 minutes

4 eggs, beaten
3 tablespoons milk
½ teaspoon salt
freshly ground black pepper
15 g/½ oz butter

Mix the eggs, milk, salt and pepper to taste until well blended.

Place the butter in a 25-cm/10-in pie plate and cook for ½ minute to melt. Brush the melted butter over the plate and pour in the egg mixture. Cover with cling film, snipping two holes in the top to allow the steam to escape. Cook for 1½ minutes, then, using a fork or spatula, move the cooked egg from the edge of the dish to the centre. Re-cover and cook for 1¼–1½ minutes, then allow to stand for 1½–2 minutes. Loosen the omelette with a spatula and fold it in half to serve.

VARIATIONS

Crispy Bacon Omelette Coarsely chop 3 rashers of rindless bacon. Place in a bowl and cook for 2–3 minutes until crisp and brown. Allow to cool. Crumble the bacon into the egg mixture, then prepare and cook as above. *Total cooking time* 5¼–6½ minutes.

Cheese Omelette Prepare and cook as above, then add 50 g/2 oz grated cheese to the omelette before leaving it to stand. Fold in half and cook for a further ½ minute. *Total cooking time* 3¾–4 minutes

Onion Omelette Peel and chop 1 small onion. Place in a bowl with 15 g/½ oz butter and cook for 2 minutes. Add to the egg mixture, then prepare and cook as above. *Total cooking time* 5¼–5½ minutes

Tomato Omelette *(Illustrated on page 152)* Prepare and cook the omelette as above. Peel and coarsely chop 100 g/4 oz tomatoes and place them in a bowl with 15 g/½ oz butter. Cook for 1 minute. Add the tomatoes to the cooked omelette, fold over and serve. *Total cooking time* 4¼–4½ minutes.

Ham Omelette Prepare and cook the omelette as above. Finely chop 100 g/4 oz cooked ham. Place in a bowl with 15 g/½ oz butter and cook for 1½ minutes. Add to the cooked omelette, fold over and serve. *Total cooking time* 4¾–5 minutes

Mushroom Omelette Prepare and cook the omelette as above. Place 100 g/4 oz sliced mushrooms in a bowl with 25 g/1 oz butter. Cover and cook for 2–3 minutes, add to the cooked omelette, then fold over and serve. *Total cooking time* 5¼–6½ minutes

Quick Spanish Omelette Peel and finely chop 1 onion, then place in a bowl with 25 g/1 oz butter. Remove the seeds from a small red or green pepper, then chop and add it to the onion. Cook for 3 minutes. Mix with 1 large cooked potato, diced, and 1 peeled and chopped tomato. Add to the omelette mixture before cooking. Prepare and cook as above allowing an extra ½–1 minute cooking time if necessary. *Total cooking time* 6¾–7½ minutes

HAM, EGG AND COTTAGE CHEESE SCRAMBLE

(Illustrated on page 152)
Power setting FULL
Total cooking time 9½–12 minutes

40 g/1½ oz butter
1 small onion, peeled and finely chopped
9 eggs, beaten
350 g/12 oz cooked ham, cubed
100 g/4 oz cottage cheese

Place the butter and onion in a large bowl and cook for 2 minutes. Stir, add the eggs and mix well, then add the ham and cook for 7–9 minutes, stirring every ½ minute.

Stir in the cottage cheese and cook for a further ½–1 minute before serving with hot buttered toast.

SPEEDY ITALIAN PIZZAS

(Illustrated on pages 30/31)
Serves 4
Power setting FULL
Total cooking time 4 minutes

4 (15-cm/6-in) ready-baked pizza bases
100 g/4 oz tomato paste with basil or 1 (141-g/5-oz) can tomato purée and 2 teaspoons dried basil
175 g/6 oz Cheddar cheese, grated
1 (56-g/2-oz) can anchovy fillets, drained
16–24 black olives

Place the pizza bases on a large baking sheet and spread each evenly with the tomato paste. Top with the grated cheese, anchovy fillets and black olives. Cook for 4 minutes, giving the dish a half turn halfway through the cooking time.

CHEESE FONDUE

Serves 4
Power setting FULL and MEDIUM
Total cooking time 7–8 minutes

250 ml/8 fl oz dry white wine
2 tablespoons kirsch (optional)
275 g/10 oz Gruyère cheese, grated
275 g/10 oz Emmental cheese, grated
3 tablespoons plain flour
pinch of freshly ground black pepper

Place the wine and kirsch, if used, in a fondue dish or casserole. Cook on FULL POWER for 4 minutes, until very hot.

Toss the cheeses with the flour and pepper until well coated. Quickly stir or whisk the cheese into the wine and cover. Cook on MEDIUM POWER for 3–4 minutes, stirring briskly every 1 minute, until the cheese is just melted.

Serve at once with cubes of crispy French bread for dipping.

CHEESY RAREBIT

Serves 3–4
Power setting FULL and MEDIUM
Total cooking time 7–10 minutes

225 g/8 oz Double Gloucester or strong Cheddar cheese, grated
15 g/½ oz butter
¼ teaspoon salt
¼ teaspoon mustard powder
½ teaspoon Worcestershire sauce
pinch of cayenne pepper
3 tablespoons double cream
1 egg yolk, beaten
toasted bread to serve

Place the cheese and the butter in a bowl and cook on FULL POWER for 2–3 minutes, stirring every 1 minute, until the cheese is smooth.

Add the remaining ingredients, stirring well. Cook on MEDIUM POWER for 5–7 minutes, stirring every 1 minute, until hot and smooth. Serve on hot toasted bread.

Toasted Cheese Sandwich

Makes 1
Power setting MEDIUM/HIGH
Total cooking time 1–1½ minutes

2 slices bread, toasted
25–40 g/1–1½ oz cheese, grated

Sandwich the toasted bread slices together with the cheese. Place on a plate in the microwave and cook for 1–1½ minutes until melted.

Prawn and Tomato Savoury Cheesecake

(Illustrated on page 149)
Serves 8
Power setting FULL
Total cooking time 9½ minutes

3 tablespoons lemon juice
15 g/½ oz gelatine
450 g/1 lb cottage cheese
2 tablespoons mayonnaise
2–3 tablespoons tomato ketchup
4 small tomatoes, peeled, seeds removed and chopped
100 g/4 oz peeled prawns
1 tablespoon snipped chives
salt and freshly ground black pepper
100 g/4 oz butter
4 slices white or brown bread, crusts removed and cubed
GARNISH (optional)
parsley sprigs
1 tomato, cut in half and then into wedges
whole unpeeled prawns

Place the lemon juice in a small bowl and sprinkle over the gelatine. Leave for 2–3 minutes to soften, then cook in the microwave for ½ minute to dissolve. Mix the gelatine liquid with the cottage cheese, mayonnaise, tomato ketcup, tomato, prawns, chives and seasoning to taste. Spoon into a greased 20-cm/8-in spring-form tin or loose-bottomed cake tin.

Melt the butter in a large bowl by cooking for 2 minutes. Add the bread cubes and toss in the butter. Cook for 3½ minutes, stir and cook for a further 3½ minutes. Cover with foil and allow to stand for 2 minutes.

Top the savoury cheesecake mixture with the bread croûtons, pressing them down gently to form a base. Chill well to set.

Invert the cheesecake on to a serving plate. Garnish with parsley sprigs, tomato wedges and whole unpeeled prawns (if used). Cut into wedges to serve.

Rice, Pasta and Cereals

There are dozens of different and delicious ways of serving rice, pasta and cereals but these ingredients are often quickly pushed aside at the thought of sticky bubbling pans and steamy kitchens. They can, however, come to the fore again with the help of the microwave oven. Cooking rice, pasta and cereals in the microwave couldn't be easier – simply follow the chart on page 147 for quantities and cooking times and remember to use a large deep bowl which will give the foods room to expand as they cook.

Always cover the food with either a tight-fitting lid or a piece of cling film while cooking, but snip two holes in the film to allow the steam to escape. If you're cooking the larger size pasta, spaghetti or lasagne for example, soften it in the boiling water so that it can be completely immersed before cooking. Observe the standing times for rice and pasta to make sure the water or liquid used is absorbed.

Cooking rice and pasta in the microwave takes about the same length of time as conventional cooking, so what are the benefits? A good flavour and firm 'al dente' texture is guaranteed, no more sticky saucepans, and you can cook and serve in the same dish. But perhaps the most valuable way to use the microwave for cooking pasta and rice is when reheating. Reheated by conventional means, pasta and rice will dry out unless you add more water, and the extra liquid will probably overcook them. Tightly covered with cling film, pasta and rice can be reheated in the microwave to give a freshly cooked flavour and texture. The same is true of cooked rice taken straight from the freezer – simply cover with cling film and reheat until hot. If you are cooking fresh pasta, then halve the cooking and standing times given in the table for perfect results.

Delicious ways with rice Rice, like pasta, comes in various shapes and sizes from round-grain to long-grain and from wild to easy-cook, so you should have little trouble in providing plenty of variety in rice-type meals. Sometimes a meal calls for something a little more than plain boiled rice. When such an occasion occurs why not try one of the following suggestions.

Chicken or beef-flavoured rice Cook the rice according to the table, but add boiling stock – either beef or chicken – instead of the water.

Herb-flavoured rice Cook the rice according to the table but add a large pinch of dried mixed herbs before cooking.

Peppered rice Place ½ chopped green pepper, ½ chopped red pepper and 4 tablespoons chopped spring onions in a bowl with 25 g/1 oz butter. Cook on FULL POWER for 2 minutes, then add to the rice ingredients before cooking.

Curried rice Place 25 g/1 oz butter in a bowl with 2 small peeled and chopped onions, a pinch of ground nutmeg and ½–1 teaspoon curry powder, according to taste. Cook on FULL POWER for 3–4 minutes until soft and golden. Add to the cooked rice with 100 ml/4 fl oz single cream and reheat on FULL POWER for 1 minute.

Risotto alla Milanese Place 25 g/1 oz butter in a bowl with 1 peeled and finely chopped onion and a little powdered saffron or turmeric. Cook on FULL POWER for 2 minutes. Add to the rice, substituting an equal quantity of dry white wine for a quarter of the water. Cook the rice according to the table and serve sprinkled with Parmesan cheese.

Herbed orange rice Place 50 g/2 oz butter in a bowl with 2 chopped sticks celery and 2 tablespoons grated onion. Cook on FULL POWER for 2 minutes. Add to the rice with 1 tablespoon grated orange rind and substitute an equal quantity of unsweetened orange juice for half of the water. Cook the rice according to the table.

Vegetable rice Cook the rice according to the table, then add 100 g/4 oz cooked chopped French beans, 100 g/4 oz cooked peas and 2 teaspoons snipped chives.

Delicious ways with pasta There is nothing more delicious than pasta tossed with a knob of butter to give a golden buttery glaze, seasoned to taste and topped with freshly grated Parmesan cheese. But here are more ideas to try – simply return the pasta to the oven with one of the following flavourings and cook for 1 minute on FULL POWER.

Add a little chopped garlic and 1–2 tablespoons double cream and toss well.

Add a few snipped chives or parsley and toss well.

For a crunchy effect, add a few poppy or caraway seeds and toss well.

Place 25 g/1 oz flaked almonds in a shallow dish with 15 g/½ oz butter. Cook on FULL POWER for 2–4 minutes until golden brown. Add to the pasta and toss well.

Place ½ small chopped green pepper and 1 small peeled and chopped onion in a bowl with 25 g/1 oz butter and cook on FULL POWER for 2 minutes. Add to the pasta and toss well.

Mix 1 egg yolk with 4 tablespoons double cream and stir into the cooked pasta. Do not reheat.

Place 50 g/2 oz sliced mushrooms in a bowl with 15 g/½ oz butter. Cover and cook on FULL POWER for 2 minutes. Add to the pasta with 50 g/2 oz shredded cooked ham and toss well.

Place 15 g/½ oz butter in a bowl with 1 small peeled and chopped onion and cook on FULL POWER for 2 minutes. Add 2 tablespoons concentrated tomato purée and 2 tablespoons water and stir to mix. Add to the pasta and toss.

Top the cooked pasta with Minted Ratatouille (page 126) and sprinkle with grated cheese. No need to reheat.

Add about 75 g/3 oz freshly cooked summer green vegetables – like beans, broccoli, courgettes or asparagus – and a sprinkling of chopped fresh parsley and toss well.

Guide to Cooking Rice and Pasta

Rice	*Quantity*	*Preparation*	*Cooking time in minutes on* FULL POWER	*Standing time*
Brown rice	225 g/8 oz	*Place in a deep, covered container with 600 ml/1 pint boiling salted water.*	20–25	5–10
American easy-cook rice	225 g/8 oz	*Place in a deep, covered container with 600 ml/1 pint boiling salted water.*	12	5–10
Long-grain patna rice	225 g/8 oz	*Place in a deep, covered container with 600 ml/1 pint boiling salted water and 1 tablespoon oil.*	10	5–10

Pasta	*Quantity*	*Preparation*	*Cooking time in minutes on* FULL POWER	*Standing time*
Egg noodles and tagliatelle	225 g/8 oz	*Place in a deep, covered container with 600 ml/1 pint boiling salted water and 1 tablespoon oil.*	6	3
Macaroni	225 g/8 oz	*Place in a deep, covered container with 600 ml/1 pint boiling salted water and 1 tablespoon oil.*	10	3
Pasta shells and shapes	225 g/8 oz	*Place in a deep, covered container with 900 ml/1½ pints salted water and 1 tablespoon oil.*	12–14	5–10
Spaghetti	225 g/8 oz	*Hold in a deep, covered container with 1 litre/1¾ pints boiling salted water to soften, then submerge or break in half and add 1 tablespoon oil.*	12	5–10

PAELLA

Serves 6
Power setting FULL
Total cooking time 17–18 minutes

25 g/1 oz butter
1 onion, peeled and finely chopped
1 clove garlic, peeled and finely chopped
$\frac{1}{2}$ teaspoon turmeric
225 g/8 oz long-grain rice
600 ml/1 pint boiling fish or chicken stock
100 g/4 oz cooked chicken, cut into bite-sized pieces
100 g/4 oz peeled prawns
75 g/3 oz cooked mussels
50 g/2 oz frozen peas
2 tomatoes, peeled, seeds removed and chopped
50 g/2 oz garlic sausage, cubed
salt and freshly ground black pepper
a few unpeeled prawns and cooked mussels in their shells to garnish

Place the butter in a large bowl with the onion and garlic. Cook for 2 minutes. Add the turmeric, rice and stock. Cover and cook for 12 minutes. Allow to stand for 5 minutes until the rice has absorbed most of the stock.

Add the chicken, prawns, mussels, peas, tomato, garlic sausage and seasoning to taste. Cover and cook for 3–4 minutes, stirring after 2 minutes.

Serve hot, garnished with whole unpeeled prawns and mussels.

Top: Spinach and Cheese Soufflé (page 140); *Below:* Savoury Prawn and Tomato Cheesecake (page 144)
Overleaf Page 150 French Country Pâté (page 43)
Page 151 *Top left:* Lasagne with Sausages and Tomatoes (page 158); *Right:* Tropical Chicken and Rice (page 153); *Below:* Paella

TROPICAL CHICKEN AND RICE

(Illustrated on pages 150/151)
Serves 4
Power setting FULL
Total cooking time 19 minutes

25 g/1 oz butter
1 medium onion, peeled and chopped
225 g/8 oz long-grain rice
pinch of salt
750 ml/1¼ pints boiling water
100 g/4 oz button mushrooms, sliced
350 g/12 oz cooked chicken, cut into bite-sized pieces
40 g/1½ oz dry-roasted peanuts
100 g/4 oz fresh or canned pineapple, diced
2 small bananas, sliced
DRESSING
juice of ½ lemon
4 tablespoons lemon mayonnaise
salt and freshly ground black pepper

Place the butter in a small bowl and heat for 1 minute to melt. Add the onion and cook for a further 3 minutes. Allow to cool.

Place the rice in a large deep dish. Add the salt and boiling water. Cook uncovered, for 15 minutes, stirring halfway through the cooking time, then drain. Add the onion and mushrooms to the hot rice and allow to cool.

Add the chicken, peanuts and pineapple to the rice. Toss the bananas in a little of the lemon juice from the dressing ingredients, then add to the rice.

Stir the remaining lemon juice into the mayonnaise and season to taste. Stir the mayonnaise into the rice mixture and spoon into a serving dish. Serve with a salad made of curly endive, thinly sliced cucumber, radish curls or slices, green pepper rings and water melon balls.

Top: Tomato Omelette (page 141); *Below:* Ham, Egg and Cottage Cheese Scramble (page 142)

SAVOURY TOMATO RICE

(Illustrated on pages 30/31)
Serves 4–6
Power setting FULL
Total cooking time $26\frac{1}{2}$–29 minutes

4 rashers rindless bacon
1 (398-g/14-oz) can peeled tomatoes, chopped
100 g/4 oz long-grain rice
6 tablespoons chilli sauce
1 small green pepper, seeds removed and chopped
1 small onion, peeled and finely chopped
1 teaspoon soft brown sugar
1 teaspoon salt
freshly ground black pepper
$\frac{1}{2}$ teaspoon Worcestershire sauce
475 ml/16 fl oz hot water

Place the bacon on a plate or bacon rack and cover with absorbent kitchen paper. Cook for $3\frac{1}{2}$–4 minutes until brown and crispy. Allow to cool, then crumble into a large casserole.

Add the tomatoes and their juice and all the remaining ingredients. Cover and cook for 23–25 minutes, stirring every 8 minutes, until the rice is cooked. Allow to stand for 5–10 minutes before serving.

PILAF WITH BACON AND PEAS

(Illustrated on page 109)
Serves 4–6
Power setting FULL
Total cooking time $16\frac{1}{2}$–19 minutes

4 rashers rindless streaky bacon, chopped
1 small onion, peeled and finely chopped
225 g/8 oz long-grain rice
600 ml/1 pint boiling chicken stock
350 g/12 oz frozen peas
salt and freshly ground black pepper

Place the bacon in a large casserole and cook for $3\frac{1}{2}$–4 minutes until crisp. Remove with a slotted spoon and set aside. Add the onion to the bacon drippings and cook for 2 minutes. Add the rice, stock, peas and seasoning to taste. Cover and cook for 12–14 minutes. Allow to stand, covered, for 5–10 minutes until all the stock has been absorbed by the rice.

Add the bacon to the rice and cook for 1 minute to reheat.

SPEEDY SPANISH RICE

Serves 4–6
Power setting FULL
Total cooking time 13–17 minutes

450 g/1 lb minced beef
225 g/8 oz cooked long-grain rice
1 (398-g/14-oz) can tomatoes, coarsely chopped with their juice
1 small onion, peeled and chopped
1–2 tablespoons chilli powder (according to taste)
2 teaspoons salt
freshly ground black pepper

Place the beef in a large casserole and cook for 5–6 minutes, stirring and breaking up the meat halfway through the cooking time. Drain away any excess fat. Add the remaining ingredients, cover and cook for 8–11 minutes, stirring after 4 minutes.

Leave to stand, covered, for 5–10 minutes before serving.

PASTA WITH CREAMED SPINACH AND WALNUTS

Serves 4
Power setting FULL
Total cooking time 17–18 minutes

175 g/6 oz pasta twistetti
450 ml/¾ pint boiling water
1 teaspoon oil
100 g/4 oz frozen chopped spinach
150 ml/¼ pint soured cream
3 tablespoons single cream or top of the milk
50 g/2 oz walnut pieces, chopped
salt and freshly ground black pepper

Place the pasta in a deep bowl with the boiling water and the oil. Cover with cling film, snipping two holes in the top to allow the steam to escape, and cook for 12 minutes. Allow to stand for 10 minutes.

Meanwhile, place the frozen spinach in a bowl. Cover with cling film, snipping two holes in the top, and cook for 4–5 minutes, breaking up the block 2 or 3 times during cooking. Add the soured cream, single cream or top of the milk, walnuts and seasoning to taste.

Drain the twistetti and toss in the spinach sauce. Cook for 1 minute to reheat. This dish is delicious served as an appetiser or as an accompaniment to grills.

SPAGHETTI WITH BACON AND PESTO SAUCE

(Illustrated on pages 30/31)
Serves 4
Power setting FULL
Total cooking time 19–22 minutes

450 g/1 lb spaghetti
2.25 litres/4 pints boiling water
1 tablespoon oil
1 onion, peeled and chopped
1 (200-g/7-oz) can stuffed anchovies or 1 (56-g/2-oz) can anchovy fillets
4 rashers rindless streaky bacon
1 (200-g/7-oz) jar Pesto sauce
1 tablespoon chopped parsley
salt and freshly ground black pepper
GARNISH
tomato slices
parsley sprigs

Place the spaghetti in a deep bowl with the boiling water. Add the oil and cook, covered, for 12–15 minutes until barely cooked. Cover and leave to stand for 10–15 minutes.

Meanwhile, place the onion in a small bowl with the oil drained from the can of anchovies and cook for 1½ minutes. Place the bacon on a bacon rack or plate and cover with absorbent kitchen paper. Cook for 3½ minutes or until crisp.

Drain the spaghetti if necessary and add the onion, crumbled bacon and stuffed anchovies or anchovy fillets. Add the Pesto sauce, parsley and seasoning to taste, toss to mix. Cook for a further 2 minutes until hot. Serve garnished with tomato slices and parsley sprigs.

SPAGHETTI WITH GARLIC SAUSAGE

(Illustrated on page 162)

Serves 4

Power setting FULL

Total cooking time 22½–23½ minutes

1 tablespoon oil
1 large onion, peeled and chopped
1 clove garlic, crushed
675 g/1½ lb tomatoes, peeled, seeds removed and chopped
225 g/8 oz garlic sausage, cubed
¼ teaspoon dried basil
¼ teaspoon anchovy essence
½ teaspoon sugar
salt and freshly ground black pepper
275 g/10 oz spaghetti
1.15 litres/2 pints boiling water
1 tablespoon oil
chopped parsley to garnish
grated Parmesan cheese to serve (optional)

Place the oil in a bowl and cook for ½ minute. Add the onion and garlic and cook for 2 minutes. Add the tomatoes, garlic sausage, basil, anchovy essence, sugar and seasoning to taste. Cover with cling film, snipping two holes in the top to allow the steam to escape and cook for 6 minutes, stirring halfway through the cooking time.

Place the spaghetti in a deep bowl with the boiling water and the oil. Cover with cling film, snipping two holes in the top, and cook for 12 minutes. Leave to stand, covered, for 10 minutes, then drain and add to the sausage mixture. Place in a serving dish and cook for 2–3 minutes until hot. Serve garnished with chopped parsley and sprinkled with Parmesan cheese.

LASAGNE WITH SAUSAGES AND TOMATOES

(Illustrated on pages 150/151)
Serves 4
Power setting FULL
Total cooking time $28\frac{1}{2}$–$30\frac{1}{2}$ minutes

350 g/12 oz sausages
2 cloves garlic, peeled and finely chopped
1 (398-g/14-oz) can tomatoes, drained and chopped
175 g/6 oz canned tomato purée
$\frac{1}{2}$ teaspoon dried basil
$\frac{1}{2}$ teaspoon salt
$\frac{1}{4}$ teaspoon freshly ground black pepper
175 g/6 oz lasagne
1 litre/$1\frac{3}{4}$ pints boiling water
1 teaspoon oil
225 g/8 oz button mushrooms, sliced
225 g/8 oz ricotta cheese
350 g/12 oz Mozzarella cheese, sliced
25 g/1 oz Parmesan cheese, grated

Prick the sausages and arrange them in a circle on a plate. Cover with a piece of absorbent kitchen paper and cook for $4\frac{1}{2}$–$5\frac{1}{2}$ minutes, giving the plate a half turn after 2 minutes. Remove and slice thinly. Place the sausage slices in a large bowl with the garlic, tomatoes, tomato purée, basil, salt and pepper. Cover with cling film, snipping two holes in the top to allow the steam to escape. Cook for 4 minutes, stirring halfway through the cooking time.

Place the lasagne in a large, deep dish with the boiling water and oil. Cook for 6 minutes, making sure that the pasta is completely immersed and stirring once during the cooking time. Cover and leave to stand for 10 minutes, then drain.

Meanwhile, place the mushrooms in a small bowl with 2 tablespoons water. Cook for 2–3 minutes then drain. Fill a large oblong dish with alternate layers of lasagne, sausage and tomato sauce, ricotta, Mozzarella and mushrooms, finishing with a layer of sauce. Sprinkle with the Parmesan cheese and cook for 12 minutes, giving the dish a half turn halfway through the cooking time. Serve hot with a green salad.

MACARONI CHEESE

(Illustrated on page 129)
Serves 4
Power setting FULL
Total cooking time 15 minutes

225 g/8 oz quick-cook macaroni
600 ml/1 pint boiling water
salt and freshly ground black pepper
50 g/2 oz butter
2 tablespoons plain flour
1 teaspoon made mustard
450 ml/$\frac{3}{4}$ pint milk
100 g/4 oz Cheddar or Double Gloucester cheese, grated
parsley sprigs to garnish

Place the macaroni in a deep bowl with the water and a pinch of salt. Cover with cling film, snipping two holes in the top to allow the steam to escape. Cook for 8 minutes, stirring halfway through the cooking time, then drain and keep warm.

Place the butter in a large jug and cook for 1 minute. Add the flour and mustard, mixing well. Gradually add the milk and season to taste. Cook for 4 minutes, stirring every 1 minute, then add most of the cheese and stir to melt.

Mix the macaroni with the cheese sauce. Place in a serving dish and cook for 2 minutes. Serve hot, topped with the remaining cheese and garnished with parsley.

HOME-MADE CRUNCHY MUESLI

(Illustrated on page 161)
Serves 6–8
Power setting FULL
Total cooking time $3\frac{1}{2}$ minutes

2 tablespoons clear honey
1 tablespoon sunflower oil
100 g/4 oz rolled oats
2 tablespoons wheatgerm
25 g/1 oz hazelnuts, chopped
25 g/1 oz dried apricots, chopped
25 g/1 oz flaked almonds
25 g/1 oz stoned dates, chopped
25 g/1 oz raisins

Place the honey and oil in a large bowl and cook for $\frac{1}{2}$ minute. Add the oats, wheatgerm and hazelnuts, mixing well to coat the ingredients in the honey and oil. Spread the mixture on a shallow microwave baking sheet and cook for 3 minutes, stirring frequently to ensure the mixture browns evenly. Add the apricots, almonds, dates and raisins and leave to stand, covered, for 1 minute. Serve with fresh fruit, milk or yogurt.

PORRIDGE

Porridge oats are generally available in two varieties – the traditional type and the quick-cook type. They should both be cooked in a mixture of half milk and half water, or all water for good results in the microwave. Recipes using all milk tend to boil over and spoil the appearance and taste of the dish. Always cook porridge in a deep bowl: a deep individual cereal bowl is ideal for cooking a single portion so that you can cook and serve in one simple operation. Cover three-quarters of the bowl with cling film – this will enable you to stir the cereal easily without removing its cover. The times given in the table are a basic guideline – for a softer porridge leave to stand, covered, for 2–3 minutes before serving.

No of servings	*Water*	*Salt*	*Cereal*	*Cooking time in minutes on* FULL POWER	*Cooking time in minutes on* LOW POWER
			Traditional oatmeal / slow-cook oatmeal		
1	175 ml/6 fl oz	$\frac{1}{4}$ teaspoon	30 g/$1\frac{1}{4}$ oz	3–5	10
2	350 ml/12 fl oz	$\frac{1}{2}$ teaspoon	65 g/$2\frac{1}{2}$ oz	6–7	10
4	750 ml/$1\frac{1}{4}$ pints	$\frac{3}{4}$ teaspoon	125 g/$4\frac{1}{2}$ oz	8–9	12
			Quick cook oatmeal		
1	175 ml/6 fl oz	$\frac{1}{4}$ teaspoon	30 g/$1\frac{1}{4}$ oz	1–2	5
2	350 ml/12 fl oz	$\frac{1}{2}$ teaspoon	65 g/$2\frac{1}{2}$ oz	2–3	5
4	750 ml/$1\frac{1}{4}$ pints	$\frac{3}{4}$ teaspoon	125 g/$4\frac{1}{2}$ oz	5–6	7–8

Top left: Home-made Crunchy Muesli (page 159); *Top right:* Three-fruit Marmalade (page 224); *Right:* White Bread Bap (page 203); *Below:* Scrambled eggs (page 138) with bacon (cooking chart on page 95) and tomato

Sauces

A well-flavoured sauce can often lift an ordinary dish into the luxury class. Sauces are especially easy to make in the microwave – they are not always speedier to cook than their traditionally made counterparts, but they do afford greater success. Microwave-cooked sauces rarely go lumpy as it is so easy to control the smoothness of the sauce by stirring once or twice during cooking instead of constantly stirring over a hot stove. But the microwave oven does save time in reheating – prepare a sauce or gravy well ahead, refrigerate it, then quickly reheat it in just a couple of minutes on FULL POWER, remembering to stir halfway through the cooking time.

Sauce making seems less of a chore, too, if all you have to do is simply defrost and reheat a batch-made sauce in under 5 minutes; or prepare a quick dessert sauce for topping ice cream by melting chocolate and cream together without fear of burning or scorching. And the advantages don't stop there – you can make your sauce in the serving jug or boat, or prepare it in the measuring jug to save washing up. Since the microwave gives greater control, even those tricky sauces – hollandaise and béarnaise, for example – will join the ranks of the never-fail, simply prepared favourites.

Top: Spaghetti with Garlic Sausage (page 157); *Below:* Sausage Pizza Flan (page 207)

BASIC WHITE POURING SAUCE

Makes 300 ml/½ pint
Power setting FULL
Total cooking time 4½–5 minutes

25 g/1 oz butter
25 g/1 oz plain flour
300 ml/½ pint milk
salt and freshly ground black pepper

Place the butter in a jug and cook for 1 minute to melt. Add the flour mixing well, then gradually add the milk with seasoning to taste. Cook for 3½–4 minutes stirring every 1 minute until the sauce is smooth and thickened.

VARIATIONS

Basic White Coating Sauce Prepare and cook as above but increase both the butter and flour to 50 g/2 oz.

Cheese Sauce Add 50–75 g/2–3 oz grated cheese and a pinch of mustard powder and cayenne pepper to the white pouring or coating sauce for the last 2 minutes cooking time. Stir these ingredients in to make sure they are well blended.

Parsley Sauce Add 1 tablespoon chopped fresh parsley to the pouring or coating sauce for the last 2 minutes cooking time; stir thoroughly.

Caper Sauce Add 1–2 tablespoons chopped capers to the sauce for the last 2 minutes cooking time. Stir thoroughly.

Onion Sauce Place 15 g/½ oz butter in a bowl with 100 g/4 oz chopped onion and cook for 2 minutes. Add to the white pouring or coating sauce, stirring and blending well, for the last 2 minutes cooking time. *Total cooking time* 6½–7 minutes

Mushroom Sauce Place 100 g/4 oz sliced mushrooms in a bowl with 1 tablespoon water. Cook for 2 minutes. Drain and add, stirring, to the white pouring or coating sauce for the last 2 minutes cooking time. *Total cooking time* 6½–7 minutes

Curry Sauce Prepare the white pouring or coating sauce as above, adding 4 tablespoons very finely chopped onion, 2 teaspoons curry powder (strength according to taste) and ¾ teaspoon sugar with the flour. Just before serving stir in 1 teaspoon lemon juice.

Hot Thousand Island Sauce Prepare the white pouring or coating sauce as above, then mix 4 tablespoons mayonnaise and 4 tablespoons mild chilli sauce together and stir into the white sauce before serving.

Lemon Sauce Stir in the finely grated rind of 1 small lemon and 1 tablespoon lemon juice to the white pouring or coating sauce for the last 2 minutes cooking time.

Anchovy Sauce Prepare the white pouring or coating sauce as above. Stir in 2 tablespoons anchovy essence and 1 teaspoon lemon juice before serving.

Prawn or Shrimp Sauce Mix 50 g/2 oz finely chopped peeled prawns or whole prepared shrimps, ½ teaspoon mustard powder with 2 teaspoons lemon juice and ½ teaspoon anchovy essence. Stir into the white pouring or coating sauce for the last 2 minutes cooking time.

Egg Sauce Stir in 1 finely chopped, hard-boiled egg to the white pouring or coating sauce for the last 2 minutes cooking time.

BÉCHAMEL SAUCE

Makes 300 ml/$\frac{1}{2}$ pint
Power setting FULL or DEFROST
Total cooking time 7$\frac{1}{2}$–8 minutes or 12$\frac{1}{2}$–14 minutes

1 small onion, peeled
6 cloves
1 bay leaf
6 peppercorns
1 small carrot, peeled
300 ml/$\frac{1}{2}$ pint milk
25 g/1 oz butter
25 g/1 oz plain flour
salt and freshly ground black pepper

Stud the onion with the cloves and place in a bowl with the bay leaf, peppercorns, carrot and milk. Cook on DEFROST POWER for 10–11 minutes until hot. Alternatively, cook on FULL POWER for 3 minutes, allow to stand for 3 minutes, then cook for a further 2 minutes and allow to stand for 2 minutes.

Place the butter in a jug and cook on FULL POWER for 1 minute. Stir in the flour and seasoning to taste. Gradually add the strained milk, stirring continuously, and cook on FULL POWER for 1$\frac{1}{2}$–2 minutes until smooth and thick.

VARIATIONS

Aurore Sauce Prepare and cook as above, then add 2 tablespoons concentrated tomato purée and $\frac{1}{2}$ teaspoon caster sugar before serving.
Chaud-froid Sauce Prepare and cook as above. Dissolve 3 teaspoons gelatine in 150 ml/$\frac{1}{4}$ pint hot water. Cook on FULL POWER for 1 minute. Stir into the hot sauce. Use when cold and almost at setting point. Total cooking time 8$\frac{1}{2}$–9 minutes or 13$\frac{1}{2}$–15 minutes.
Cucumber Sauce Prepare and cook as above but add 4 tablespoons finely grated peeled cucumber and a large pinch of ground nutmeg to the sauce before serving.
Hot Horseradish Sauce Prepare and cook as above but add 2 tablespoons grated horseradish, $\frac{1}{2}$ teaspoon sugar and 1 teaspoon vinegar to the sauce for the last 2 minutes cooking time, stirring and blending well.
Mornay Sauce Prepare and cook as above but add 1 egg yolk mixed with 2 tablespoons double cream and 50 g/2 oz very finely grated Cheddar cheese to the hot sauce. Whisk until the cheese melts and the sauce is smooth.
Hot Tartar Sauce Prepare and cook as above but add 1 egg yolk mixed with 2 tablespoons double cream, 1 tablespoon finely chopped parsley, 2 teaspoons finely chopped gherkins and 2 teaspoons finely chopped capers, stirring and blending well.

HOLLANDAISE SAUCE

(Illustrated on pages 50/51)
Serves 4
Power setting FULL and MEDIUM
Total cooking time 2½ minutes

100 g/4 oz butter
juice of 1 medium lemon
½ teaspoon mustard powder
2 egg yolks
salt and freshly ground black pepper

Place the butter in a large jug and heat on FULL POWER for 1½ minutes. Mix the lemon juice with the mustard and egg yolks and whisk into the hot butter. Whisk well to blend smoothly, then season to taste. Cook on MEDIUM POWER for 1 minute, taking care to ensure the sauce does not boil. Serve hot with poached salmon, globe artichokes or vegetables.

BÉARNAISE SAUCE

Makes about 100 ml/4 fl oz
Power setting FULL
Total cooking time 1–2 minutes

100 g/4 oz butter
4 egg yolks
1 teaspoon minced or grated onion
1 teaspoon tarragon vinegar
1 teaspoon white wine

Place the butter in a jug and cook for 1–2 minutes until hot and bubbly. Place the egg yolks, onion, vinegar and wine in a blender. Turn on to the highest setting and add the hot butter, blending until the sauce is creamy and thickened. Serve with steaks, poached eggs on toast or with green vegetables.

CRANBERRY SAUCE

Makes 750–900 ml/1¼–1½ pints
Power setting FULL
Total cooking time 18–20 minutes

350 g/12 oz sugar
6 tablespoons cold water
450 g/1 lb fresh cranberries

Place the sugar, water and cranberries in a large bowl. Cover with cling film, snipping two holes in the top to allow the steam to escape. Cook for 18–20 minutes, stirring every 6 minutes. Serve warm or cold.

APPLE SAUCE

Makes 300 ml/½ pint
Power setting FULL
Total cooking time 6–8 minutes

450 g/1 lb cooking apples, peeled, cored and sliced
15 g/½ oz butter
1 teaspoon lemon juice
2–4 teaspoons caster sugar
1 tablespoon water

Place the apples, butter, lemon juice, sugar to taste and water in a bowl. Cover with cling film, snipping two holes in the top to allow the steam to escape, and cook for 6–8 minutes until the apples are soft. Beat until smooth or press through a sieve, or blend in a liquidiser. Serve with pork, duck, game or goose.

VARIATION

Quince and Apple Sauce Prepare a half quantity of the apple sauce and cook for 3–4 minutes until soft. Beat until smooth, or sieve or blend in a liquidiser. Meanwhile peel, core and thinly slice 2 small quinces, place in a bowl with 5 tablespoons cider and 2 tablespoons sugar. Cover with cling film, snipping two holes in the top to allow the steam to escape, and cook for 6–7 minutes until tender. Combine the apple sauce with the cooked quince mixture and cook, uncovered, for a further 2–3 minutes until thick. Serve with pork, duck, game or goose. *Total cooking time* 11–14 minutes

BREAD SAUCE

Makes about 450 ml/¾ pint
Power setting FULL
Total cooking time 7 minutes

1 onion, peeled
4 cloves
300 ml/½ pint milk
pinch of ground nutmeg
65 g/2½ oz fresh white breadcrumbs
15 g/½ oz butter
1 tablespoon cream or top of the milk
salt and freshly ground black pepper

Stud the onion with the cloves and place in a deep dish with the milk and nutmeg. Cook, uncovered, for 4 minutes.

Add the breadcrumbs and cook, uncovered, for 2 minutes, then remove the onion. Add the butter and cream or top of the milk. Cook for 1 minute, stirring halfway through the cooking time. Season to taste and serve hot with poultry.

SWEET AND SOUR SAUCE

(Illustrated on page 229)
Makes about 300 ml/½ pint
Power setting FULL
Total cooking time 5–7 minutes

100 g/4 oz sugar
4½ teaspoons cornflour
4 tablespoons cold water
1 (227-g/8-oz) can crushed pineapple
1 small green pepper, seeds removed and chopped
100 g/4 oz canned pimiento, chopped
1 clove garlic, crushed
6 tablespoons cider vinegar
4½ teaspoons soy sauce
dash of Tabasco sauce

Blend the sugar with the cornflour and water in a large bowl. Add the pineapple, pepper, pimiento, garlic, cider vinegar, soy sauce and Tabasco. Cook for 5–7 minutes, stirring every 2 minutes, until clear and thickened. Allow to stand for 5 minutes to allow the flavours to develop before serving.

BARBECUE SAUCE

Makes about 300 ml/½ pint
Power setting FULL
Total cooking time 8–10 minutes

25 g/1 oz butter
1 teaspoon oil
1 onion, peeled and finely chopped
3 tablespoons boiling water
2 tablespoons vinegar
1 tablespoon Worcestershire sauce
2 tablespoons lemon juice
2 teaspoons soft brown sugar
2 teaspoons made mustard
½ teaspoon salt
½ teaspoon paprika
¼ teaspoon chilli powder

Place the butter and oil in a bowl and cook for 1 minute. Add the onion and cook for 2 minutes. Add the remaining ingredients, cover and cook for 5–7 minutes, stirring after 3 minutes. Serve hot.

ITALIAN TOMATO SAUCE

Makes 450 ml/$\frac{3}{4}$ pints
Power setting FULL
Total cooking time 7$\frac{1}{2}$–9 minutes

1 onion, peeled and chopped
1$\frac{1}{2}$ tablespoons oil
1 clove garlic, peeled and crushed
1 (398-g/14-oz) can tomatoes or tomato sauce
1 (141-g/5-oz) can tomato purée
4 tablespoons red wine, beef stock or tomato juice
1 tablespoon brown sugar
1 teaspoon Worcestershire sauce
$\frac{1}{2}$ teaspoon dried oregano
$\frac{1}{2}$ teaspoon dried basil
$\frac{1}{2}$ teaspoon salt
$\frac{1}{4}$ teaspoon freshly ground black pepper

Place the onion, oil and garlic in a large bowl. Cook for 1$\frac{1}{2}$–2 minutes. Add the remaining ingredients, mixing well. Cover and cook for 6–7 minutes, stirring halfway through the cooking time.

VARIATIONS

Italian Tomato and Mushroom Sauce *(Illustrated on page 229)* Prepare and cook the sauce as above. Place 450 g/1 lb sliced mushrooms in a bowl with 4 tablespoons water. Cover and cook for 4–5 minutes. Add to the tomato sauce and serve with pasta, meatballs or chicken. *Serves* 4–6 *Total cooking time* 11$\frac{1}{2}$–14 minutes

Italian Bolognese-style Sauce Prepare and cook the sauce as above. Preheat a browning skillet for 5 minutes or according to the manufacturer's instructions. Quickly stir 450 g/1 lb lean minced beef in the dish until evenly browned. Cook for 8–9 minutes, breaking up the meat with a fork and stirring occasionally during cooking. Add to the tomato sauce and serve with pasta. *Serves* 4–6 *Total cooking time* 20$\frac{1}{2}$–23 minutes

SAVOURY RAISIN SAUCE

Makes about 300 ml/½ pint
Power setting FULL
Total cooking time 4–6 minutes

150 g/5 oz soft brown sugar
4½ teaspoons cornflour
1½ teaspoons made mustard
pinch of ground cloves
250 ml/8 fl oz dry cider
4½ teaspoons lemon juice
50 g/2 oz raisins
25 g/1 oz butter

Place the sugar, cornflour, mustard and cloves in a large jug and mix well. Add the cider and lemon juice and blend until smooth. Add the raisins and butter and cook for 4–6 minutes, stirring every 2 minutes until clear and thickened. Serve with ham or pork.

SIMPLE CUSTARD SAUCE

Makes about 300 ml/½ pint
Power setting FULL
Total cooking time 3–4 minutes

1–2 tablespoons sugar
1 tablespoon custard powder
300 ml/½ pint milk
few drops vanilla essence (optional)

In a large jug, mix the sugar to taste with the custard powder and a little of the milk. Gradually blend in the remaining milk and cook for 3–4 minutes until thick and smooth, stirring or whisking every 1 minute. Add a few drops of vanilla essence before serving.

VARIATION

Brandy or Sherry Sauce Prepare as above but use 1 tablespoon cornflour instead of the custard powder. When the sauce is cooked, stir in 1 tablespoon brandy or sherry instead of the vanilla essence.

BUTTERSCOTCH SAUCE

Makes 350 ml/12 fl oz
Power setting FULL
Total cooking time 3½–4½ minutes

1 tablespoon cornflour
275 g/10 oz light soft brown sugar
6 tablespoons single cream
4½ teaspoons light corn or maple syrup
pinch of salt
50 g/2 oz butter
1 teaspoon vanilla essence

Mix the cornflour with the sugar, single cream, corn or maple syrup, salt and butter. Cover and cook for 3½–4½ minutes, stirring after 2 minutes. Add the vanilla and stir until smooth and well blended. Serve warm or cold over pancakes, ice cream or waffles.

VARIATION

Maple Walnut Butterscotch Sauce Prepare as above using maple syrup and add 40 g/1½ oz chopped walnuts to the cooked sauce.

JAM SAUCE

Makes 450 ml/¾ pint
Power setting FULL
Total cooking time 4–5½ minutes

300 ml/½ pint water or fruit juice
225 g/8 oz jam
1 tablespoon cornflour or arrowroot powder
4 tablespoons cold water
lemon juice to taste

Place the water or fruit juice in a large jug and cook for 2–2½ minutes until hot, then stir in the jam. Blend the cornflour or arrowroot powder with the cold water and stir into the jam mixture, blending well. Cook for 2–3 minutes, stirring every 1 minute. Add lemon juice to taste and serve.

VARIATIONS

Marmalade Sauce Prepare as above but use 225 g/8 oz marmalade instead of the jam.
Syrup Sauce Prepare as above but use 225 g/8 oz golden syrup instead of the jam.

MOCHA SAUCE

(Illustrated on page 229)
Makes 450 ml/$\frac{3}{4}$ pint
Power setting FULL
Total cooking time 2$\frac{1}{2}$–4 minutes

175 g/6 oz plain dessert chocolate
1 teaspoon butter
3–4 tablespoons golden syrup
2 teaspoons coffee essence or chicory extract
150 ml/$\frac{1}{4}$ pint single cream

Break up the chocolate and place it in a bowl with the butter, golden syrup and coffee essence or chicory extract. Cook for 2–3 minutes until melted, stirring halfway through the cooking time.

Stir in the cream and cook for $\frac{1}{2}$–1 minute to heat through without boiling. Serve hot or cold with puddings and desserts.

FUDGE SAUCE

(Illustrated on pages 190/191)
Makes about 350 ml/12 fl oz
Power setting FULL
Total cooking time 5–6 minutes

225 g/8 oz sugar
$\frac{1}{4}$ teaspoon salt
1 (170-g/6-oz) can evaporated milk
50 g/2 oz plain dessert chocolate, broken into pieces
25 g/1 oz butter
1 teaspoon vanilla essence

Place the sugar, salt and milk in a bowl and mix well. Cook for 5–6 minutes until the sauce is boiling rapidly. Carefully stir in the chocolate, butter and vanilla. Serve warm.

CHOCOLATE MINT SAUCE

Makes about 250 ml/8 fl oz
Power setting LOW
Total cooking time 3–5 minutes

175 g/6 oz chocolate mint creams
3 tablespoons whipping cream

Place the chocolate mint creams and whipping cream in a bowl. Cover and cook for 3–5 minutes, stirring every 1 minute until smooth. Serve warm, poured over ice cream.

Puddings and Desserts

Feeding a family can be one of the most difficult of tasks, because it is not just feeding them, it's pleasing them too! And that often means preparing a pudding or dessert to round off a meal. Your microwave oven will arm you with a wealth of quick and easy puddings and desserts ranging from wholesome and hearty custards, fruit puddings, pies and sponges to lighter cheesecakes, mousses, ice creams and sorbets. You'll find all the old favourites here – for example Christmas Pudding, a rice pudding and Jam Roly-poly – alongside new ideas like Strawberry and Pistachio Shortcake, Chocolate and Whisky Syllabub Shells and Armenian Kishmish; and all cooked in a fraction of the time it takes to cook them conventionally.

You're bound to be impressed with suet puddings cooked in minutes rather than hours, smooth creamy custards that don't need the careful stirring and intense concentration that conventional cooking demands or dried fruit dishes, like compotes, that don't need the traditional pre-soaking. You will also find that simple poached fruit retains a full, fresh flavour because it is cooked so quickly with the minimum water.

It is difficult to give firm ground rules for cooking puddings and desserts – their variety almost denies any generalisation. The individual recipes will themselves give the tips for success. However, do remember to score or prick whole fruit before baking to prevent it bursting and turn, rearrange or rotate puddings halfway through the cooking time. Cover the fruit with a lid, cling film or greaseproof paper and snip two holes in the top of cling film to allow the steam to escape. Always observe, too, a 5–10 minute standing time so that the residual heat in the food is used.

Guide to Defrosting Fruit

Defrost fruits in their covered freezer containers, if suitable, for the times given below, or transfer the fruit to a suitable covered dish first. The times given will partially defrost the fruit: it should then be allowed to stand at room temperature to completely thaw by means of the residual heat. The times given are approximate and will depend upon the freezing method used, the type and shape of the container and the variety of the fruit. During defrosting gently shake or stir the contents to ensure even heat distribution.

Quantity of fruit and freezing method	*Time in minutes on* FULL POWER	Time in minutes on DEFROST POWER
450 g/1 lb fruit, dry packed with sugar	4–8	—
450 g/1 lb fruit packed with sugar syrup	8–12	—
450 g/1 lb free-flow fruit (open frozen)	—	4–8

Guide to Cooking Fruit

Fruit – type and quantity	*Preparation*	*Cooking time in minutes on* FULL POWER
450 g/1 lb apricots	*Stone and wash, then sprinkle with 100 g/4 oz sugar.*	6–8
450 g/1 lb cooking apples	*Peel, core and slice, then sprinkle with 100 g/4 oz sugar.*	6–8
450 g/1 lb goose-berries	*Top and tail, then sprinkle with 100 g/4 oz sugar.*	4
4 medium-sized peaches	*Stone and wash, then sprinkle with 100 g/4 oz sugar.*	4–5
6 medium-sized pears	*Peel, halve and core. Dissolve 75 g/3 oz sugar in a little water and pour over the pears.*	8–10
450 g/1 lb plums, cherries, damsons or greengages	*Stone and wash. Sprinkle with 100 g/4 oz sugar and the grated rind of ½ lemon.*	4–5
450 g/1 lb soft berry fruits	*Top and tail or hull. Wash and add 100 g/4 oz sugar.*	3–5
450 g/1 lb rhubarb	*Trim and cut into short lengths. Add 100 g/4 oz sugar and the grated rind of 1 lemon.*	8–10

CHRISTMAS PUDDING

(Illustrated on pages 190/191)
Serves 4–6
Power setting FULL
Total cooking time 8 minutes

75 g/3 oz fresh breadcrumbs
75 g/3 oz plain flour
pinch of mace
pinch of nutmeg
pinch of cinnamon
75 g/3 oz shredded beef suet
50 g/2 oz soft brown sugar
50 g/2 oz caster sugar
50 g/2 oz candied peel
75 g/3 oz currants
50 g/2 oz sultanas
150 g/5 oz raisins
40 g/1½ oz blanched almonds, chopped
1 small cooking apple, peeled, cored and chopped
grated rind and juice of ½ lemon
1 tablespoon brandy
1 large egg, beaten
3 tablespoons brown ale or stout
1 tablespoon milk
1½ tablespoons black treacle

In a large mixing bowl mix the breadcrumbs with the flour, mace, nutmeg, cinnamon, suet and sugars. Add the peel, currants, sultanas, raisins, almonds and apple, mixing well. Blend the lemon rind and juice with the brandy, egg, ale or stout, milk and treacle. Add to the dry ingredients, mixing to make a mixture with a soft dropping consistency – add a little extra milk if necessary. Cover the mixture and leave overnight or for 6–8 hours.

Turn into a greased 1.15-litre/2-pint pudding basin. Cover loosely with cling film and cook for 8 minutes. Leave to rest in the basin for 5 minutes before turning out and serving with custard, cream or brandy butter.

If the pudding is cooked in advance and needs reheating, cook for 2–3 minutes, then serve.

SYRUP SUET PUDDING

Serves 4–6
Power setting FULL
Total cooking time 4–4½ minutes

100 g/4 oz self-raising flour
50 g/2 oz shredded beef suet
50 g/2 oz caster sugar
1 teaspoon vanilla essence
1 egg, beaten
100 ml/4 fl oz milk
3 tablespoons golden syrup

Line a 1.15-litre/2-pint pudding basin with cling film, or grease well.

Mix the flour with the suet and sugar and, using a fork, gradually add the vanilla essence, egg and milk to make a soft batter. Make sure the mixture is well blended without actually beating it.

Place the syrup in the base of the prepared basin and carefully spoon the suet mixture on top, cover with cling film and snip two holes in the top to allow the steam to escape. Cook for 4–4½ minutes or until the pudding rises to the top of the basin.

Remove the cling film carefully and invert the pudding on to a serving plate. Cut into wedges, and serve with a sweet sauce or custard.

VARIATIONS

Jam Suet Pudding Prepare and cook as above, but use 3 tablespoons jam instead of the syrup.

Fair Lady Pudding Prepare and cook the pudding as above, but add the finely grated rind of 1 orange to the mixture and omit the syrup.

Four-fruit Pudding Prepare and cook as above, but omit the syrup and add 25 g/1 oz chopped dates, 25 g/1 oz chopped figs, 25 g/1 oz chopped prunes and 25 g/1 oz chopped mixed peel to the mixture.

Marmalade Suet Pudding Prepare and cook as above, but substitute 3 tablespoons marmalade for the syrup.

Spotted Dick Suet Pudding Prepare and cook as above, but omit the syrup and add 75 g/3 oz currants and 25 g/1 oz chopped mixed peel to the mixture.

JAM ROLY-POLY PUDDING

(Illustrated on pages 190/191)
Serves 6
Power setting FULL
Total cooking time 8½ minutes

SUET PASTRY
225 g/8 oz self-raising flour
pinch of salt
100 g/4 oz shredded suet
150 ml/¼ pint cold water
flour for dusting
FILLING AND TOPPING
100 g/4 oz jam
2 teaspoons lemon juice
2 tablespoons caster sugar
½ teaspoon cinnamon

Sift the flour with the salt and stir in the suet. Add the cold water and mix to form a soft but manageable dough. Roll out the dough on a lightly floured surface to form a 23-cm/9-in square.

Mix the jam with the lemon juice in a small bowl and heat for ½ minute. Spread evenly over the suet pastry square, leaving a 1-cm/½-in border around the edge, and carefully roll up like a Swiss roll. Place joined-side down on a large piece of greaseproof paper and roll the greaseproof up loosely around the pastry roll, allowing plenty of space for the roly-poly to rise. Carefully tie the ends of the paper with string or elastic bands and cover loosely with cling film.

Cook in the microwave for 8 minutes until well risen and cooked through. Test by inserting a skewer into the centre of the roly-poly – the skewer should come out clean of the pastry dough.

Mix the sugar with the cinnamon. Remove the cling film and greaseproof paper from the roly-poly and place on a serving dish. Sprinkle with the cinnamon sugar. Serve hot with a simple Custard Sauce or Jam Sauce (see pages 170 and 171).

BLACKBERRY AND APPLE CRUMBLE

Serves 4
Power setting FULL
Total cooking time 11–13 minutes

225 g/8 oz fresh or frozen blackberries, hulled and thawed if necessary
225 g/8 oz cooking apples, peeled, cored and sliced
sugar to taste
100 g/4 oz butter
175 g/6 oz plain flour
50 g/2 oz soft brown sugar
grated rind of $\frac{1}{2}$ lemon

Place the blackberries and apples in a heatproof dish and sprinkle with sugar to taste.

Rub the butter into the flour until the mixture resembles fine breadcrumbs. Stir in the sugar and lemon rind. Carefully spoon on top of the fruit and cook for 11–13 minutes, giving the dish a quarter turn every 3 minutes. Place under a hot grill to brown further if liked. Serve hot with cream or custard.

VARIATIONS

Bramble Crumble Prepare and cook as above but use redcurrants, blackcurrants, raspberries, blueberries or loganberries – or a mixture – instead of the apple and blackberries.

Gooseberry and Orange Crumble Prepare and cook as above but use 450 g/1 lb topped and tailed gooseberries with the grated rind of 1 orange instead of the apples and blackberries. Prick gooseberries before cooking.

Rhubarb Crumble Prepare and cook as above but use 450 g/1 lb prepared rhubarb, cut into chunks, instead of the apples and blackberries.

Cherry and Lemon Crumble Prepare and cook as above but use the drained black cherries from a 425-g/15-oz can with the grated rind of 1 lemon instead of the apples and blackberries.

Damson and Cinnamon Crumble Prepare and cook as above. Omit the apples and blackberries but use 450 g/1 lb halved and stoned damsons mixed with $\frac{1}{2}$ teaspoon ground cinnamon.

Crunchy Nut Crumble Prepare and cook as above using 450 g/1 lb fresh, frozen or canned fruit. Add 25 g/1 oz chopped nuts to the crumble topping.

Oaten Crumble Prepare and cook as above using 450 g/1 lb fresh, frozen or canned fruit. Add 25 g/1 oz porridge oats to the crumble topping.

Top: Blackberry and Apple Crumble; *Below:* Crème Caramel
(page 187)

JAM SPONGE PUDDING

Serves 6
Power setting FULL
Total cooking time 6–7 minutes

100 g/4 oz butter or margarine
100 g/4 oz caster sugar
2 eggs, beaten
100 g/4 oz self-raising flour
pinch of salt
1–2 tablespoons hot water
3 tablespoons jam

Line a 900-ml/1½-pint pudding basin with cling film, or grease well.

Cream the butter with the sugar until light and fluffy. Add the eggs, blending well. Sift the flour with the salt and fold into the mixture. Add the hot water to make a dropping consistency.

Place the jam in the base of the prepared basin and carefully spoon the sponge mixture on top, cover with cling film, snipping two holes in the top to allow the steam to escape. Cook for 6–7 minutes, giving the basin a half turn after 3 minutes. Leave to stand for 5–10 minutes before inverting on to a serving plate. Cut into wedges to serve.

VARIATIONS

Syrup Sponge Pudding Prepare and cook as above but use 3 tablespoons golden syrup instead of the jam.

Fruit Sponge Pudding Prepare and cook as above but omit the jam and add 3 tablespoons mixed dried fruit and 1 tablespoon chopped mixed peel to the sponge mixture.

Chocolate Sponge Pudding *(Illustrated on pages 190/191)* Prepare and cook as above but omit the jam. Sift 75 g/3 oz self-raising flour with the salt, 15 g/½ oz cornflour and 15 g/½ oz cocoa instead of the 100 g/4 oz self-raising flour.

Coconut Sponge Pudding Prepare and cook as above, adding 40 g/1½ oz desiccated coconut to the creamed mixture. Omit the jam if liked.

Top: French Fresh Orange Mousse (page 197); *Below:* Summer Port Compote (page 187)

HONEY PLUM COBBLER

Serves 4–6
Power setting FULL
Total cooking time 14–15 minutes

1 kg/2 lb ripe plums, halved and stoned
4–6 tablespoons clear honey
225 g/8 oz self-raising flour
25 g/1 oz sugar
50 g/2 oz butter or margarine
1 egg, beaten
5–6 tablespoons milk
2 teaspoons demerara sugar
1 teaspoon cinnamon

Place the plums and honey in a shallow pie dish. Cover loosely with cling film and cook for 5 minutes, stirring halfway through the cooking time.

Meanwhile, mix the flour with the sugar. Rub in the butter or margarine until the mixture resembles fine breadcrumbs. Using a knife, gradually stir in the egg and milk to form a fairly soft dough, reserving a little of the milk to brush the cobbler topping. Roll out on a floured surface to about 1.5 cm/$\frac{3}{4}$ in thick. Cut out 16 (5-cm/2-in) rounds with a biscuit cutter. Place the scones in an overlapping circle on top of the plums and brush with the reserved milk. Mix the sugar with the cinnamon and sprinkle over the top of the scones. Cook, uncovered, for 9–10 minutes until the scones are cooked. Serve piping hot with fresh cream.

BAKED STUFFED APPLES OR PEARS

Serves 1–4
Power setting FULL

allow 1 large whole apple or pear per person
FOR EACH FRUIT
25 g/1 oz brown sugar
pinch of cinnamon
25 g/1 oz currants, raisins, dates or sultanas
1 teaspoon butter
4$\frac{1}{2}$ teaspoons water

Remove the cores and cut a slit all around the middle of the fruit with a sharp knife to prevent the skin from bursting during cooking.

Place the fruit in a casserole. Mix the sugar, cinnamon and dried fruit together and press this mixture into the centre of each apple or pear. Dot with the butter. Pour the water around the fruit and cook 1 apple or pear for 2–4 minutes, 2 for 4–5$\frac{1}{2}$ minutes, 3 for 6–8 minutes or 4 for 9–10 minutes.

HONEY AND APRICOT COLLEGE PUDDING

Serves 6
Power setting FULL
Total cooking time 6–7 minutes

100 g/4 oz butter or margarine
100 g/4 oz caster sugar
2 eggs, beaten
100 g/4 oz self-raising flour
1 teaspoon baking powder
100 g/4 oz dried apricots, chopped
6 tablespoons clear honey
TO SERVE
Jam Sauce (page 171)
or **Simple Custard Sauce (page 170)**

Cream the butter with the sugar until light and fluffy. Add the eggs and mix well, then fold in the flour, baking powder and apricots making sure the mixture is evenly mixed. Place the honey in a greased 900-ml/1½-pint pudding basin and spoon in the apricot mixture.

Cover with cling film, snipping two holes in the top to allow the steam to escape. Cook for 6–7 minutes, then leave to stand for 5–10 minutes before inverting on to a serving plate. Serve with jam or custard sauce.

VARIATION

Individual Honey and Apricot College Puddings Prepare the apricot mixture as above. Place a little of the honey in the bases of 6 lightly-greased microwave muffin pans: you will need half the above quantity of honey for this. Divide half of the apricot mixture between the moulds and cook for 2½ minutes, giving the dish a half turn after 1 minute. Leave to stand for 2 minutes before turning out. Repeat with the remaining honey and apricot mixture. Serve two puddings per portion. *Total cooking time* 5 minutes

BUTTERSCOTCH BANANAS

Serves 2
Power setting FULL
Total cooking time 5–7 minutes

100 g/4 oz brown sugar
3 tablespoons brown rum
50 g/2 oz butter
2 large ripe, firm bananas, peeled

Place the sugar, rum and butter in a 1.15-litre/2-pint dish. Cover and cook for 4–5 minutes, stirring after 2 minutes, until the sugar has dissolved.

Cut the bananas in half lengthwise, then across to make eight pieces. Add the pieces of banana to the sugar syrup and toss to coat, then cook for 1–2 minutes until hot. These bananas are delicious served with ice cream.

Bread and Butter Pudding

Serves 4
Power setting FULL
Total cooking time 12–14 minutes

6 slices white bread, crusts removed
75 g/3 oz butter
50 g/2 oz sultanas or currants
3 eggs, beaten
40 g/1½ oz caster sugar
450 ml/¾ pint milk
few drops of vanilla essence
1 teaspoon nutmeg

Lightly grease a 1.15-litre/2-pint pie dish. Spread the bread slices with butter, then cut each in half diagonally. Layer the bread pieces evenly in the dish with the sultanas or currants. Beat the eggs with the sugar. Pour the milk into a jug and cook for 1 minute. Add the vanilla essence and then pour into the egg mixture, mixing well. Pour the egg and milk mixture over the bread and cook, uncovered, for 3 minutes.

Press the bread down into the custard and leave to stand for 5 minutes. Cook, uncovered, for a further 5 minutes, then leave to stand for 15 minutes. Cook, uncovered, for a further 3–5 minutes until the custard has set. Sprinkle with nutmeg and place under a hot grill until golden. Serve hot or warm.

Creamy Rice and Raisin Pudding

Serves 3–4
Power setting FULL and DEFROST
Total cooking time 35 minutes

50 g/2 oz round-grain rice
450 ml/¾ pint boiling water
¼ teaspoon nutmeg
strip of lemon rind
25 g/1 oz sugar
1 (170-g/6-oz) can evaporated milk
1 teaspoon butter
50 g/2 oz raisins
150 ml/¼ pint double cream, whipped

Place the rice, water, nutmeg and lemon rind in a large deep dish and cook on FULL POWER for 10 minutes, stirring occasionally. Remove the lemon rind, add the sugar and evaporated milk and cook on DEFROST POWER for 20 minutes, stirring occasionally. Stir in the butter and raisins and continue to cook on DEFROST POWER for a further 5 minutes.

Allow to cool for 5 minutes, then fold in the whipped cream. Serve warm or cold.

SEMOLINA, SAGO OR GROUND RICE PUDDING

Serves 2–3
Power setting FULL and LOW
Total cooking time 17–23 minutes

600 ml/1 pint milk
4 tablespoons semolina, sago or ground rice
2 tablespoons caster sugar

Place the milk, semolina, sago or ground rice and sugar in a large bowl. Cook on FULL POWER for 5–6 minutes or until the milk boils. Stir well, then cover with cling film, snipping two holes in the top to allow the steam to escape. Cook on FULL POWER for 2 minutes, then reduce to LOW POWER and cook for 10–15 minutes until cooked, stirring every 5 minutes.

Allow to stand for 5 minutes before serving.

VARIATIONS

Lemon Semolina, Sago or Ground Rice Pudding Prepare and cook as above, but add 2 teaspoons finely grated lemon rind to the ingredients prior to cooking.
Orange Semolina, Sago or Ground Rice Pudding Prepare and cook as above, but add 2 teaspoons finely grated orange rind to the ingredients prior to cooking.
Chocolate Semolina, Sago or Ground Rice Pudding Prepare and cook as above but add 25 g/1 oz grated plain dessert chocolate to the pudding when cooked. Stir well to melt.
Fruit Semolina, Sago or Ground Rice Pudding Prepare and cook as above but add 50 g/2 oz seedless raisins halfway through the cooking time.

CHOCOLATE FONDUE

Serves 3–4
Power setting MEDIUM
Total cooking time 8–10 minutes

100 g/4 oz plain dessert chocolate
250 ml/8 fl oz whipping cream
225 g/8 oz sugar
½ teaspoon vanilla essence

Place the chocolate and cream in a fondue or casserole dish and cook for 5–6 minutes, or until the chocolate melts. Stir well, add the sugar and vanilla essence, then cook for 3–4 minutes, or until sugar has dissolved.

Serve with marshmallows, pieces of fresh fruit, cake cubes, sponge fingers or biscuits.

ARMENIAN KISHMISH

Serves 4
Power setting FULL
Total cooking time 12–14 minutes

450 g/1 lb mixed dried fruits, for example apricots, apples, prunes and figs
450 ml/$\frac{3}{4}$ pint cold water
4 tablespoons clear honey
4 tablespoons brandy
1 cinnamon stick
3–4 cloves
$\frac{1}{4}$ teaspoon ground allspice
strip of lemon rind

Combine all the ingredients in a large deep dish, cover and leave to stand for 2 hours.
Cover loosely with cling film and cook for 12–14 minutes or until the fruit is tender, giving the dish an occasional shake during cooking. Remove the cinnamon stick, cloves and lemon rind and serve hot or chilled. Top with yogurt, soured cream, whipped cream or ice cream if liked.

JAMAICAN BANANA, FIG AND PINEAPPLE COMPOTE

Serves 4
Power setting FULL
Total cooking time 7 minutes

50 g/2 oz butter
100 g/4 oz demerara sugar
3 tablespoons lemon juice
$\frac{1}{2}$ teaspoon mixed spice
675 g/1$\frac{1}{2}$ lb firm bananas, peeled and thickly sliced
2 large fresh figs, peeled and chopped *or* 100 g/4 oz dried figs, chopped
1 medium pineapple, peeled, cored and cubed
4 tablespoons dark rum
25 g/1 oz walnuts, coarsely chopped

Place the butter in a large dish and cook for 1 minute. Stir in the sugar, lemon juice and spice and cook for a further 2 minutes. Add the bananas, figs and pineapple and toss well to coat in the spice mixture. Cover the dish tightly and cook for a further 3 minutes, then add the rum, re-cover and cook for a final 1 minute. Remove from the oven and sprinkle with the walnuts. Serve hot with soured cream or single cream.

SUMMER PORT COMPOTE

(Illustrated on page 180)
Serves 4–6
Power setting FULL
Total cooking time 4 minutes

1 kg/2 lb prepared soft summer fruits (for example, strawberries, raspberries, redcurrants, blackcurrants, gooseberries, plums, cherries and peaches)
150 ml/¼ pint port
100 g/4 oz caster sugar
whipped cream to serve

Place the fruits in a large bowl and pour over the port. Leave to macerate, covered, in the refrigerator for 2–4 hours.

Add the sugar and mix until well blended. Cover with cling film, snipping two holes in the top to allow the steam to escape and cook for 4 minutes, stirring halfway through the cooking time. Remove the cling film, cool and chill. Serve with whipped cream.

CRÈME CARAMEL

(Illustrated on page 179)
Serves 4–6
Power setting FULL and LOW
Total cooking time 24–29 minutes

CARAMEL
100 ml/4 fl oz water
100 g/4 oz granulated sugar
CUSTARD
3 eggs
50 g/2 oz sugar
1 teaspoon vanilla essence
pinch of salt
350 ml/12 fl oz milk

First prepare the caramel by placing the water and sugar in a heatproof jug; stir well. Cook on FULL POWER for 10–12 minutes until golden. Do not allow the syrup to become too brown as it will continue to cook after you have removed it from the oven. Pour quickly into an 18-cm/7-in soufflé dish, then allow to cool and harden.

Whisk the eggs with the sugar, vanilla and salt until well blended and the sugar has dissolved. Place the milk in a heatproof glass jug and cook on FULL POWER for 4 minutes. Gradually add to the egg mixture, blending well. Pour or strain the mixture over the caramel. Cover and stand in a shallow dish. Pour enough hot water into the outer dish to come 2.5–5 cm/1–2 in up the outside of the soufflé dish. Cook on LOW POWER for 10–13 minutes, giving the dish a quarter turn every 3 minutes, until set. Chill thoroughly.

To serve, invert the crème caramel on to a serving dish.

STRAWBERRY AND PISTACHIO SHORTCAKE

Serves 4–6
Power setting DEFROST
Total cooking time 8 minutes

225 g/8 oz plain flour
50 g/2 oz icing sugar
150 g/5 oz unsalted butter, softened
$\frac{1}{4}$ teaspoon vanilla essence
TOPPING
450 g/1 lb strawberries, hulled
2 tablespoons red wine
2 tablespoons caster sugar
300 ml/$\frac{1}{2}$ pint double cream
2 tablespoons pistachio nuts

Sift the flour and sugar together until well blended. Rub in the butter until the mixture resembles fine breadcrumbs, then stir in the vanilla. Line the base of a 23-cm/9-in shallow dish with greaseproof paper. Spoon the shortcake mixture into the dish and smooth down evenly with the back of a spoon. Cook for 8 minutes or until a skewer inserted into the centre of the shortcake comes out clean. Give the dish a quarter turn every 2 minutes while cooking. Leave to cool in the dish for at least 1 hour.

Meanwhile place half the strawberries in a dish with the red wine and sugar. Leave to macerate, turning from time to time, for about 1 hour.

Turn the shortcake out on to a serving plate and remove the greaseproof paper. Top with the drained strawberries. Whip the cream until it stands in soft peaks. Pipe or spoon the cream on top of the strawberries. Decorate with the remaining strawberries and pistachio nuts. Serve on the day of making.

Top: Strawberry and Pistachio Shortcake; *Below:* Chocolate and Whisky Syllabub Shells (page 195)
Overleaf *Left:* Jam Roly-poly Pudding (page 177); *Top centre:* Orange Zabaglione (page 196); *Right:* Chocolate Sponge Pudding (page 181) with Fudge Sauce (page 172); *Below:* Christmas Pudding (page 175)

BLACKCURRANT CONDÉ

Serves 4
Power setting FULL and DEFROST
Total cooking time 39–40½ minutes

50 g/2 oz round-grain rice
450 ml/¾ pint boiling water
¼ teaspoon nutmeg
strip of lemon rind
25 g/1 oz granulated sugar
1 (170-g/6-oz) can evaporated milk
1 teaspoon butter
350 g/12 oz fresh or frozen blackcurrants, topped and tailed
3 tablespoons redcurrant jelly
3 tablespoons caster sugar
3 tablespoons cold water
1½ teaspoons arrowroot powder
1½ tablespoons Kirsch
150 ml/¼ pint double cream, whipped

Place the rice, water, nutmeg and lemon rind in a large deep dish and cook on FULL POWER for 10 minutes, stirring occasionally. Remove the lemon rind, add the sugar and evaporated milk and cook on DEFROST POWER for 20 minutes, stirring occasionally. Stir in the butter and cook on DEFROST POWER for a further 5 minutes. Allow to cool.

Place the blackcurrants in a bowl with the redcurrant jelly, caster sugar and the cold water. Cover with cling film, snipping two holes in the top to allow the steam to escape, and cook for 3–4 minutes or until the fruit softens and pops. Blend the arrowroot to a smooth paste with a little water and stir into the blackcurrant mixture. Cook, uncovered, for 1–1½ minutes or until clear and thickened, stirring occasionally. Cool, then stir in the Kirsch.

Fold the whipped cream into the cooled rice. Layer the rice with the blackcurrant mixture in individual stemmed glasses and chill before serving.

Clockwise from the top: Blackcurrant Sorbet (page 199), Tutti-frutti Ice Cream, Raspberry Ice Cream and Cointreau and Orange Ice Cream (page 198)

Sherry and Blackcurrant Trifle

Serves 6
Power setting FULL and MEDIUM
Total cooking time 11 minutes

8 trifle sponges
3 tablespoons raspberry jam
275 g/10 oz raspberries, hulled
5 tablespoons undiluted blackcurrant health drink
5 tablespoons medium sherry
1 large egg
40 g/1½ oz plain flour
25 g/1 oz soft brown sugar
¼ teaspoon vanilla essence
600 ml/1 pint milk
Decoration
300 ml/½ pint whipping cream, whipped
2 tablespoons chopped hazelnuts
few angelica leaves

Slice the trifle sponges in half and sandwich back together with the raspberry jam. Place in the base of a trifle dish or glass bowl and top with the raspberries, reserving a few for decoration. Mix the blackcurrant health drink and sherry together and pour over the trifle sponges. Leave to soak for 30 minutes.

Meanwhile, beat the egg, flour, sugar and vanilla essence together. Place the milk in a large bowl and heat on FULL POWER for 4 minutes. Pour on to the egg mixture, whisking continuously, then strain this custard back into the bowl and cook on MEDIUM POWER for 7 minutes, whisking every 2 minutes. Allow to cool slightly before pouring over the trifle sponges. Chill to set.

Decorate the trifle with the whipped cream, the reserved raspberries, hazelnuts and angelica leaves.

CHOCOLATE AND WHISKY SYLLABUB SHELLS

(Illustrated on page 190/191)
Serves 6
Power setting FULL
Total cooking time 2–2½ minutes

150 g/5 oz plain dessert chocolate
1 lemon
6 tablespoons whisky
75 g/3 oz caster sugar
300 ml/½ pint double cream
25 g/1 oz walnuts, finely chopped
DECORATION
chocolate leaves (optional)
julienne strips of lemon rind

Place the chocolate in a small bowl and cook for 2–2½ minutes until melted. Use the melted chocolate to coat the insides of six paper case cases, then turn them upside down, so that the edges stay thicker than the base. Chill until set. When well chilled, carefully peel off the paper cases.

Meanwhile, finely grate the lemon rind into a deep bowl. Add the whisky and sugar and leave to stand for 15 minutes. Whip the cream until it stands in soft peaks, then gradually whisk into the whisky mixture, keeping the cream stiff. Carefully fold in the chopped walnuts. Spoon or pipe the syllabub into the chocolate shells. Chill before serving decorated with chocolate leaves and julienne strips of lemon rind.

CHOCOLATE DREAM CREAMS

Serves 6
Power setting FULL
Total cooking time 2 minutes

175 g/6 oz plain dessert chocolate
300 ml/½ pint double cream
1 egg
pinch of salt
½ teaspoon vanilla essence

Break the chocolate into small pieces and place in a liquidiser. Place the cream in a large jug and cook for 2 minutes, then pour over the chocolate and blend until smooth. Add the egg, salt and vanilla essence and blend for 15 seconds. Pour into six individual ramekin dishes and chill for 6–8 hours – the chocolate dream creams will be smooth and creamy for serving.

HUNGARIAN WITCH'S FROTH

Serves 6
Power setting FULL
Total cooking time 7–8 minutes

6 cooking apples, peeled, cored and sliced
150 ml/$\frac{1}{4}$ pint lemon juice
225 g/8 oz caster sugar
$1\frac{1}{2}$ tablespoons brandy
3 egg whites
25 g/1 oz walnuts, coarsely chopped

Place the apple and lemon juice in a large dish. Cover with cling film, snipping two holes in the top to allow the steam to escape, and cook for 7–8 minutes until soft. Stir in the sugar while still hot and mix to dissolve. Blend in a liquidiser until smooth or press the fruit through a fine sieve. Add the brandy and chill.

Whisk the egg whites until they stand in stiff peaks and fold into the apple purée. Spoon into individual serving dishes, sprinkle with the walnuts and serve chilled.

ORANGE ZABAGLIONE

(Illustrated on pages 190/191)
Serves 4
Power setting FULL and LOW
Total cooking time 3 minutes

1 large egg
2 large egg yolks
50 g/2 oz caster sugar
150 ml/$\frac{1}{4}$ pint sweet sherry
1 tablespoon finely grated orange rind
8 sponge fingers or langue de chat biscuits

Place the egg and egg yolks in a large bowl and whisk until creamy. Add the sugar and whisk until almost thick.

Place the sherry and orange rind in a jug and heat on FULL POWER for $1\frac{1}{2}$ minutes until just boiling. Pour on to the eggs, whisking continuously. The mixture will thicken. Cook the mixture on LOW POWER for $1\frac{1}{2}$ minutes. Whisk, using an electric mixer, for about 4 minutes until thick and frothy. Serve at once in warmed glasses with the sponge fingers or langue de chat biscuits.

FRENCH FRESH ORANGE MOUSSE

(Illustrated on page 180)
Serves 6
Power setting FULL
Total cooking time 2 minutes

15 g/½ oz gelatine
3 tablespoons water
6–7 medium oranges
2–3 tablespoons lemon juice
300 ml/½ pint double cream
215 g//7½ oz caster sugar
4 egg whites
DECORATION
150 ml/¼ pint double cream, whipped
1 orange, pared and sliced

Mix the gelatine with the water in a small jug and leave until the liquid is absorbed. Heat in the microwave for ½ minute to dissolve the gelatine. Allow to cool slightly.

Meanwhile, finely grate and reserve the rind from two of the oranges. Squeeze all the oranges to make 450 ml/¾ pint juice. Strain the orange juice, then add the lemon juice to taste and the dissolved gelatine, stirring well. Heat in the microwave for 1½ minutes. Cool, then chill in the refrigerator until syrupy – about 30 minutes.

Whip the cream until it stands in soft peaks, then fold in 175 g/6 oz of the sugar and the reserved orange rind. Using a metal spoon fold the cream into the orange jelly.

Whisk the egg whites until they stand in stiff peaks. Gradually add the remaining sugar, whisking continuously, until very glossy. Fold the egg whites into the orange mixture and pour into a wetted 1.5-litre/2¾-pint mould or individual glasses and chill until set.

To serve, dip the mould briefly in hot water and turn out on to a flat serving dish. Decorate the individual dishes, or the turned-out mousse with the whipped cream and twisted orange slices.

VANILLA ICE CREAM

Serves 4
Power setting FULL
Total cooking time 6 minutes

2 eggs, beaten
450 ml/¾ pint milk
175 g/6 oz sugar
1 tablespoon vanilla essence
300 ml/½ pint double cream

Mix the eggs, milk and sugar in a medium-sized bowl and cook for 6 minutes, until lightly thickened, stirring every 2 minutes. Allow to cool, then add the vanilla essence and cream.

Pour into a freezing tray and freeze until almost solid. Remove, allow to stand for 15–30 minutes, then whisk until smooth. Return to the freezer and freeze until firm.

Place in the refrigerator for about ½–1 hour to soften slightly before serving. Serve scooped into individual dishes or glasses.

VARIATIONS

Almond Ice Cream Prepare and cook as above but use 2 teaspoons almond essence instead of the vanilla essence.

Pistachio Ice Cream Prepare and cook as above but stir 25 g/1 oz finely chopped pistachio nuts and a little green food colouring into the ice cream before the second freezing.

Ginger Ice Cream Prepare and cook as above but reduce the sugar by 15 g/½ oz and omit the vanilla essence. Add 40 g/1½ oz very finely chopped preserved ginger and 1 tablespoon ginger wine or ginger syrup to the ice cream before the second freezing.

Chocolate Ice Cream Prepare and cook as above but while the mixture is freezing for the first time, mix 2 tablespoons cocoa to a smooth paste with 3 tablespoons boiling water. Leave to cool. Add to the ice cream, whisking in well, before the second freezing.

Maraschino Cherry Ice Cream Prepare and cook as above but reduce the sugar by 15 g/½ oz and omit the vanilla essence. Add 2–3 tablespoons coarsely chopped maraschino cherries and 1 tablespoon of maraschino syrup to the ice cream before the second freezing.

Cointreau and Orange Ice Cream *(Illustrated on page 192)* Prepare and cook as above but reduce the sugar by 15 g/½ oz and omit the vanilla essence. Add 1 tablespoon finely grated orange rind and 1 tablespoon Cointreau to the ice cream before the second freezing.

Praline Ice Cream Prepare and cook as above but omit the vanilla essence. Add 50 g/2 oz finely crushed nut brittle to the ice cream before the second freezing.

Chocolate Chip Ice Cream Prepare and cook as above but add 50 g/2 oz coarsely grated plain chocolate or chocolate chips to the ice cream before the second freezing.

Tutti-frutti Ice Cream *(Illustrated on page 192)* Prepare and cook as above but add 50 g/2 oz coarsely chopped coloured glacé cherries, 2 drained and coarsely chopped canned pineapple slices and 1 small sliced banana to the ice cream before the second freezing.

Banana Ice Cream Prepare and cook as above but add 2 mashed or puréed bananas to the ice cream before the second freezing.

Coffee Ice Cream Prepare and cook as above, omitting the vanilla essence. While the mixture is freezing for the first time, mix 1 tablespoon instant coffee in 1 tablespoon hot water and 1 tablespoon rum. Leave to cool. Add to the ice cream, whisking in well, before the second freezing.

Raspberry or Strawberry Ice Cream *(Illustrated on page 192)* Prepare and cook as above, omitting the vanilla essence. Add 5 tablespoons raspberry or strawberry purée and 100 g/4 oz whole or sliced raspberries or strawberries to the ice cream before the second freezing.

Chestnut Ice Cream Prepare and cook as above, but add 225 g/8 oz chestnut purée to the ice cream, whisking in well, before the second freezing.

BLACKCURRANT SORBET

(Illustrated on page 192)
Serves 6
Power setting FULL
Total cooking time 6–8 minutes

1 kg/2 lb blackcurrants, topped and tailed
4 tablespoons clear honey
225 g/8 oz sugar
300 ml/½ pint water
2 egg whites

Place the blackcurrants in a large bowl with the honey, sugar and water. Cover with cling film, snipping two holes in the top to allow the steam to escape. Cook for 6–8 minutes until the blackcurrants are cooked, stirring halfway through the cooking time. Rub through a fine sieve and freeze until half frozen.

Whisk the egg whites until they stand in firm peaks. Fold into the blackcurrant purée. Return to the freezer and freeze until firm. Scoop into individual glasses or dishes to serve.

Baking and Confectionery

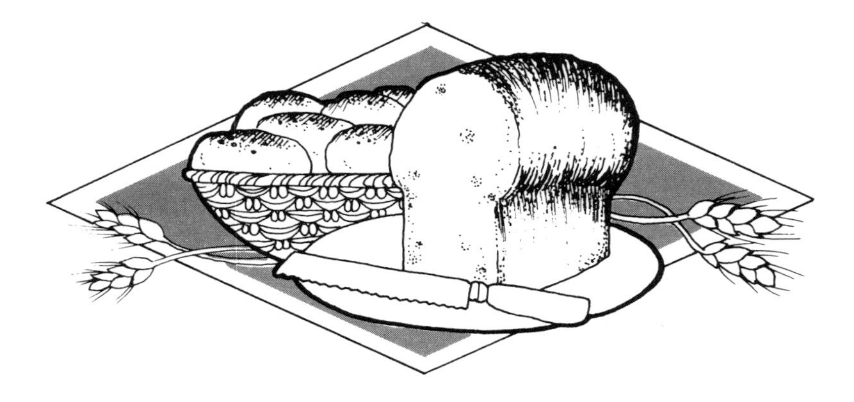

The microwave oven can be used to cook all the traditional British cakes, breads and biscuits. This area of microwave cooking is, however, perhaps the most controversial. Most of us expect a cooked cake, pastry or bread to have a handsome brown crust. Because of the speed of microwave cooking and the lack of prolonged applied surface heat, cakes, bread and biscuits remain pale. You can add colourings such as brown sugar or treacle to the basic mixture, a quick dusting of icing sugar can be added after cooking a cake, or bread and biscuits can be quickly browned under the grill.

Metal containers cannot be used in the microwave so forget your traditional bakeware. The microwave does, however, open up great scope for using other containers. For round cakes consider soufflé dishes or other round dishes with straight sides. Square cakes can be cooked in glass dishes or a cling film lined cardboard box – a shoe box or cake box, for example, can be used with great success! Small cakes in paper cake cases should be placed in microwave muffin containers, teacups or mugs to prevent them spreading. If you bake on a regular basis it may be worthwhile investing in a range of purpose-made microwave bakeware.

Always follow the specific recipe for container preparation and cooking information. In addition, the following basic information may help you to achieve the very best results.

Cooking bread It's a sad fact that most people adore home-baked bread yet they seldom get around to making it. Conventional bread-making can be such a lengthy operation because of the time needed to prove the dough in a warm place. Bread can be made in the microwave oven in less than half the time. Give the dough short bursts of energy for about 15 seconds, then allow to stand for 5–10 minutes – this gives a good speedy rise. Cover with cling film to prevent the dough from drying out – it is ready if it springs back when lightly touched with the fingertips.

Bake for the times recommended in the recipes. Microwave-cooked bread will not have a golden crust but you can brush it with oil or egg and top with poppy seeds, sesame seeds, nibbed or cracked wheat for a good appearance. If you really like a golden crust, place the bread under the grill for 2–3 minutes to brown. Alternatively, prove your bread in the microwave, then cook it conventionally. If you do choose to do this, remember not to place the bread in a metal container to prove. The time savings will still be substantial even if you prove the bread conventionally in its baking tin for the second rising.

Cooking cakes The microwave is ideal for cooking plain, fancy and rich cakes. Textures in sponge cakes are light and airy while rich fruit cakes stay moist. Liquid is often the all-important ingredient – wetter cake mixtures are the most successful, so be prepared for mixtures with a softer dropping consistency.

The cooking containers can be prepared in one of two ways. Either line them with cling film, greased greaseproof paper or parchment, or just grease the dish with a little oil or fat. *Never* grease and flour the container or you will simply end up with an awful looking and unpleasant tasting floury film around the cake. Put the mixture in the container, remembering not to fill the container more than half full if you are making a fast-rising sponge cake. If your microwave oven does not have a turntable, then give the dish a quarter turn every few minutes to ensure even rising.

There is a terrible temptation to overcook cakes for the simple reason that when a cake is cooked in the microwave the top will appear slightly wet. This wet surface will dry out with the residual heat left in the cake mixture. A fine skewer or wooden cocktail stick inserted into the cake is the true test to see if the cake is cooked: it should come out clean of mixture.

Allow the cake to cool in its container for 10–15 minutes to make use of the residual heat. To avoid cakes sticking to the container during this standing period, rotate the cake dish, gently tapping the sides, after cooking – this brings the cake away from the sides and gives a good, neat cooking edge.

The highest power setting (often the only one available with early microwave ovens) is too fast for cooking rich fruit cake mixtures, but they are delicious if cooked on lower settings like LOW, MEDIUM or DEFROST. The specific recipe will give the ideal power setting. Cooked on a slower power setting, these cakes also have the opportunity to brown slightly.

Sweet and savoury toppings for cakes or breads

Top savoury breads with crumbled cooked bacon and grated cheese before cooking.

Browned onions, finely chopped green pepper and paprika can be used for topping savoury breads before cooking.

Brush breads with gravy browning before cooking.

Sprinkle breads or cakes with a mixture of ground cinnamon and demerara sugar before cooking.

Sprinkle chopped nuts over bread or cakes before or after cooking.

Bran, nibbed wheat, porridge oats, crunchy ceral or poppy seeds can all be sprinkled on breads or cakes, before or after cooking.

Sweet breads and cakes can be topped with toasted coconut before or after cooking.

Dust cakes and sweet tea breads with icing sugar after cooking.

Coat cakes or sweet tea breads with icing, marzipan or frosting after cooking.

Brush honey or golden syrup over cakes or sweet breads, then top with colourful, chopped candied fruits after cooking.

Cooking pastry Most types of pastry can be cooked successfully in the microwave, for example shortcrust, flaky, puff and strudel pastry can all be successfully cooked. Choux is not successful since it is difficult to get a crisp texture. It is also difficult to cook pies with a double crust since the filling tends to bubble out and overcook before the pastry is ready, but single crust pies are quite successful. The best use of pastry in microwave recipes is when it is pre-cooked or baked blind first, as in flans or tartlets.

To line a flan dish for microwave cooking roll out the pastry to a round large enough to line the dish and come about 5 mm/$\frac{1}{4}$ in above the rim. This allows for any shrinkage that may occur with such fast cooking. Prick the base very well with a fork. Line the inside, upright edge of the flan dish with a long, sturdy strip of double foil. This helps to protect the vulnerable outer edge from overcooking. Line the base with a double thickness of absorbent kitchen paper, carefully pushing it into the edge to keep the foil in place. Cook on FULL POWER for 4–4$\frac{1}{2}$ minutes, giving the dish a quarter turn every 1 minute (unless you have an oven with a turntable). Remove the kitchen paper (but not the foil) and cook for a further 1–2 minutes.

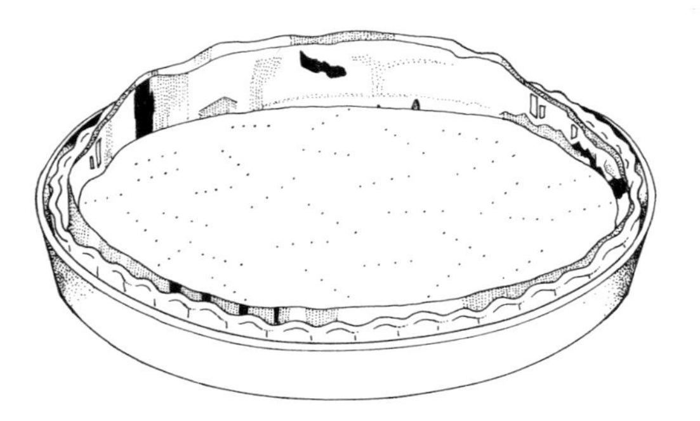

Individual pastry tart cases can be made by covering the bases of inverted ramekins, teacups or other small dishes. First place a piece of greaseproof paper over the base of the inverted container, then mould the rolled-out pastry rounds over the top.

To cook, arrange in a circle on the base of the microwave, four at a time, and cook on FULL POWER for 4–5 minutes, rearranging halfway through the cooking time. Allow to stand for 5 minutes before carefully removing the pastry from the dishes.

Cooking sweets The microwave makes extremely light work of sweet preparation and cooking. Conventional methods, with their laborious stirring and temperature checking, become a thing of the past. Similarly, accidental burns from hot, syrupy mixtures are reduced through less handling. Remember, however, to use a large container to allow the mixture to rise on boiling, and use protective gloves both to stir the mixture and remove the container from the oven. The dish will become hot through conduction so use heatproof dishes for cooking these items.

WHITE BREAD

Makes 1 (1-kg/2-lb) loaf
Power setting FULL or LOW
Total cooking time 5½ or 8½–10½ minutes

1 teaspoon sugar
1 teaspoon dried yeast
300 ml/½ pint warm water
450 g/1 lb plain flour
½ teaspoon salt
40 g/1½ oz butter or margarine
2 teaspoons oil
1 tablespoon poppy seeds

Mix the sugar with the yeast and half the water. Leave to stand in a warm place for 10 minutes until frothy.

Place the flour and salt in a large mixing bowl and cook on FULL POWER for ½ minute or until warm. Rub in the butter or margarine, add the yeast liquid and remaining water then mix to a pliable dough. Knead on a lightly floured surface until smooth and elastic – about 5–10 minutes. Return the dough to the bowl, cover with cling film and leave in a warm place until doubled in size. To hasten the rising process cook for 5 seconds occasionally if liked.

Knead the dough for a further 2–3 minutes, then shape and place in either a greased 1-kg/2-lb glass loaf dish or a greased 15-cm/6-in soufflé dish. Leave in a warm place until doubled in size.

Lightly brush the bread with the oil and sprinkle with the poppy seeds. Cook on FULL POWER for 5 minutes, giving the dish a half turn twice during the cooking time. Alternatively, cook on FULL POWER for 1 minute, then on LOW POWER for 7–9 minutes, giving the dish a half turn three times during the cooking time. Leave to stand for 10 minutes before turning out to cool on a wire rack. If a brown crust is liked, place the loaf under a hot grill for a few minutes.

VARIATIONS

White Bread Rolls Prepare, knead and allow the bread dough to rise once, as above, but shape into sixteen small rolls. Prove until doubled in size, then cook in two batches on a greased microwave baking tray, or on a piece of greased greaseproof paper, on FULL POWER for 2 minutes, rearranging halfway through the cooking time. Cook the second batch in the same way. If a brown crust is liked, place the rolls under a hot grill for a few minutes. *Total cooking time* 4½ minutes

White Bread Baps *(Illustrated on page 161)* Prepare the bread dough as above but shape into six oval-shaped baps. Prove until doubled in size, then cook in two batches on a greased microwave baking tray or on a piece of greased greaseproof paper. Dust with flour and cook on FULL POWER for 2 minutes, rearranging halfway through the cooking time. Cook the second batch in the same way. Place on a wire rack to cool. *Total cooling time* 4½ minutes

WHOLEWHEAT LOAF

Makes 1 (450-g/1-lb) loaf
Power setting FULL
Total cooking time 6½ minutes

1 teaspoon caster sugar
1 teaspoon dried yeast
300 ml/½ pint warm water
450 g/1 lb wholewheat flour
½ teaspoon salt
15 g/½ oz butter or margarine
1 tablespoon bran, nibbed wheat or porridge oats

Mix the sugar with the yeast and 100 ml/4 fl oz of the water. Leave to stand for 10 minutes until risen and frothy.

Place the flour and salt in a large mixing bowl and cook for ½ minute or until warm. Rub in the butter or margarine, then add the yeast liquid and remaining water, mixing to a pliable dough. Add 1–2 extra tablespoons water if the dough seems too dry. Knead on a lightly floured surface until smooth and elastic – about 5–10 minutes. Shape and place in a greased 450-g/1-lb glass loaf dish, cover with cling film or place in a polythene bag and leave in a warm place until doubled in size. To hasten the rising process cook for 5 seconds occasionally if liked.

Remove the cover, sprinkle with bran, nibbed wheat or porridge oats and cook for 6 minutes, giving the dish a quarter turn every 2 minutes. Remove from the dish and allow to cool on a wire rack. If a crisp brown crust is liked, place the loaf under a hot grill for a few minutes.

SESAME WHOLEMEAL ROLLS

(Illustrated on page 209)
Makes 16
Power setting FULL
Total cooking time 6½–7½ minutes

1 teaspoon caster sugar
2 teaspoons dried yeast
300 ml/½ pint warm water
350 g/12 oz wholemeal flour
100 g/4 oz plain flour
1 teaspoon salt
2 teaspoons malt extract
2 tablespoons oil
beaten egg to glaze
2 tablespoons sesame seeds

Mix the sugar with the yeast and water, then leave to stand for 10 minutes until frothy.

Place the flours and salt in a large mixing bowl and cook for ½ minute or until warm. Make a well in the centre of the flour and add the yeast liquid, malt extract and half the oil, then mix to a pliable dough. Knead on a lightly floured surface until smooth and elastic – about 5–10 minutes. Return to the bowl, cover with cling film and leave in a warm place until doubled in size. To hasten the rising process cook for 5 seconds if liked.

Knead again for 2–3 minutes, then divide the dough into sixteen pieces. Shape each piece into a small roll and brush with the remaining oil. Leave to rise again for 20–30 minutes or until well risen and springy to the touch. Place on a greased baking sheet or a piece of greased greaseproof paper and bake in two batches. Cook for 3–3½ minutes, turning over halfway through the cooking time. Cook the second batch in the same way.

Brush immediately with a little beaten egg and sprinkle with the sesame seeds. Allow to cool on a wire rack. If you prefer a crisp brown crust on the rolls, then place them under a hot grill for a few minutes.

OLD-FASHIONED SODA BREAD

Serves 4
Power setting MEDIUM and FULL
Total cooking time 8 minutes

450 g/1 lb wholemeal flour
2 teaspoons bicarbonate of soda
2 teaspoons cream of tartar
1 teaspoon salt
25 g/1 oz lard
2 teaspoons caster sugar
300 ml/$\frac{1}{2}$ pint milk
1 tablespoon lemon juice
25 g/1 oz porridge oats

Mix the flour with the bicarbonate of soda, cream of tartar and salt. Rub in the lard until the mixture resembles fine breadcrumbs, then stir in the sugar. Mix the milk with the lemon juice and add to the dry ingredients. Form into a soft dough and knead until smooth. Shape into a round and mark into four sections with a sharp knife. Place on a plate or non-metallic baking sheet and cook on MEDIUM POWER for 5 minutes. Cook on FULL POWER for a further 3 minutes. Allow to stand for 10 minutes before cooling on a wire rack.

GARLIC BREAD

Serves 4–6
Power setting FULL
Total cooking time $1\frac{1}{2}$ minutes

1 short, crusty French stick
100 g/4 oz butter
3 cloves garlic, crushed *or* 1 teaspoon garlic powder

With a sharp knife cut the stick into 2.5-cm/1-in slices, leaving them attached at the base. Mix the butter with the garlic or garlic powder, blending well. Spread evenly between the slices of bread and re-form the loaf in a neat shape. Protect the thin ends of the stick with small pieces of foil and cover the whole stick with dampened greaseproof paper.

Cook for $1\frac{1}{2}$ minutes or until the butter has just melted and the bread is warm. Pull the slices apart to serve.

VARIATIONS

Onion Bread Prepare and cook the French stick as above but replace the garlic with 1 small minced onion or 2 teaspoons onion powder.
Herb Bread Prepare and cook the French stick as above but replace the garlic with 1 tablespoon chopped fresh herbs or 2 teaspoons dried mixed herbs.

SAUSAGE PIZZA FLAN

(Illustrated on page 162)
Serves 6
Power setting FULL
Total cooking time 17 minutes

FILLING
25 g/1 oz butter
1 onion, peeled and chopped
¼ teaspoon dried mixed herbs
50 g/2 oz plain flour
1 (227-g/8-oz) can tomatoes
1 tablespoon tomato ketchup
150 ml/¼ pint milk
salt and freshly ground black pepper
SCONE DOUGH
225 g/8 oz self-raising flour
½ teaspoon salt
50 g/2 oz butter
7 tablespoons milk
TOPPING
4 large sausages, cooked and sliced
parsley sprigs to garnish

Place the butter in a bowl, add the onion and herbs and cook for 2 minutes. Add the flour and cook for 1 minute. Stir in the tomatoes with their juice, tomato ketchup, milk and seasoning to taste. Cook for 2 minutes, stirring halfway through the cooking time, then allow to cool completely.

Meanwhile make the scone dough by sifting the flour with the salt. Add the butter and rub in until the mixture resembles fine breadcrumbs. Add the milk all at once and mix well with a fork until a soft dough is formed. Turn out on to a lightly floured surface and knead lightly. Roll out and use to line a 28 × 18-cm/11 × 7-in rectangular flan dish. Pour the filling into the scone case and cook for 12 minutes, giving the dish a quarter turn every 2 minutes. Cut into squares to serve.

Slice the cooked sausages and arrange in rows down the centre of each portion of the flan. Garnish with sprigs of parsley.

VICTORIA SANDWICH

Serves 6–8
Power setting FULL
Total cooking time $6\frac{1}{2}$–$7\frac{1}{2}$ minutes

175 g/6 oz butter or margarine
175 g/6 oz caster sugar
3 eggs, beaten
175 g/6 oz plain flour
pinch of salt
2 teaspoons baking powder
2 tablespoons hot water
5 tablespoons strawberry jam
icing sugar to dust

Line a 20-cm/8-inch cake dish or soufflé dish with cling film, or lightly grease and line the base of the dish with greaseproof paper.

Cream the butter with the sugar until light and fluffy. Add the eggs, a little at a time, beating well. Sift the flour with the salt and baking powder and fold into the creamed mixture together with the hot water. Spoon into the prepared dish and cook for $6\frac{1}{2}$–$7\frac{1}{2}$ minutes, giving the dish a half turn every 2 minutes. The cake will be slightly moist on top when cooked, but it will dry out with the residual heat in the cake. Test by inserting a wooden cocktail stick into the cake, the cake is cooked when the cocktail stick comes out clean of mixture. Allow to stand for 5 minutes before turning out to cool on a wire rack.

When cool, split the cake in half horizontally and sandwich together with the jam. Dust the top with sifted icing sugar. Cut into wedges to serve.

From the top: Banana and Walnut Loaf (page 218), Honey Gingerbread (page 214) and a Sesame Wholemeal Roll (page 205) filled with salad
Overleaf *From the left:* Coffee House Gâteau (page 216), Quick Honey Christmas Cake Ring (page 217), Coconut and Maraschino Cherry Cake (page 215) and Dundee Cake (page 213)

DUNDEE CAKE

(Illustrated on previous page)
Serves 6–8
Power setting DEFROST
Total cooking time 43 minutes

175 g/6 oz butter
175 g/6 oz dark soft brown sugar
3 eggs
2 tablespoons golden syrup
1 tablespoon water
1 tablespoon milk
100 g/4 oz self-raising flour
100 g/4 oz plain flour
2 teaspoons mixed spice
pinch of salt
50 g/2 oz almonds, chopped
50 g/2 oz glacé cherries, quartered
675 g/1½ lb dried mixed fruit
about 20 split blanched almonds

Cream the butter and sugar together until pale and fluffy. Add the eggs, syrup, water and milk, blending well. Sift the flours with the spice and salt and fold into the egg mixture with the almonds, cherries and dried fruit. Spoon the mixture into a greased and greaseproof-paper lined 19-cm/7½-in straight-sided container. Stand the cake on an upturned pie dish in the microwave and cook for 20 minutes, giving the dish a half turn halfway through the cooking time.

Arrange the almonds, split side down on top of the cake and cook for a further 23 minutes, giving the dish a half turn halfway through the cooking time. Leave to stand for 30 minutes before turning out on to a wire rack to cool. Store in an airtight tin.

From the top: Coffee Honey Crackles (page 220), Crunchy Peanut Brittle and Tia Maria Truffle Logs (page 221)

GENOESE SPONGE

Serves 6–8
Power setting FULL
Total cooking time $5\frac{1}{2}$–$6\frac{1}{2}$ minutes

4 eggs
100 g/4 oz caster sugar
100 g/4 oz plain flour
pinch of salt
50 g/2 oz butter
5 tablespoons jam
150 ml/$\frac{1}{4}$ pint double cream, whipped
icing sugar to dust

Line a 20-cm/8-in cake dish or soufflé dish with cling film or lightly grease, and line the base with greaseproof paper. Whisk the eggs with the sugar until very light and fluffy and trebled in volume. Sift the flour and salt together. Place the butter in a bowl and cook for 1–$1\frac{1}{2}$ minutes to melt. Sprinkle the flour over the egg mixture and pour in the butter in a slow steady stream. Fold in carefully with a metal spoon until evenly mixed. Pour into the prepared dish and cook for $4\frac{1}{2}$–5 minutes, giving the dish a quarter turn every $1\frac{1}{2}$–2 minutes. Leave to stand for 5–10 minutes before turning out on to a wire rack to cool.

Split in half horizontally and fill with the jam and cream. Sandwich together and dust with icing sugar. Cut into wedges to serve.

HONEY GINGERBREAD

(Illustrated on page 209)
Serves 6–8
Power setting FULL and MEDIUM/HIGH
Total cooking time 12–13 minutes

100 g/4 oz butter
100 g/4 oz soft brown sugar
4 tablespoons thick honey
2 eggs, beaten
225 g/8 oz plain flour
1 tablespoon ginger
1 teaspoon bicarbonate of soda
25 g/1 oz dried mixed fruit

Place the butter, sugar and honey in a bowl and cook on FULL POWER for 3 minutes until melted. Beat in the eggs. Sift the flour with the ginger and bicarbonate of soda, then fold into the egg mixture with the dried fruit.

Line an 18-cm/7-in square dish with cling film, grease and base-line with greaseproof paper. Spoon in the mixture, smoothing the top, then cook on MEDIUM/HIGH POWER for 9–10 minutes, giving the dish a quarter turn every $2\frac{1}{2}$ minutes. Turn out on to a wire rack to cool. Cut into slices to serve.

COCONUT AND MARASCHINO CHERRY CAKE

(Illustrated on pages 210/211)
Serves 6–8
Power setting FULL
Total cooking time $10\frac{1}{2}$–$12\frac{1}{2}$ minutes

175 g/6 oz long-thread coconut
5 g/8 oz self-raising flour
pinch of salt
100 g/4 oz butter or margarine
100 g/4 oz soft brown sugar
175 g/6 oz desiccated coconut
2 eggs, beaten
a little milk
600 ml/1 pint double cream
1 (227-g/8-oz) jar maraschino cherries, drained

Place the long-thread coconut on a plate and cook for 5 minutes, stirring frequently, until golden. Allow to cool.

Line a 20-cm/8-in cake dish or soufflé dish with cling film, or lightly grease the dish and line the base with greaseproof paper.

Sift the flour with the salt and rub in the butter or margarine until the mixture resembles fine breadcrumbs. Stir in the sugar and desiccated coconut, mixing well. Mix in the eggs and enough milk to give a soft dropping consistency. Spoon into the prepared dish and cook for $5\frac{1}{2}$–7 minutes, giving the dish a half turn every 2 minutes. The cake will be slightly moist on top when cooked but it will dry with the residual heat in the mixture. Test by inserting a wooden cocktail stick into the cake, the cake is cooked when the cocktail stick comes out clean. Allow to stand for 5 minutes before turning out to cool on a wire rack.

Whip the cream until it stands in soft peaks. Reserve a few maraschino cherries and fold the remainder into one-third of the cream.

Split the cake in half horizontally and sandwich together with the cherry cream. Spread a second third of the cream over the top and sides of the cake. Press almost all of the long-thread coconut on to the sides of the cake. Place the remaining cream in a piping bag fitted with a large star nozzle and pipe swirls of cream on top of the cake. Decorate each swirl alternately with a cherry or a few strands of coconut. Cut into wedges to serve.

VARIATION

Banana and Apricot Cake Prepare and cook the cake as above but add two peeled and mashed bananas to the dry ingredients instead of the desiccated coconut. Coat the sides of the cake with 175 g/6 oz chopped nuts, reserving a few for decoration. Substitute 175 g/6 oz sliced canned or fresh apricots for the cherries. Decorate the top with a few reserved sliced apricots and the remaining nuts. *Total cooking time* $5\frac{1}{2}$–7 minutes

COFFEE HOUSE GÂTEAU

(Illustrated on pages 210/211)
Serves 6–8
Power setting FULL
Total cooking time 12–14 minutes

CAKE
4 eggs
100 g/4 oz caster sugar
100 g/4 oz plain flour
pinch of salt
50 g/2 oz butter
FILLING AND TOPPING
40 g/1½ oz cornflour
450 ml/¾ pint milk
2 tablespoons instant coffee granules
215 g/7½ oz light soft brown sugar
350 g/12 oz butter
65 g/2½ oz walnuts, finely chopped
thin plain chocolate squares or wafers to decorate

Line a 20-cm/8-in cake dish or soufflé dish with cling film or lightly grease, and line the base with greaseproof paper.

Whisk the eggs with the sugar until very pale and creamy and trebled in volume. Sift the flour and salt together. Place the butter in a bowl and cook for 1–1½ minutes to melt. Sprinkle the flour and salt over the egg mixture and pour in the butter in a slow, steady stream. Fold in carefully with a metal spoon until evenly mixed. Pour into the prepared dish and cook for 4½–5 minutes, giving the dish a quarter turn every 1½–2 minutes. Leave to stand for 5–10 minutes before turning out on to a wire rack to cool. When cold carefully cut the cake horizontally into three equal layers.

Make the filling and topping by blending the cornflour with a little of the milk in a bowl to form a smooth paste. Place the remaining milk in a jug with the coffee and sugar. Cook for 1½ minutes. Add to the blended cornflour, stirring well to mix. Cook for 5–6 minutes until thick, stirring occasionally to keep the sauce smooth. Cover the surface of the sauce with dampened greaseproof paper and leave to cool completely.

Beat the butter until creamy. Gradually add the cold coffee sauce, beating well to form a smooth mixture.

Mix one-third of the coffee filling with 25 g/1 oz of the walnuts. Sandwich the sponge layers together with this walnut and coffee filling. Spread the top and sides of the cake with about half of the remaining coffee mixture. Press the remaining walnuts on to the sides of the cake. Place the remaining coffee mixture in a piping bag fitted with a large star nozzle and pipe swirls on top of the cake. Decorate with halved and whole chocolate squares or wafers and cut into wedges to serve.

QUICK HONEY CHRISTMAS CAKE RING

Serves 8–12
Power setting LOW
Total cooking time 30–40 minutes

225 g/8 oz butter or margarine
175 g/6 oz soft brown sugar
3 tablespoons thick honey
250 g/9 oz plain flour
1 teaspoon baking powder
1 teaspoon nutmeg
½ teaspoon cinnamon
½ teaspoon ground cloves
5 eggs, lightly beaten
100 g/4 oz chopped mixed peel
50 g/2 oz blanched almonds
100 g/4 oz glacé cherries, chopped
225 g/8 oz currants
225 g/8 oz raisins
225 g/8 oz sultanas
3–5 tablespoons brandy, rum or sherry
ICING AND DECORATION
225 g/8 oz icing sugar, sifted
1 tablespoon lemon juice
1 tablespoon warm water
4 glacé cherries, halved
16 angelica leaves

Cream the butter or margarine with the sugar and honey until very soft and light. Sift the flour with the baking powder, nutmeg, cinnamon and cloves. Gradually beat the eggs into the creamed mixture, adding a little of the sifted flour and spices with each addition to prevent the mixture from curdling. Fold in the sifted dry ingredients, then stir in the mixed peel, almonds, cherries and remaining dried fruit.

Grease a 30-cm/12-in glass cake ring, or line it with cling film, and spoon the mixture into it, carefully smoothing over the top. Cook for 30–40 minutes, or until a wooden cocktail stick inserted into the middle of the cake comes out clean of mixture. Leave to stand for 30 minutes before turning out to cool on a wire rack.

Prick the surface of the cool cake with a skewer and sprinkle the brandy over. Cover with foil and store in an airtight tin until required.

To decorate the cake, mix the icing sugar with the lemon juice and water to make a smooth, fairly thick, pouring icing. Pour this over the cake, allowing it to run down the sides. Decorate with glacé cherries and angelica leaves.

BANANA AND WALNUT LOAF

(Illustrated on page 209)
Makes 1 (1-kg/2-lb) loaf
Power setting FULL
Total cooking time 5–6 minutes

175 g/6 oz self-raising flour
pinch of salt
pinch of bicarbonate of soda
40 g/1½ oz butter or margarine
75 g/3 oz caster sugar
1 egg, beaten
175 g/6 oz bananas, peeled and mashed
75 g/3 oz walnuts, coarsely chopped
a little milk

Lightly grease a 1-kg/2-lb glass loaf dish and line the base with greaseproof paper.

Sift the flour with the salt and bicarbonate of soda into a bowl. Rub in the butter or margarine until the mixture resembles fine breadcrumbs. Stir in the sugar, egg, bananas and walnuts, mixing until all the ingredients are blended. Add a little milk if necessary to make a soft consistency. Spoon into the prepared dish and cook for 5–6 minutes, giving the dish a half turn halfway through the cooking time.

Leave to stand for 10 minutes before turning out on to a wire rack to cool. Serve sliced and buttered.

CHOCOLATE AND HAZELNUT LOAF CAKE

Serves 6–8
Power setting FULL
Total cooking time 8½–9 minutes

100 g/4 oz golden syrup
100 g/4 oz dark soft brown sugar
100 g/4 oz butter or margarine
175 g/6 oz self-raising flour
50 g/2 oz cocoa
1 egg, beaten
150 ml/¼ pint milk or single cream
50 g/2 oz hazelnuts, chopped
100 g/4 oz plain dessert chocolate
150 ml/¼ pint double cream, whipped
chocolate curls to decorate

Line a 23-cm/9-in glass loaf dish with greaseproof paper.

Place the syrup, sugar and butter or margarine in a large bowl and cook for 2 minutes or until melted. Add the flour and cocoa and mix well. Beat in the egg and milk and fold in the hazelnuts. Spoon into the prepared dish and cook for 5–5½ minutes, giving the dish a half turn halfway through the cooking time. The cake is cooked when a wooden cocktail stick inserted into the centre comes out clean. Leave to stand for 5 minutes before turning out on to a wire rack to cool.

Break the chocolate into small pieces and place in a small bowl. Cook for $1\frac{1}{2}$ minutes to melt. Spread the cake with the chocolate, allowing it to run down the sides. Leave to set.

Decorate the cake with piped swirls of cream and chocolate curls. Slice to serve.

VARIATION

Chocolate and Orange Loaf Cake Prepare and cook the cake as above but use the finely grated rind of 2 oranges instead of the hazelnuts. Decorate the chocolate-coated cake with piped swirls of cream and orange slices.

COBURG BUNS

Makes 12
Power setting FULL
Total cooking time 4 minutes

12 split blanched almonds
150 g/5 oz plain flour
1 teaspoon bicarbonate of soda
$\frac{1}{2}$ teaspoon ground allspice
$\frac{1}{2}$ teaspoon ginger
$\frac{1}{2}$ teaspoon cinnamon
50 g/2 oz butter
50 g/2 oz caster sugar
1 egg, beaten
1 tablespoon golden syrup
5 tablespoons milk

Place an almond in the base of each of twelve double thickness paper cake cases. Sift the flour with the bicarbonate of soda and spices. Cream the butter with the sugar until light and fluffy and beat in the egg. Fold in the dry ingredients. Mix the syrup with the milk and add to the butter mixture, folding lightly until blended.

Divide the mixture evenly between the bun cases taking care to keep the almonds in position. Place six in a microwave bun tray or on a plate and cook for 2 minutes, giving the tray or plate a half turn halfway through the cooking time. The tops of the cakes will still be moist when the cooking time is complete, but they will dry out with the residual heat of the cakes.

Repeat with the remaining six cakes. Allow to cool slightly before peeling away the paper cases. Serve the buns almond side uppermost.

TRADITIONAL SHORTBREAD

Makes 8 pieces
Power setting FULL
Total cooking time 3–4 minutes

175 g/6 oz plain flour
50 g/2 oz ground rice
pinch of salt
150 g/5 oz butter
50 g/2 oz caster sugar

Line an 18-cm/7-in fluted flan dish with cling film. Sift the flour into a bowl and add the ground rice and salt. Rub in the butter until the mixture resembles fine breadcrumbs. Stir in half of the sugar and knead the ingredients together lightly to form a dough.

Press into the prepared flan dish and smooth the top with the back of a metal spoon. Mark into 8 wedges and prick well. Cook for 3–4 minutes, giving the dish a quarter turn every 1 minute. Sprinkle with the remaining sugar, cool slightly, then cut into wedges. Turn out and allow to cool on a wire rack.

VARIATIONS

Hazelnut Shortbread Prepare and cook as above, but add 25 g/1 oz finely chopped hazelnuts to the basic mixture.
Orange or Lemon Shortbread Prepare and cook as above, but add the finely grated rind of one lemon or orange to the basic mixture.
Currant Shortbread Prepare and cook as above, but add 25 g/1 oz currants to the basic mixture.

COFFEE HONEY CRACKLES

(Illustrated on page 212)
Makes 30
Power setting FULL
Total cooking time 2–2½ minutes

2 tablespoons clear honey
75 g/3 oz butter
2 teaspoons powdered instant coffee
175 g/6 oz icing sugar
100 g/4 oz rice krispies

Place the honey and butter in a large bowl and cook for 2–2½ minutes until melted. Stir in the remaining ingredients, mixing well to coat the cereal. Spoon into about 30 paper cake cases and leave to set. Store in an airtight container and eat within two days of making.

CRUNCHY PEANUT BRITTLE

(Illustrated on page 212)
Makes about 450 g/1 lb
Power setting FULL
Total cooking time 8–11 minutes

225 g/8 oz sugar
6 tablespoons golden syrup
200 g/7 oz salted peanuts
7 g/¼ oz butter
1 teaspoon vanilla essence
1 teaspoon baking powder

Place the sugar and syrup in a large heatproof bowl, mix well and cook for 4 minutes.

Add the peanuts and stir well to blend. Cook for 3–5 minutes or until light brown. Add the butter and vanilla, mixing well, then cook for 1–2 minutes. Add the baking powder and stir gently until light and foamy.

Pour on to a lightly-greased baking tray and leave until set. Break up and store in an airtight tin.

TIA MARIA TRUFFLE LOGS

(Illustrated on page 212)
Makes 15
Power setting FULL
Total cooking time 1½ minutes

75 g/3 oz plain dessert chocolate
1 teaspoon single cream
1 egg yolk
7 g/¼ oz butter
1 teaspoon Tia Maria
40 g/1½ oz chocolate vermicelli

Break the chocolate into small pieces and place in a bowl. Cook for 1½ minutes to melt. Add the cream, egg yolk, butter and Tia Maria, mixing well. Beat until cool and thick – about 5–10 minutes. Chill until lightly set.

Divide the mixture into 15 portions and shape each into a small log. Roll in the chocolate vermicelli and place in small paper sweet cases if liked.

QUICK CHOCOLATE FUDGE

Makes about 36 squares
Power setting FULL
Total cooking time 2 minutes

450 g/1 lb icing sugar, sifted
50 g/2 oz cocoa
pinch of salt
3 tablespoons milk
1 tablespoon vanilla essence
100 g/4 oz butter

Place the icing sugar, cocoa, salt, milk and vanilla essence in a large heatproof bowl and mix together thoroughly. The mixture should still be very dry. Make a well in the centre of the dry ingredients and place the butter, in one piece, in the middle. Cook for 2 minutes, then stir vigorously until smooth. Pour into a small, greased and greaseproof paper lined, shallow square tin. Mark into squares and leave until set.

VARIATION

Quick Chocolate and Nut Fudge Prepare and cook as above, then stir in 100 g/4 oz chopped nuts after cooking.

OLD-FASHIONED CHOCOLATE NUT FUDGE

Makes about 450 g/1 lb
Power setting FULL and MEDIUM/HIGH
Total cooking time 20–22 minutes

450 g/1 lb sugar
pinch of salt
175 ml/6 fl oz milk
50 g/2 oz bitter dessert chocolate
50 g/2 oz butter
2 teaspoons vanilla essence
50 g/2 oz chopped nuts

Place the sugar, salt and milk in a large heatproof bowl and mix well. Add the chocolate and butter, cover and cook on FULL POWER for 6 minutes, until hot and bubbly. Stir thoroughly, then cook, uncovered on MEDIUM/HIGH POWER for 14–16 minutes, stirring every 5 minutes. Test to see if the mixture forms a soft ball when a few drops of it are placed in a cup of cold water. Cool until lukewarm.

Add the vanilla essence and beat until thick. Quickly fold in the nuts and pour into a small, greased and greaseproof paper lined, shallow square tin. Mark into squares and leave until set.

Preserves

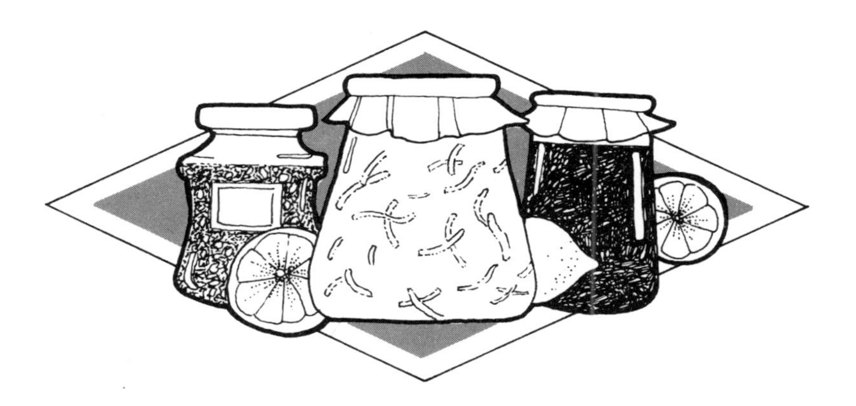

Making your own preserves is great fun, and a few shelves of really individual and fresh-flavoured jams, jellies, chutneys, pickles and spreads are a source of infinite satisfaction and variety the whole year round. There is nothing more rewarding than an unusual pot of jam or marmalade at breakfast or tea, a laden jar of fruit for a pudding or pie, a home-made pickle or chutney to cheer up a cold joint, or to add flavour to stews and curries.

But all too often it seems too much trouble to make your own preserves – either through lack of time, reluctance to cope with a steamy hot kitchen or the bother of sterilising dozens of jars. The microwave takes care of all of these problems – and you are unlikely to be faced with long cooking sessions, sticky pans, steamy kitchens and burnt fingers. The biggest advantage, however, must be speed: jams, jellies, marmalades, chutneys and relishes can be made in a fraction of the time it takes to make them conventionally, and they cook quite safely in the microwave oven, requiring only the occasional stir. Because microwave energy heats from all sides, not just the bottom, sugar mixtures do not scorch as easily, so they need less stirring. And because there is generally less evaporation you should also obtain a greater yield.

The preparation and procedures remain the same – you will still need to use a large cooking container, since mixtures bubble up high. Test the set of jams, jellies and marmalades in the usual way and spoon into warm, dry, sterilised jars. Seal and label in the traditional way.

The microwave oven can be used to sterilise empty preserving jars. Simply pour a little water into each jar and heat individually on FULL POWER for 2–3 minutes, depending upon the size and thickness of the glass. Drain jars upside down on absorbent kitchen paper.

Mixtures must reach a good rolling boil to ensure a good set – if in doubt add commercial pectin according to the manufacturer's instructions. Test jams, jellies and marmalades for set by placing a little on a cold saucer. Allow to cool then push with the finger. If the surface wrinkles, setting point has been reached.

BLACKCURRANT JAM

Makes about 1 kg/2 lb
Power setting FULL
Total cooking time 13–16 minutes

450 g/1 lb caster sugar
150 ml/$\frac{1}{4}$ pint hot water
675 g/1$\frac{1}{2}$ lb blackcurrants, topped and tailed

Place the sugar and water in a large bowl and cook for 3 minutes or until the sugar has dissolved. Add the blackcurrants and cook for 8–10 minutes, stirring halfway through the cooking time. Test for setting, by placing a little of the jam on a cold saucer. Leave for 1–2 minutes: a skin should form on the surface of the jam and it will wrinkle when pushed with the forefinger. If a skin does not form, microwave for a further 2–3 minutes. Ladle into warmed jars, cover, seal and label.

VARIATION

Blackberry Jam Prepare and cook as above but use 675 g/1$\frac{1}{2}$ lb blackberries instead of blackcurrants.

THREE-FRUIT MARMALADE

(Illustrated on page 161)
Makes 2.25–2.75 kg/5–6 lb
Power setting FULL
Total cooking time 50–60 minutes

3 lemons
2 oranges
2 grapefruit
900 ml/1$\frac{1}{2}$ pints boiling water
1.5 kg/3$\frac{1}{2}$ lb granulated or preserving sugar

Squeeze and reserve the juice from the lemons, oranges and grapefruit. Cut away the peel and shred it coarsely. Place the remaining pith and pips into a piece of muslin and tie to secure.

Place the reserved juice, the muslin bag and shredded peel into a large bowl. Add 300 ml/$\frac{1}{2}$ pint of the water and leave to stand for $\frac{1}{2}$ hour.

Add the remaining water and cover with cling film, snipping two holes in the top to allow the steam to escape. Cook for 25 minutes. Uncover, squeeze out then discard the muslin and stir in the sugar, cook, uncovered, for about 25–35 minutes or until setting point is reached, stirring every 5 minutes. Allow to stand for 5 minutes. Ladle into warm jars, cover, seal and label.

LEMON CURD

Makes 675 g/1½ lb
Power setting FULL and LOW
Total cooking time 17–19 minutes

100 g/4 oz butter
grated rind and juice of 3 lemons
225 g/8 oz granulated sugar
3 eggs
1 egg yolk

Place the butter, lemon rind and juice in a large bowl and cook on FULL POWER for 3 minutes. Stir in the sugar and cook on FULL POWER for 2 minutes. Stir until the sugar dissolves. Beat the eggs and egg yolk together. Add the egg mixture to the lemon mixture and cook, uncovered, on LOW POWER for 12–14 minutes, stirring occasionally, until the curd thickens and will coat the back of a spoon.

Spoon into dry sterilised jars, cover, seal and label. Store in a cool place for up to 2 weeks.

VARIATION

Orange Curd Prepare and cook as above but use the finely grated rind and juice of 2 medium oranges and 1 lemon instead of the 3 lemons.

APPLE JELLY

Makes about 1 kg/2 lb
Power setting FULL
Total cooking time 17–21 minutes

475 ml/16 fl oz unsweetened apple juice
800 g/1¾ lb sugar
5 tablespoons commercial pectin
few drops of green food colouring (optional)

Place the apple juice and sugar in a 3-litre/5-pint bowl. Mix well, cover and cook for 12–14 minutes, stirring after 6 minutes.

Stir in the pectin, mixing thoroughly. Cover and cook for 4–6 minutes until the mixture boils. Boil the jelly for 1 minute, stir and remove any foam. Colour with green food colouring if liked. Ladle into clean warmed jars, cover, seal and label.

CHAMPAGNE JELLY

(Illustrated on pages 230/231)
Makes about 1.5 kg/3 lb
Power setting FULL
Total cooking time 9–11 minutes

400 ml/14 fl oz Champagne or sparkling wine
675 g/1½ lb sugar
5 tablespoons commercial pectin
3 bunches green grapes, washed

Place the Champagne or sparkling wine in a 3-litre/5-pint bowl with the sugar. Cover and cook for 8–10 minutes, until the mixture begins to boil, then boil for 1 minute. Add the pectin, stirring well. Place each bunch of grapes in a separate, warmed clean jar. Ladle the jelly into the jars, cover, seal and label. Store this jelly in the refrigerator and eat within a week.

VARIATIONS

Port Wine Jelly Prepare and cook as above but use port instead of the Champagne or sparkling wine. Use red grapes instead of green ones.
Rosé Wine Jelly Prepare and cook as above but use rosé wine instead of the Champagne or sparkling wine. Use red grapes instead of green ones.
Red Wine Jelly Prepare and cook as above but use red wine instead of the Champagne or sparkling wine. Use red grapes instead of green ones.
White Wine Jelly Prepare and cook as above but use white wine instead of the Champagne or sparkling wine.

BOTTLED PLUMS

(Illustrated on pages 230/231)
Makes 1 (1.75-kg/4-lb) jar
Power setting FULL and MEDIUM
Total cooking time 14 minutes

450 g/1 lb caster sugar
300 ml/½ pint hot water
1 kg/2 lb plums, washed, halved and stoned

Place the sugar and water in a 1.75-kg/4-lb preserving jar. Cook, uncovered, on FULL POWER for 4 minutes. Pack the plums into the jar with the syrup and cover with cling film. Cook on FULL POWER for 5 minutes, then reduce to MEDIUM POWER and cook for 5 minutes.

Remove from the oven, cover, seal and label. Check that the jar is sealed when cold.

BOTTLED APPLES

Makes 1 (1.75-kg/4-lb) jar
Power setting FULL and MEDIUM
Total cooking time 8½ minutes

450 g/1 lb caster sugar
300 ml/½ pint hot water
1 kg/2 lb cooking apples, peeled, cored and sliced

Place the sugar and water in a 1.75-kg/4-lb preserving jar, then cook, uncovered, on FULL POWER for 4 minutes. Pack the apples into the jar with the syrup and cover with cling film. Cook on FULL POWER for 2½ minutes, then reduce to MEDIUM POWER and cook for 2 minutes.

Remove from the oven, cover, seal and label. Check that the jar is sealed when cold.

CORN RELISH

(Illustrated on pages 230/231)
Makes about 1.5 kg/3 lb
Power setting FULL
Total cooking time 20–22 minutes

225 g/8 oz sugar
4 teaspoons cornflour
½ small onion, peeled and chopped
1 tablespoon mustard seeds
1 teaspoon celery seeds
¼ teaspoon turmeric
250 ml/8 fl oz vinegar
200 ml/7 fl oz hot water
3 (362-g/11½-oz) cans sweet corn with peppers

Place the sugar, cornflour, onion, mustard seeds, celery seeds and turmeric in a 3-litre/5-pint bowl or container and mix well. Add the vinegar and water blending well. Cover and cook for 5 minutes.

Add the corn, mixing well to blend. Cover and cook for 15–17 minutes, stirring halfway through the cooking time. Ladle into warmed, clean jars, then seal and label.

TOMATO HAMBURGER RELISH

Makes about 750 ml/$1\frac{1}{4}$ pints
Power setting FULL
Total cooking time 3 minutes

1 tablespoon made mustard
1 tablespoon dark soft brown sugar
2 teaspoons white vinegar
$\frac{1}{2}$ teaspoon salt
6 tomatoes, peeled and chopped
50 g/2 oz chopped celery
1 green pepper, seeds removed and chopped
1 bunch spring onions, trimmed and finely chopped

Place the mustard, brown sugar, vinegar and salt in a 1.4-litre/$2\frac{1}{2}$-pint bowl and cook for 1 minute.

Add the remaining ingredients and cook for 2 minutes, uncovered, stir well, then cool and refrigerate before serving. Store any leftovers in the refrigerator for up to 1 week.

SPICY COLESLAW RELISH

Makes about 750 ml/$1\frac{1}{4}$ pints
Power setting FULL
Total cooking time $7\frac{1}{2}$–$9\frac{1}{2}$ minutes

25 g/1 oz butter
150 g/5 oz white cabbage, finely shredded
1 green pepper, seeds removed and chopped
1 small onion, peeled and chopped
2 tomatoes, peeled and chopped
5 teaspoons vinegar
2 teaspoons made mustard
1 teaspoon Worcestershire sauce
$\frac{1}{2}$ teaspoon salt
$\frac{1}{4}$ teaspoon Tabasco sauce
freshly ground black pepper

Place the butter in a 1.75-litre/3-pint bowl and cook for $\frac{1}{2}$ minute. Add the remaining ingredients, mixing together well, then cover and cook for 7–9 minutes, stirring halfway through the cooking time. Serve hot with hot dogs or continental sausages. Store any leftover relish in the refrigerator for up to 3 days.

Clockwise from the top: Mocha Sauce (page 172), Sweet and Sour Sauce (page 168) and Italian Tomato and Mushroom Sauce (page 169)
Overleaf *Top:* Champagne Jelly (page 226); *Left:* Corn Relish (page 227); *Right:* Bottled Plums (page 226)

Beverages

Microwave owners often remember the fascination they experienced when they made their first cup of tea or coffee in the microwave oven. The idea of putting a cup of cold water or milk in the microwave complete with flavourings is quite novel, and to see it emerge steaming just some $1\frac{1}{2}$–2 minutes later is amazing. And the 'magic' doesn't stop there – if you leave a cup to go just a little too cold for drinking, simply reheat it on FULL POWER for $\frac{1}{2}$ minute. Gone are the days of steamy kitchens, burnt milk pans and mounds of washing up.

It isn't necessary to cover beverages during heating but do remember to leave room for expansion between the liquid and the brim of the cup, glass or mug. Remember, too, to place drinking containers in a ring pattern if heating more than one at a time.

Observe the rule to avoid metal by ensuring that you do not use lead crystal glasses and those mugs or cups with glued-on handles should not be used. Never attempt to defrost or heat beverages in narrow-necked bottles, as pressure builds up in the lower part of the bottle, causing it to shatter.

Opposite page *From the left:* Lemonade (page 237), Hot Honey Fruit Punch (page 237) and Irish Coffee (page 235)

Guide to Heating Coffee and Milk

	Time in minutes on FULL POWER
Black coffee	
600 ml/1 pint (cold)	4½–5
1.15 litres/2 pints (cold)	7–7½
Milk	
150 ml/¼ pint (cold)	1–1½
300 ml/½ pint (cold)	2–2½

	Time in minutes on FULL POWER
Coffee and milk together	
600 ml/1 pint coffee and 150 ml/¼ pint milk (both cold)	5–5½
1.15 litres/2 pints coffee and 300 ml/½ pint milk (both cold)	8–8½

COCOA

Serves 4
Power setting FULL
Total cooking time 4–4½ minutes

50 g/2 oz sugar
3 tablespoons cocoa
900 ml/1½ pints milk

Place the sugar in a large jug with the cocoa. Add 150 ml/¼ pint of the milk and mix well. Cook for 1–1½ minutes until very hot. Add the remaining milk, whisking well and cook for 3 minutes until hot and steaming.

DUTCH CHOCOLATE CUPS

Serves 4
Power setting FULL
Total cooking time 4–4½ minutes

300 ml/½ pint milk
150 ml/¼ pint single cream
150 ml/¼ pint hot water
4 tablespoons drinking chocolate
¼ bottle advocaat or egg flip
pinch of cinnamon

Place the milk, cream and water in a jug and cook for 4–4½ minutes or until very hot. Whisk in the drinking chocolate and advocaat or egg flip. Pour into four mugs or cups and sprinkle lightly with cinnamon.

CAPPUCCINO

Serves 4
Power setting FULL
Total cooking time 3 minutes

450 ml/$\frac{3}{4}$ pint milk
40 g/1$\frac{1}{2}$ oz plain dessert chocolate, grated
4 teaspoons sugar
2 teaspoons instant coffee granules or powder
100 ml/4 fl oz brandy
150 ml/$\frac{1}{4}$ pint whipping cream, lightly whipped
chocolate curls to decorate

Place the milk in a large jug and cook for 3 minutes. Whisk in the chocolate, sugar and coffee. Pour into individual heatproof glasses or mugs and divide the brandy equally between them. Do not stir. Top each with a little whipped cream and decorate with chocolate curls.

IRISH COFFEE

(Illustrated on page 232)
Serves 1
Power setting FULL
Total cooking time 1$\frac{1}{2}$–2 minutes

2–3 tablespoons Irish whiskey
1–2 tablespoons sugar, according to taste
175 ml/6 fl oz cold, made coffee
1–2 tablespoons double cream

Place the whiskey, sugar and coffee in a stemmed, heatproof glass. Cook for 1$\frac{1}{4}$–2 minutes until very hot but not boiling. Stir to dissolve all the sugar.

Whip the cream lightly, then pour over the back of a spoon on to the coffee so that it forms a layer on the surface. Serve at once.

VARIATIONS

Russian Coffee Prepare as above but use vodka instead of whiskey.
French Coffee Prepare as above but use brandy instead of whiskey.
Jamaican or Caribbean Coffee Prepare as above but use rum instead of whiskey.
Spanish Coffee Prepare as above but use sherry instead of whiskey.
German Coffee Prepare as above but use Kirsch instead of whiskey.
Normandy Coffee Prepare as above but use Calvados instead of whiskey.
Calypso Coffee Prepare as above but use Tia Maria instead of whiskey.

LEMON TEA

Serves 4
Power setting FULL
Total cooking time 4½–5 minutes

750 ml/1¼ pints weak China tea, strained
1 lemon, finely sliced

Place the tea in a large jug and cook for 4½–5 minutes until very hot. Add the lemon slices, cover and leave to stand for 5 minutes. Pour into heated glasses and serve.

GLÜHWEIN

Serves 4
Power setting FULL
Total cooking time 4 minutes

600 ml/1 pint dry or medium red wine
75 g/3 oz demerara sugar
2 cinnamon sticks
1 lemon
6 cloves
100 ml/4 fl oz brandy

Place the wine, sugar and cinnamon sticks in a large heatproof bowl or jug. Stud the lemon with the cloves and add to the wine mixture. Cook for 4 minutes or until boiling.

Add the brandy and leave to stand, covered, for 5 minutes. Strain and serve warm.

HOT HONEY AND WINE TODDY

Serves 6–8
Power setting FULL
Total cooking time 4 minutes

1 bottle medium dry white wine
thinly pared rind and juice of 1 lemon
1 orange, thinly sliced
4 tablespoons clear honey
1 cinnamon stick
4 tablespoons brandy

Combine the wine, lemon rind and juice, orange slices, honey and cinnamon in a large bowl and cook for 4 minutes until nearly boiling. Remove the lemon rind and cinnamon stick and add the brandy. Serve warm.

HONEYED POSSET

Serves 4
Power setting FULL and LOW
Total cooking time 3 minutes

3 egg yolks
2 tablespoons clear honey
150 ml/¼ pint medium white wine
grated rind of 1 orange

Whisk the egg yolks with the honey until pale and thick. Place the wine and orange rind in a jug and heat on FULL POWER for 1½ minutes, until just boiling. Pour on to the eggs, whisking continuously – the mixture will thicken. Cook on LOW POWER for 1½ minutes. Remove and whisk until thick and frothy. Pour into individual glasses and serve at once.

HOT HONEY FRUIT PUNCH

(Illustrated on page 232)
Serves 8
Power setting FULL
Total cooking time 6 minutes

1 litre/1¾ pints unsweetened apple juice
6 tablespoons lemon juice
12 cloves
3 tablespoons clear honey
1 dessert apple, cored and thinly sliced
1 lemon, thinly sliced

Combine the apple juice, lemon juice, cloves, honey, apple and lemon in a large jug and cook for 6 minutes until nearly boiling. Serve warm.

LEMONADE

(Illustrated on page 232)
Serves 6–8
Power setting FULL
Total cooking time 4 minutes

3 tablespoons water
grated rind of 2 lemons
juice of 4 lemons
225 g/8 oz granulated sugar

Place all the ingredients in a large jug and mix well. Cook for 4 minutes, stirring twice during cooking, then cool and chill before serving.

Dilute 50 ml/2 fl oz of the lemonade with 300 ml/½ pint iced water to serve.

Index